T0269715

Richer and More Equal

Richer and More Equal

A New History of Wealth in the West

Daniel Waldenström

polity

First published in 2024 by Polity Press

Polity Press
65 Bridge Street
Cambridge CB2 1UR, UK

Polity Press
111 River Street
Hoboken, NJ 07030, USA

ISBN-13: 978-1-5095-5778-3

A catalogue record for this book is available from the British Library.

Library of Congress Control Number: 2023950839

Typeset in 10.5 on 13pt Swift
by Cheshire Typesetting Ltd, Cuddington, Cheshire

For further information on Polity, visit our website:
politybooks.com

Contents

Preface

Over recent decades, private wealth in the Western world has multiplied, making us richer than ever. However, a hasty glance at the soaring number of billionaires – some of whom double as international celebrities – prompts the question: are we also living in a time of unparalleled inequality?

A widely accepted narrative argues that, yes, we are. This story paints wealth as an instrument of power and inequality. It traces a path from nineteenth-century Europe, where low taxes and minimal market regulation allowed for unchecked capital accumulation, to the two world wars and subsequent progressive taxation policies that diminished the fortunes of the wealthy. Yet, the narrative continues, a wave of market-friendly policies in the late twentieth century reversed this trend, sending wealth inequality back towards historic highs.

This tale, though intriguing, is largely flawed.

My goal in this book is to reframe the conversation around the history of wealth. Leveraging new historical data along with existing research, I contend that the main catalysts for wealth equalization are neither the devastations of war nor progressive tax regimes. While these elements have had their effects, they do not account for the broader and more potent forces shaping wealth. Instead, I will demonstrate that the real game-changer has been the expansion of asset ownership among everyday citizens, driven largely by the rise of homeownership and pension savings.

Another, broader purpose of this book is to contribute to a better understanding of the role that economic policies can

play for promoting the growth of wealth in the entire population, from the economically disadvantaged to the super-rich.
As we confront challenges such as technological disruption,
climate change, and potential retrenchment in global trade,
private wealth takes center stage. It serves as an investment
engine, a cushion against financial shocks, and a revenue
base for public initiatives. My hope is that, by exploring the
economic history of the West, we can identify policies that
encourage new wealth creation and avoid those that put it
at risk.

In the course of writing this book, I have incurred con-
siderable debts that I wish to acknowledge. Special thanks
for valuable discussions and comments on drafts of the
book or its earlier related writings go to Anders Björklund,
Bertrand Garbinti, Branko Milanović, Charlotte Bartels,
Clara Martínez-Toledano, Daron Acemoğlu, David Splinter,
David Weil, Enea Baselgia, Enrico Rubolino, Eric Zwick,
Erik Bengtsson, Isabel Martínez, Gabriel Zucman, Guido
Alfani, Jacob Lundberg, Jakob Madsen, James Davies, James
Heckman, James Robinson, Johan Norberg, John Sabelhaus,
Lucas Chancel, Jesse Bricker, Mikael Elinder, Neil Cummins,
Olle Hammar, Peter Lindert, Rodney Edvinsson, Rolf
Aaberge, Salvatore Morelli, Thilo Albers, Thomas Helleday,
and Thomas Piketty. I have also received constructive feed-
back during presentations at workshops and seminars at
Bonn University, the Harris School of Public Policy and the
Lifecycle Working Group at the University of Chicago, the
Norwegian University of Science and Technology, the Federal
Reserve Bank of Chicago, Örebro University, the Paris School
of Economics, the Research Institute of Industrial Economics
(IFN) in Stockholm, Statistics Norway, Stockholm University,
and Uppsala University.

In addition, my understanding of wealth inequality and
history has benefited greatly from discussions with Andreas
Peichl, Anthony Atkinson, Anthony Shorrocks, Ariell Reshef,
Enrico Rubolino, Facundo Alvaredo, Frank Cowell, Ignacio
Flores, Henry Ohlsson, Jean-Laurent Rosenthal, Jeffrey G.
Williamson, Jesper Roine, Leandro Prados de la Escosura, Luis

Bauluz, Magnus Henrekson, Marc Morgan, Moritz Schularick, Roberto Iacono, Spencer Bastani, and Yonatan Berman. I have also appreciated help with data from Bertrand Garbinti, Charlotte Bartels, Clara Martínez-Toledano, Eric Zwick, Facundo Alvaredo, Jakob Madsen, Miguel Artola Blanco, Rodney Edvinsson, and Thilo Albers.

At Polity Press, my editor, Ian Malcolm, has given me support with the project and excellent guidance at every step in the process. I was fortunate to receive advice from two reviewers who helped me anticipate a number of important questions about the argument and the evidence. Of course, the final word, and any errors that may appear, are solely my responsibility.

Finally, I wish to thank my wife Nina for her advice and sufferance throughout the long gestation of this book.

1

Uncovering a Positive Story

Over many decades, the distribution of wealth has been a topic of fascination and contention. It has stirred emotions and sparked debates among scholars, policymakers, and the public alike. The answers to questions such as how wealth is accumulated, distributed, and inherited are important for understanding economic growth, social mobility, and the overall wellbeing of a society. And, as for any other complex subject, our understanding of wealth distribution is evolving whenever new evidence and interpretations come to light.

Calls to reduce the ever-present disparities between rich and poor may be as old as the disparities themselves, and in recent years they have grown louder. The ambition to reduce inequality, however, should not distract us from a positive aspect to the narrative, which is largely untold. Over the past century, people in Western countries have become both richer and more equal. This unseen wealth revolution has profoundly transformed the lives of millions. To understand the origins and implications of this large-scale change is vital in our quest for a more equitable and prosperous future.

The numbers are striking: today, we are more than three times richer in purchasing power than we were in 1980, and we are nearly a staggering tenfold richer than a century ago. Such growth in wealth is extraordinary by historical standards, and it begs the question: what has driven this remarkable change, and why has wealth become increasingly equally distributed? The answer, as we shall see, lies in the broadening of wealth ownership among ordinary people primarily through homeownership and pension savings.

Old Narrative Challenged by New Data

Wealth is defined as the total value of all assets in housing, land ownership, and financial holdings less the value of debts. For much of human history, wealth has been concentrated in the hands of a few, leaving the vast majority with limited resources and opportunities. The past century, however, has witnessed a dramatic shift, with wealth becoming increasingly accessible to the bottom and middle strata of society. This phenomenon has had a profound impact on wealth inequality, helping to narrow the gap between the richest and the rest.

In this volume, I offer an in-depth exploration of the historical trajectory of wealth in the Western world. Drawing upon the latest discoveries of long-term patterns and determinants of aggregate wealth accumulation as well as wealth inequality, I examine detailed and comparable data for all relevant countries. Some of the data series were produced by me and my research associates, but other researchers have produced many of the series used here. However, this book does not just present a compilation of already known evidence; it also introduces new estimates of aggregate wealth–income ratios and wealth inequality.

The analysis reassesses a previously established narrative on the history of wealth, perhaps most notably associated with the works of the French economist Thomas Piketty, and offers a comprehensive historical and political account to shed light on the dynamics of equality within the capitalist economy. In the following sections, I elaborate on the intricacies of Piketty's work and explain how my own narrative builds upon but also revises the overarching history of wealth distribution. It should be noted that measuring household wealth and its distribution is difficult, as I will explain in more detail below. Estimating historical trends in wealth inequality puts extraordinary requirements on data quality. However, the newer evidence produced in recent years benefits from a closer examination of the sources and analytical choices, and this gives it a clear advantage over earlier works.

Homes and Pensions, Not Wars

Contrary to the old scholarly narrative, this book will demonstrate that the primary drivers of wealth equalization have not been the destruction wrought by wars or the redistributive effects of capital taxation. While these factors have undoubtedly played a role, they are based on presumptions that building wealth is a zero-sum game, and they therefore fail to account for the broader and more fundamental forces at work. Instead, I will show that the expansion of wealth ownership among ordinary citizens, materialized through widespread homeownership and pension savings, has been the real engine of change.

At the turn of the twentieth century, owning a decent home and saving for retirement were luxuries enjoyed by only a select few – maybe a couple of tens of millions in Western countries. Fast forward to today, and these once elusive dreams have become a reality for several hundreds of millions of people. This massive increase in both homeownership and retirement savings, made possible by expanding educational attainment, elevated labor incomes, and financial development, has effectively democratized wealth. It has lifted the fortunes of the bottom and middle segments of society and contributed significantly to the reduction of wealth inequality. In addition, owning one's home has historically offered high long-term investment returns at low risk and is generally associated with a lower depreciation of housing capital compared to rented homes.

Bidding Farewell to the Zero-Sum Game

Yet this critical aspect of our recent history, with ordinary people building personal wealth at an unprecedented pace, has been largely overshadowed by the prevailing focus among some academics and policymakers on the fortunes of the super-rich and on the role of wars and capital taxation in addressing wealth inequality. This book seeks to redress this imbalance, shedding light on the transformative power of wealth creation, challenging the conventional wisdom that views wealth equalization as a zero-sum game.

Wealth accumulation is a positive, welfare-enhancing force in free market economies. It is closely linked to the growth of successful businesses, which leads to new jobs, higher incomes, and more tax revenue for the public sector. Throughout the following chapters, I will explore the historical, social, and economic factors that have contributed to the rise of wealth accumulation in the middle class, home-ownership and pension savings, as key drivers of wealth equalization. I will explore how governments, businesses, and individuals have collaborated to create the conditions for this unprecedented democratization of wealth. And I will examine the far-reaching consequences of this transformation, including the implications for social mobility, economic growth, and the prospects for future generations.

As we embark on this journey, it is important to recognize that the story of wealth equalization is not one of unmitigated success. There are still significant disparities in wealth within and among nations, generating instability and injustice. Over the past years, wealth concentration has increased in some countries, most notably in the US. However, by acknowledging the progress that has been made and understanding the mechanisms that have driven it, we can lay the foundation for further advancements in our quest for a more just and prosperous world.

1.1 THE PREVIOUS NARRATIVE ARGUING THAT WARS AND PROGRESSIVE TAXES SHAPED A CENTURY OF WEALTH INEQUALITY

In his bestselling book *Capital in the Twenty-First Century* (2014), Thomas Piketty described the historical development of capital and wealth inequality in the Western world. His work built on the research by a large international collective of scholars, including several studies by me and my coauthors. The book quickly gained attention from both academics and policymakers. Piketty's unique approach in combining historical data with a simple yet thought-provoking analysis that also has an ideological bent has been appealing to many.

In this book, I will refer to Piketty's narrative as "the previous narrative," although it has not been told for more than a couple of decades.[1] However, the aging process of narratives can be quick, as new insights and revisions continue to emerge from the ever-growing body of research on the history of wealth.[2]

The narrative that is primarily associated with Piketty describes wealth accumulation and concentration over the past century as following a U-shaped pattern. Wealth levels and concentration peaked in the late nineteenth century and up to World War I. This was the result of an unchecked capitalism that had little regulation, taxation, or democratic influence. Europe's aggregate wealth–income ratios at that time were estimated to be extraordinarily high, with capital values of around 600 to 800 percent of national income. These levels then dropped significantly during the 1920s, and even more after World War II. Wealth–income ratios began to rise again in the 1980s, marking the completion of the U-shaped pattern and leading Piketty to declare: "Capital is back!"

Wealth inequality according to this narrative is also described as following a U-shaped pattern. High levels of inequality in the past dropped sharply during the twentieth century, driven primarily by the shocks to capital during the two world wars and the rise of progressive taxation. Wealth was slashed, particularly among the rich, by wartime capital

destruction and through regulations, and postwar redistributive taxation prevented the emergence of new fortunes and
thus the rise of wealth concentration. After 1980, this narrative claims, neoliberal policies deregulated markets and
lowered taxes. That led to a boosting of capital values, mainly
benefiting a small wealth-holding elite, and it elevated wealth
inequality towards historical levels.[3]

In summary, this account views the history of wealth as a
story about the consequences of restraining capitalism and
the failure of doing so. Wars and redistributive policies tem-
pered the natural tendencies of capitalism to accumulate
and concentrate wealth. The dismantling of the restrictions
through the liberalization of Western economies in the 1980s
reawakened these forces.[4]

1.2 A NEW HISTORICAL NARRATIVE: RICHER AND MORE EQUAL

The scholarly dialogue that emerged in the wake of Piketty's
Capital concentrated largely on its theoretical constructs and
the paradigms it employed. Although the debate was rigorous
in questioning the theoretical underpinnings and proposing
alternative models of capital and inequality, there was a con-
spicuous absence of scrutiny of Piketty's historical data and
the empirical conclusions that were drawn from it.[5] This void
in critical appraisal is of course well deserved, but it may also
be attributed to a prevalent disinterest in economic history
and lack of attention to details in historical data within the
mainstream economic community.

While it may be partially understandable that many economists are concerned principally with contemporary phenomena, this focus undermines a nuanced understanding
of historical trends and their contemporary implications.
This relative neglect not only impedes a critical evaluation
of historical research but also, inadvertently, cedes an almost
monopolistic influence to those researchers who do engage
deeply with historical data.

Therefore, the emergence of new research initiatives in recent years that interrogate the historical dimensions is particularly encouraging. Notably, these new contributions not only corroborate or challenge earlier data but also extend the empirical base by incorporating previously unexplored countries. Some studies have revisited the historical datasets of countries such as Germany and the United Kingdom to offer revisions, while others have unveiled new empirical evidence for countries hitherto lacking in this type of data.

In this book, I collect the updated data series and pieces of evidence presented in the recent research literature to build a new analysis of the history of wealth and wealth inequality in the West. The data show that we are both richer and more equal today than in the past, and the accumulation of housing wealth and pension savings among the middle classes emerge as the main factor behind this development. At its core, the new narrative thus hinges on the interdependence of wealth accumulation among average citizens and the equalization of wealth.[6] Wealth creation is here regarded as inherently positive for a country's economic development, reflecting the successful outcomes of business ventures and other private and public investments, and providing the means to advance new structures and set up buffers against unexpected future shocks.

To present the main empirical results of the book, this storyline can be distilled into three overarching facts.

The New Wealth Narrative in Three Facts

Fact #1: We Are Richer Today

To gauge a country's affluence, the wealth in the population serves as a comprehensive metric. Higher average wealth permits greater consumption of goods and services, more savings and investment for future prosperity, and an insurance against unforeseen events. Figure 1.1 illustrates a marked growth in the average real per capita wealth in the Western world over the last 130 years. Particularly since the end of

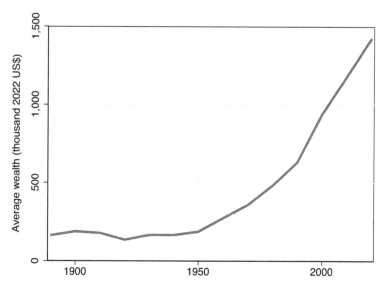

Figure 1.1 Rising Real Average Wealth in the Western World

Note: Wealth is expressed in real terms, meaning that it is adjusted for the rise in consumer prices and thus expresses change in purchasing power. The line is an unweighted mean of the average wealth in the adult population in six countries (France, Germany, Spain, Sweden, the UK, and the US) expressed in constant 2022 US$. For further details and sources, see chapter 2.

World War II, the average wealth in the population has risen substantially, amplifying sevenfold from 1950 to 2020.

In essence, it is notable that each postwar decade has witnessed an augmentation in wealth. This affirms the robustness of the first fact in the new wealth narrative: we are wealthier today than at any previous point in modern history.

Fact #2: Wealth Is Different Today

Over the course of a century, the asset composition that constitutes private wealth has undergone a monumental shift. A century ago, in the early twentieth century, wealth comprised primarily agricultural and business assets, largely concentrated among the affluent. If we look at the situation today, the majority of personal wealth is tied up in housing

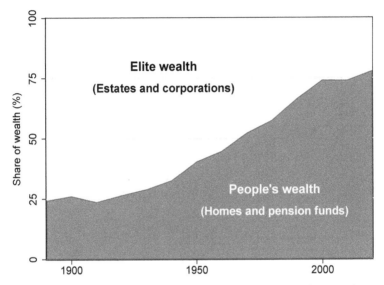

Figure 1.2 The Changing Nature of Wealth from Elite-Owned to Popular Wealth

Note: Unweighted average of six countries (France, Germany, Spain, Sweden, the UK, and the US). For further details and sources, see chapter 3.

and pension funds, assets that are more evenly distributed among the populace. Figure 1.2 visualizes this transformation by showing the average asset shares across a number of Western countries.

Hence, the second fact of the new wealth narrative: wealth has transitioned from being largely elite-centric to being widespread, diffused across the average household. This shift has profound implications for wealth distribution, as we will discuss later.

Fact #3: We Are More Equal Today

A salient goal of this book is to chart and comprehend the evolving patterns in wealth inequality. The issue that we are interested in is not confined merely to the growth of the wealth "pie" but also its equitable distribution. In fact, much of the past debates about wealth among both academics

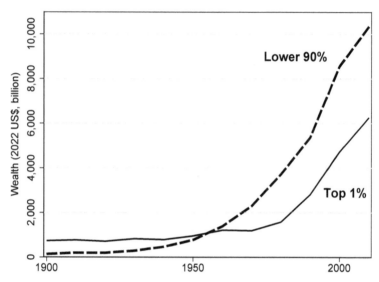

Figure 1.3 Accelerating Growth in Popular Wealth over the Twentieth Century

Note: The figure shows the total value of wealth of the lower nine decile groups ("Lower 90%") and top percentile group ("Top 1%") in each country's distribution, calculated as an unweighted average of the six countries (France, Germany, Spain, Sweden, UK, US). For further details and sources, see chapter 2 for wealth totals and chapter 5 for wealth shares.

and policymakers concerns the trends in the distribution of household wealth rather than the amount of wealth amassed over the past years. When looking at the most recent data on wealth inequality in the Western world, they reveal a substantial reduction in wealth inequality over the past century. Figure 1.3 shows that, while the wealthiest 1 percent once held quadruple the wealth of the least wealthy 90 percent, the tide has turned. As of 2010, the bottom 90 percent possess twice the wealth of the top 1 percent. Notably, the growth rate in real wealth for the least wealthy far outstripped that of the wealthiest segment.

A similar pattern is found in figure 1.4, depicting the average of the share of total wealth held by the richest percentile in Europe and the US across history. In 1910, the richest percentile held three times more wealth than in 2010.

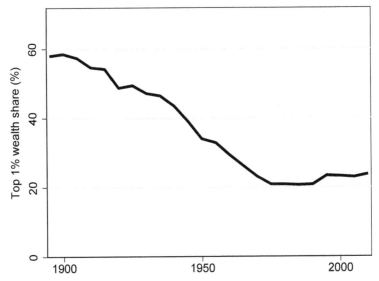

Figure 1.4 A Historic Drop in the Top 1 Percentile Wealth Share

Note: The figure shows the unweighted average of the wealth share held by the richest 1 percent of the wealth distribution in six Western countries (France, Germany, Spain, Sweden, the UK, and the US). For further details and sources, see chapter 5.

This forms the third fact in the new wealth narrative: wealth is more equally divided today than it was in the past.

I coin this phenomenon "the Great Wealth Equalization," a term that, despite its grandiosity, is grounded in empirical data. Europe, particularly France and the UK, led in this equalizing trend, moving from extreme concentrations of wealth to more modest, post-welfare-state levels. While the US started from a less unequal base a century ago, its path to equalization has been less pronounced; recently it has even regressed in terms of wealth concentration and also in more broader inequality terms. Had I presented the US and Europe separately in the figure, we would have seen an upward recent trend in wealth concentration in the US while the European trend would have been even flatter. This indicates that there is a complexity and multifaceted aspects that one needs to take into account when discussing the evolution of wealth inequality. However, taking the very long historical view, even current US levels of inequality pale in comparison to those witnessed in Europe 100 years ago.

Institutional Shifts and Expanding Wealth Definitions

Several factors contribute to the important historical accumulation of housing and pension assets in the population. However, in the new wealth narrative presented in this book, specific attention is paid to the role of political and economic institutions in society. By institutions, I mean the laws and norms that confine the rules of the game shaping decisions and interactions between people. The twentieth century saw a number of profound institutional changes that have bearing on the evolution of wealth and wealth inequality in the Western countries.

During the 1910s and 1920s, there was a broad wave of political democratization in the West as most countries experienced the introduction of universal suffrage. In its aftermath, a series of political reforms changed the economic reality of most people. Educational attainment was expanded to broader groups. Labor laws were changed to improve the rights of workers. These institutional shifts lifted the productivity of workers, and that in turn elevated their labor earnings. Meanwhile, the financial system developed by offering better services to people, increasingly backed by better regulations. All of this gave ordinary people new opportunities to acquire mortgages for purchasing their own homes. Another outcome was a general improvement of living standards that extended the lifespans of most people, and this motivated them to start saving for retirement and accumulate pension savings.

Two other important institutional developments during the twentieth century – cross-border capital flows and the advent of modern social insurance – have a bearing on what we define as wealth in the empirical analysis. Should foreign assets be part of domestic wealth? Should the present value of promised future pension incomes be counted as the pension wealth of today's citizens? How important these possible new assets may be, incorporating them into the analysis shows that the overarching findings of the book remain largely unaltered.

Specifically, one possible extension of the wealth concept is to address the impact of hidden offshore assets owned by wealthy Westerners. This issue has received much attention in the political debates, and there have been calls for improved reporting, and also the taxation, of offshore wealth. The question of tax-driven capital flight from rich countries to tax havens has been on the agenda since the liberalization of capital accounts and the emergence of new technologies for international transfers during the 1980s. In recent years, researchers and policymakers have started to examine the quantitative effects of these asset flows for wealth inequality estimates of rich countries in the event that the offshore assets are not fully disclosed to the authorities. The results, however, show only marginal effects on wealth inequality in Western countries when estimates of offshore wealth are added to the wealth of its richest individuals. The long-run historical wealth equalization in the Western world remains unchanged.[7]

Another extension examines how the vast values generated within modern welfare-state systems affect the wealth inequality trends. People's entitlements to future pensions and social insurance transfers are financed by income taxes. These taxes lower people's ability, and probably also their willingness, to save privately for social insurance. If, instead, taxes had been lowered, people would have accumulated wealth themselves. Researchers have tried to calculate the values that would have been generated by capitalizing the stream of expected future pensions and social insurance incomes. The results show that this would significantly reduce wealth inequality, since the new wealth would be owned by all wage earners. For example, top wealth shares are reduced by about half when adding this social security wealth. Since social insurance and pension systems emerged gradually over the twentieth century, this result acts to reinforce the main finding of the book, namely that the long-run wealth equalization is even more pronounced than when just counting standard, marketable wealth.

1.3 MEASURING WEALTH INEQUALITY: PROMISES AND PITFALLS

The distribution of wealth is a unique aspect of inequality analysis that has traditionally garnered less attention than the distribution of income. There are several reasons for this. We often lack individual-level data on assets and debts, making it impossible to measure wealth differences within the population. Certain assets, especially corporate assets, pension savings, and consumer durables, are also difficult to value. For some of them we lack current market prices, since they are not traded regularly and the values therefore have to be estimated. Pension assets materialize in most cases only after people retire, which means that the amounts in pension funds are not exactly equivalent in consumption terms to money deposited in the bank. Consumer durables such as cars or boats are relatively straightforward to consider as assets, but home electronics or furniture are less so, and their values need to be heavily discounted if they are added to personal wealth.

Furthermore, understanding what wealth is gets complicated by the life choices people make, such as planning for retirement, investing in education, and acquiring property. How much wealth people own is affected by the life stage they have reached. For instance, younger individuals might have fewer assets not because they are impoverished, but because they have not had the time to accumulate wealth like their older counterparts. As they educate themselves and get a job, they start investing in a home and saving for old age. Because of this, wealth increases as people grow older. After retiring, however, people begin consuming their assets, and in some cases use up everything before they die. This hump-shaped life-cycle pattern of wealth is well known and recurrently found in all countries and time periods. A specific result is that many of the asset-poor people in society are simply young people who have not yet had the time to start building wealth (I will come back to this question in chapter 5). Altogether, interpreting and analyzing wealth is a multifaceted endeavor.[8]

Defining Wealth

Wealth is the value of all the things we own. When talking about wealth, this book always refers to net wealth, or net worth, which means the sum of assets net of debts. This interpretation of wealth is the standard definition among all researchers and statistical agencies.

Assets are classified into non-financial and financial types. Non-financial assets encompass real estate – houses, summer homes – as well as land and other tangible goods such as agricultural assets. Financial assets include cash, bank savings, and investments in mutual funds, stocks, and individual-linked pension funds. The valuation of assets is typically done by using current market prices that are multiplied with the quantities of each asset component. An alternative valuation approach, which has been common in the construction of aggregate capital stock estimates in the national accounts, is the so-called perpetual inventory method. This method defines an asset's value as the sum of past years' investments net of an annual depreciation rate. In contemporary developed economies, non-financial and financial assets are approximately equal in their aggregate value.

When discussing wealth inequality, the inclusion of funded pension savings in household wealth is contentious. Advocates argue for their incorporation on the grounds of providing a complete picture of an individual's resources, ensuring international comparability, enhancing policy formulation, and reflecting behavioral economics accurately. If

funded pensions were excluded it would create inconsistencies in household budget calculations, since pension savings
have represented a large share of household net saving in
most Western countries for several decades. Critics counter
that pension savings are not readily accessible like other
assets; they pose valuation difficulties on account of their
future uncertainty, and their variability in availability may
distort wealth distribution measurements. Standard wealth
definitions nowadays cover funded pensions, both in the
wealth research literature and in the standardized national
accounting systems.

When it comes to liabilities, mortgages are the dominant
type. Approximately 80 percent of all debt in modern economies stems from home loans. They are the essential counterpart to one of the most significant non-financial assets
– residential property. Beyond this, student loans account
for roughly a tenth of total debt. Other types of debt, often
labeled as "consumer debt," make up the remainder and can
vary from auto loans to credit card balances. During earlier
historical eras, private-sector borrowing was not so dominated by mortgages, and other types of collateral, such as
corporate shares or borrowing against one's own name, were
relatively more common.

Measuring Household Wealth Today and in the Past

The pursuit of a robust understanding of wealth and its distribution is a data-intensive endeavor. The evidence in this book
draws heavily on wealth information coming from administrative registers, such as property and tax records, as well as
household surveys. Yet, as with any empirical study, such data
sources are not without their limitations and complexities.

In the contemporary context, corporate shares in closely
held firms form some of the most problematic assets to deal
with. The valuation of many closely held firms emerges as a
substantive issue. These entities, exemplified by Germany's

Mittelstand firms, lack a public trading platform, necessitating reliance on accounting data for valuation, which inevitably introduces a degree of imprecision. Furthermore, trusts – legal constructs often employed for tax-minimization purposes – complicate the picture. These trusts may or may not be openly reported in administrative registers or household surveys. While researchers have adapted methodologies to account for the muddling effects of trusts on the estimation of households' wealth and also of wealth inequality, especially in jurisdictions where trusts are pervasive, a residual degree of uncertainty remains.[9]

Turning to historical data, the absence of comprehensive digitalized registers and surveys, particularly before the 1970s, introduces additional complexities when estimating individual wealth holdings and the overall shape of wealth distribution. Researchers must often resort to alternative data sources such as probate records and estate tax returns, which have often been kept in different archives going far back in time. These records provide valuable insights into the wealth holdings of deceased individuals, offering in many contexts unique opportunities to estimate household wealth inequality. However, they necessitate additional inferential steps to generalize their findings to the broader living population, which may not exactly resemble the population of the deceased.[10]

Another data source that is often employed in historical contexts is that of wealth tax payments, often presented as tabulated distributions in official publications. Although useful, this source introduces its own set of limitations and should be interpreted with caution. In particular, if reporting one's wealth is associated with paying more taxes, there can be strong incentives to underreport the true amount of asset holdings or overreport indebtedness. If such reporting behavior is more common among the wealthier echelons, and there are good reasons to believe it is, that could bias the measured wealth inequality downwards and give a picture of society being more equal than it really is. But readers can rest assured that extensive efforts have been made in previous research to devise methods to minimize systematic biases in tax-based estimates of historical wealth inequality.[11]

Estimating the Inequality of Wealth

By far the most common statistical measure of wealth inequality in the historical literature is the top 1 percent wealth share. This metric quantifies the ratio of the wealth held by the richest hundredth of all wealth holders to the overall wealth in a given population. For instance, a 20 percent top percentile group's wealth share, a figure not uncommon in contemporary European settings, implies that the average wealth of this elite group is twenty times that of the general population.

The top 1 percent wealth share is notably convenient for historical analyses. This is because its calculation demands only an understanding of the elite's wealth holdings and an aggregate figure for a nation's total wealth. Historical tax systems, often designed with a focus on taxing the affluent, offer pertinent data, rendering this measure particularly advantageous for longitudinal assessments of wealth inequality.

Another widely employed metric is the Gini coefficient, or Gini index. This index ranges from zero to one, where zero indicates perfect equality and one denotes extreme inequality – that is, all wealth being concentrated in the hands of a single individual. The Gini coefficient's strength lies in its utilization of comprehensive population data, thus enabling it to capture nuanced shifts across the wealth distribution that may escape the top 1 percentile metric. However, individual or household wealth data covering the entire population have not been commonplace for more than a few decades, which makes the Gini coefficient less commonly employed in historical analyses.[12]

An additional perspective on wealth inequality measurement comes from viewing trends in wealth inequality using either the standard relative measures or alternative absolute measures. Relative metrics, such as the Gini index or the top 1 percent wealth share, are well established and fulfill the standard requirements on inequality measures. They remain stable when everyone's wealth grows at the same pace in percentage terms, making them useful for cross-country and historical comparisons. Absolute measures capture growing wealth gaps, focusing on changes in nominal currency (such as dollars or euros) terms and may align with some people's perceptions. Researchers, statistical agencies and policymakers rely on relative metrics when analyzing and discussing inequality trends.

There are research studies that examine whether people perceive inequality changes from a relative or an absolute perspective.[13] The main findings in these studies reveal that the majority resonates with the relative inequality measures – that is, metrics that mirror conventional approaches used in scholarly research. There is, however, a significant minority that focuses primarily on wealth gaps in absolute monetary terms.

From an academic standpoint, the advantages of using the standard relative inequality measures are many. In addition to the ones mentioned above, they facilitate comparisons with other trends in society such as economic growth or stock market increases. The focus on nominal values, as in absolute inequality measures, also implies that economic development by itself drives perceived economic disparities, and thus could make inequality-averse people refute the gains of long-run economic growth. For these reasons, this book employs the established analytical framework based on relative inequality measures throughout.

It is important to note that, despite the problems inherent in measuring wealth inequality, all data series that form the empirical backbone of this book have undergone rigorous academic peer review. Consequently, they represent the most reliable portrayals of both the current state and the historical evolution of aggregate wealth and wealth inequality extant in scholarly discourse.

Why Study the Rich?

The historical evidence on economic inequality studied in this book refers mainly to the top of the distribution. Focusing on the rich has become more commonplace in the historical literature, but it is still not so common in inequality research. Typically, researchers have preferred studying the lower ends and the particular welfare issues concerned with them. But, as the English economic historian R. H. Tawney remarked, "What thoughtful rich people call the problem of poverty, thinking poor people call, with equal justice, the problem of riches."[14] There are, in fact, several reasons why an in-depth look at the upper end of the financial spectrum is scientifically warranted.

To begin with, the rich are doubtlessly an important group in society. Many of them are successful entrepreneurs that hold considerable shares of ownership in the corporate sector. This makes them a crucial component in the factors generating economic growth and long-run welfare improvements in society. The wealthy groups also constitute an important tax base, which is particularly important in modern Western societies, where a large share of output is channeled through the public sector. Through these channels, the rich typically enjoy a disproportionate influence on the economic and political agenda. In other words, if we wish to fully understand what forces drive economic and political change, we need to keep track of the status of those with the highest incomes and fortunes.

From a purely fiscal perspective, the wealthiest in society are important since that is where the money is. The highest paid tenth of all Swedes earn one-third of all incomes before taxes, and they paid four-tenths of all direct taxes. The top wealth decile in Sweden owns over half of all personal wealth in the country. Such concentration of resources is not unique to Sweden. Quite the contrary in fact. For example, the richest decile group owned two-thirds of all wealth. Given the fiscal needs of government, studying the rich as tax objects is therefore highly relevant.

Another, more pragmatic, reason for studying the rich relates to the specific availability of historical data on the wealth top. Inequality estimates based on top wealth shares can hence span considerably longer time periods than any other of the common inequality measures used. Given the right adjustments, they are also homogeneous and comparable over time as well as across countries.

The findings in the inequality research literature in recent years suggest that the rich are not all alike but, rather, a quite heterogeneous group in society.[15] In terms both of the size and the structure of their wealth, the differences between the lower and upper parts of the top decile are substantial. Such detailed knowledge about the top can be crucial for sifting through competing explanations of what fuels inequality. For example, to differentiate between theories which focus, on the one hand, on changes in the savings out of earning income and, on the other hand, on theories that stress the importance of entrepreneurial capital formation, we must have details about top wealth holdings.

Can We Trust the Rich Lists?

Listings of named super-rich individuals or families, such as the *Forbes 400* in the US, the *Sunday Times Rich List* in the UK, or that in *Manager Magazin* in Germany, have gained popularity in recent years among the general public but also among researchers.[16] Even if these lists offer sometimes unique opportunities to address the wealth of the super-rich, they should be treated with caution.

The methods and sources that journalists use to create these lists are openly disclosed only in broad terms. Most information is derived from publicly available sources, such as newspapers, company reports, and financial market prices. Sometimes, journalists also conduct interviews with the wealthy individuals themselves. These approaches may not be reliable, however, as the super-rich may wish either to exaggerate or to underplay their wealth, depending on their interests in receiving attention or the opposite. Debts are typically unknown, leading to a systematic overvaluation of fortunes.[17]

In summary, while rich lists can provide some insight into the wealth of the super-rich, they should not be considered a definitive source for understanding wealth inequality. For a more accurate and comprehensive understanding of wealth distribution, it is essential to rely on objective data sources, such as household surveys, administrative population registers, and historical records, as well as rigorous academic research.

1.4 INEQUALITY HAS DECREASED IN OTHER OUTCOMES AS WELL

Although this book is about wealth, the discussion about economic inequality extends beyond the realm of wealth distribution. In fact, the majority of the economic and historical research on inequality, as well as the societal debate over distributional outcomes, have looked not at wealth but at other phenomena, most notably incomes. The emphasis on income inequality is driven by its direct connection to disparities in personal welfare, as well as the capacity to consume or save, both of which play a pivotal role in individuals' economic lives. This warrants a look at historical developments in other inequality outcomes.

Diminishing Inequality in Four Social and Economic Dimensions

Throughout the past century, a trend towards greater equality has been observed across multiple facets of economic and social development in Western societies. This pattern has garnered scholarly attention across a wide range of academic disciplines. In Gregory Clark's *A Farewell to Alms* (2007), which explores the broad developments in Western economic history, an overall decrease in inequality is documented along a number of important socio-economic indicators.[18]

Table 1.1 presents data from England contrasting the situation at the onset of industrialization with the contemporary era. The table shows outcomes of four distinct variables: literacy, surviving children, male stature, and life expectancy.

In the era before industrialization, there was a considerable literacy gap between the affluent and the indigent. Among the rich, 85 percent were literate, compared to only 30 percent among the poor, generating a disparity of 183 percent. Presently, this gap has significantly narrowed, with 100 percent literacy among the affluent and 95 percent among the less affluent – a mere 5 percent disparity. The rich–poor differential in the number of surviving children has likewise experienced a precipitous decline. Historically, the affluent had approximately twice as many surviving children (3.85) compared to the impoverished (1.93). Today, not only has this disparity decreased, it has even marginally reversed (1.33 versus 1.64).

Turning to male stature, the differences were marginal in

Table 1.1 How Inequality Has Fallen in Many Life-Relevant Outcomes

	Literacy (%)	Surviving children	Stature (males, cm)	Life expectancy (years)
Pre-industrial society				
Rich	85	3.85	174	39
Poor	30	1.93	168.5	31
Difference	183%	99%	3%	26%
Modern society				
Rich	100	1.33	178.2	80.8
Poor	95?	1.64	176	74.3
Difference	5%?	−19%	1%	9%

Source: Data come from England and are reported in Clark (2008, table 12.4). The literacy rate for the poor in modern times is my plausible but uncertain guess based on a reading of the results from studies of socio-economic gradients in literacy rates in today's Western countries.

the pre-industrial period and have all but vanished today. Finally, life expectancy at birth also reflects a diminished rich–poor gap. In pre-industrial England, the difference was eight years (39 versus 31), whereas today it stands at approximately six years (80.8 versus 74.3). In percentage terms, the difference has contracted from 26 percent to 9 percent.

These developments in England serve as a microcosm of broader Western trends, offering empirical validation of the pervasive shrinkage in inequality across diverse socio-economic dimensions. The length of one's life serves as a cardinal indicator of wellbeing, arguably holding more salience for many than income or wealth. Lifespan variance is shaped by an array of factors, encompassing economic determinants such as labor earnings, consumption, and asset ownership.

Historical demographic records reveal a longstanding focus of governance on the monitoring of citizens' lifespans. Figure 1.5 delineates Gini coefficients for lifespan dispersion within the aggregate population, spanning from the mid-1800s to the present. During the 1800s, the Gini coefficient for lifespan hovered around 0.5. However, it underwent a marked reduction in the twentieth century: descending to 0.3 by 1930, further declining to 0.2 by 1950, and finally stabilizing near 0.1 after 1980. This manifests a substantial contraction in lifespan inequality across Western societies, concomitant with industrialization.

The principal driver of this equalization in lifespan was an uplift at the lower end of the distribution. While today's affluent and healthy populations do experience marginally elongated lifespans compared to a century ago, this extension pales in comparison to the dramatic enhancement in life expectancy witnessed among the economically disadvantaged. Thus, the lion's share of equalization materialized through the elevation of the lower strata rather than a diminution at the upper end.

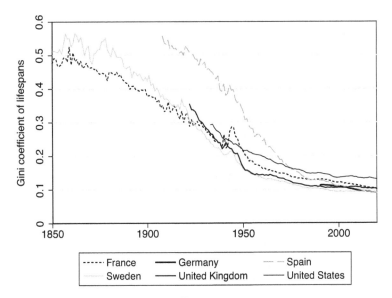

Figure 1.5 Falling Inequality in Lifespans, 1850–2020

Note: The Gini coefficient shows the inequality in expected remaining years of life (ranging between full equality at 0 to full inequality at 1), computed from data on a number of individuals and life expectancy across yearly age cohorts.

Source: Human Mortality Database.

The Long View of Income Inequality: The Increasing Role of Government

The long-term development of income inequality in Western countries reveals that inequality was high at the beginning of the twentieth century and that it has been declining up to the present day.

When one looks at incomes before taxes and transfers, inequality stopped falling in the 1980s and thereafter trends became divergent. Technological advances and freer markets led to growing income gaps, particularly in Anglo-Saxon countries such as the US and the UK. On the other hand, most other Western countries managed to keep inequality relatively at its historically low levels and saw only slight increases if at all.

But here is also where the role of government comes in. Over the last century, the share of money collected through taxes jumped from about 10 percent of GDP in 1900 to, on average, 40 percent by 2000. A large portion of these taxes goes into programs designed to balance out income disparities. The growth in government accountability represents a gigantic shift in the structure of Western economies over the twentieth century and plays a role in most of the outcomes studied in this book.

Recent studies show that, when you factor in not just income and cash transfers but also government spending on things such as healthcare and education, the income inequality numbers look quite different. The reason is that these welfare services are provided almost proportionally to all citizens, and this means that they become relatively more important for low-income earners than for high-income earners. As a result, disposable incomes that include also the non-cash transfers coming from public spending are more equally distributed. For instance, in France, the share of income going to the top 10 percent of earners dropped much more dramatically when you include these benefits, from 50 percent to 25 percent. In the US, the impact of government spending is possibly even larger. According to one study, the top income share going to the top decile falls from 55 percent to 35 percent when factoring in public expenditures, although overall trends do not change much. However, another more recent study of US top income shares finds that not only does public welfare spending make incomes more equal but it also erases much of the increasing income inequality over the post-1980 period. The reason for the different findings of the trend patterns lies in differences in assumptions about the allocation of public spending on Medicare, infrastructure, police, and so forth.[19]

Incomes have thus become substantially more equal over the last century, especially in Europe, where governments have really leaned into programs designed to balance the scales. Even in the US, where income inequality has been a stubborn issue, the role of government has made things more equal than they were in the past, even if the exact degree of this equalization is debated among scholars.

In a nutshell, one of the book's central arguments – that there has been a "Great Wealth Equalization" over the past century – fits into a larger trend. Whether you are looking at wealth, income, or other measures of people's wellbeing, the Western world has grown both richer and more equal over the last hundred years.

A Global Perspective

When we broaden our lens to include global trends, we find a pattern that is consistent with what we found for the history of the West: economic growth often goes hand in hand with reduced inequality.[20] Take the new millennium as a starting point. Since the early 2000s, the global distribution of wealth has become more equitable. The Gini index has dipped from 0.93 to 0.88, while the world's total wealth has astonishingly quadrupled.[21]

During the same timeframe, global poverty rates have experienced a dramatic decline. The number of individuals subsisting on less than approximately US$2 per day shrank from 1.8 billion in 2000 to 600 million in 2020. Put another way, the global poverty rate – representing the share of the world's population living in poverty – has tumbled from 30 percent to a mere 9 percent.[22] Moreover, the distribution of income on a global scale has steadily evened out. Since 2000, the global Gini index has dropped from about 0.70 to 0.60, all while the world's GDP has tripled. If we stretch this analysis back a century, we discover that today's inequality levels are the lowest recorded since the era before World War I.[23]

In summary, the progress towards wealthier and more equal societies in Western countries is not an isolated phenomenon. It reflects a wider global trend towards both enrichment and equality.

1.5 WHAT POLICYMAKERS CAN LEARN FROM THE HISTORY OF WEALTH

A key question arises: can this book's findings offer practical guidance for today's policymakers? While history does not exactly repeat itself, the economic settings and human behavior studied in this book are still highly relevant to current and future challenges. With that in mind, this section aims to extract several tangible policy lessons.

Wealth-Building and Inequality Reduction: A Balanced Approach
Historical patterns show that increasing personal wealth often goes hand in hand with decreasing wealth inequality. Importantly, this is not about bringing down the top earners but, rather, about promoting economic growth and institutional changes that lift up those at the bottom. Two main assets – housing and pension savings – have been instrumental in this equalization. Encouraging homeownership and long-term savings can thus serve dual goals: they are both pro-equality and pro-wealth accumulation.

Tax Strategies: Empowering Workers and Savers
Lowering labor income taxes could be a powerful tool in equitable pro-growth policies. It not only facilitates productive workers to accumulate wealth and buy homes but also encourages people, both young and older, to invest in education and career development. This, in turn, can boost their future income and potential to save.

Homeownership as a Policy Goal
Promoting policies that encourage tenant-owned housing over rental units can make a big difference in homeownership rates. This could involve reducing or eliminating subsidies for building rental apartments, particularly those that are publicly owned. In addition, tax incentives related to mortgage interest rates can further encourage home buying.

Retirement Planning: Security through Savings
Tax benefits linked to long-term saving plans, especially those connected to retirement, can have a substantial impact on wealth distribution. Rendering interest earnings from these savings tax-exempt is one way to achieve this.

Reforming Pension Systems: A Way Forward
Switching from pay-as-you-go pensions to funded, defined-contribution pensions can offer workers more tangible forms of wealth. Given the generally higher long-term returns in financial markets, this policy shift could even add value to the pension system as a whole, benefiting everyone involved. Fully funded pensions also address the demographic trend towards larger population shares of retirees seen in many Western economies by increasing the rate of accumulation of physical capital to balance the aggregate decline in human capital.

Taxing Capital Income, Not Wealth
Capital taxation can either redistribute wealth or deter its accumulation. Capital income taxes are the most prevalent and effective, adjusting to economic cycles and capturing windfall gains. Wealth taxes, by contrast, may be ideologically appealing to some but are problematic in practice. They strain entrepreneurs, perplex tax authorities, and yield low revenues. Consequently, many countries have scrapped them. Overall, capital income taxes present a more practical, empirically backed approach to mitigating wealth inequality.

1.6 OUTLINE OF THE BOOK

The book is organized into two major sections and concludes with an epilogue. In Part I, we view wealth from a bird's-eye perspective. Chapter 2 uncovers how the ratios of private wealth to national income have evolved and also maps out shifts in the kinds of assets people hold. Chapter 3 transitions to a discussion about how wealth has been transformed over time, shifting from agrarian lands and business stocks to housing and pension funds. The focus in chapter 4 is on the ascent of homeownership and pension savings, which are the cornerstone assets for most households today.

Part II shifts focus to the distribution of wealth. Chapter 5 sheds light on trends in wealth inequality for the past 130 years, examining data from various Western nations. It pays special attention to both ends of the spectrum: the super-rich and those with negligible assets. Chapter 6 explores the "why" behind these patterns of inequality. It looks at historical events such as wars, fiscal policies, and sweeping societal changes that broadened education and financial inclusion. Chapter 7 delves into the hushed world of offshore assets, which often escape official statistics but have potential implications for our understanding of wealth inequality. Chapter 8 tackles public-sector assets, notably future pensions and social security, to give a rounded view of wealth. Chapter 9 turns to the question whether fortunes are generally inherited or self-made, and what this means for wealth inequality in the long run.

Part III wraps up with chapter 10, which distills the main takeaways of the previous analyses into a revised narrative about the history of wealth distribution. The chapter closes by outlining actionable lessons for policymakers and the general public, grounded in the book's historical analysis.

Part I

Building Wealth

2

The History of Wealth Accumulation

The story of capitalism is often told through big numbers. When the Industrial Revolution swept across the Western world in the 1800s, it brought unprecedented levels of prosperity to many. New technologies increased productivity and opened up new frontiers, leading to movements between sectors, from agriculture to industry, as well as across continents.

Capital has played a central role in this economic history. As growth opportunities emerged, capital became important to finance the new endeavors. Income, saving, investment, and capital accumulation soon became intertwined in a race that led to higher levels of wealth and welfare in both industrial and service-oriented societies.

In this chapter, I examine the latest evidence on the historical evolution of wealth in Western countries. The chapter begins with a presentation of the evolution of real per capita wealth, a direct measure of how rich a country is in terms of the long-term economic potential of the average citizen. Thereafter, I continue with reporting trends in aggregate wealth–national income ratios, which has been the main measure used in recent historical wealth research.

One takeaway of this chapter is the need to revise our understanding of wealth accumulation before World War I. Contrary to the previous narrative, early European capitalism – characterized by scant regulation, low taxation, and minimal democratic oversight – did not result in exorbitant wealth levels. New data challenge the established storyline in the previous wealth literature, underscoring lower-than-anticipated wealth values.

The time-series data employed in the analysis below stem from a collaborative scholarly effort, including my own contributions on Sweden and some other countries. Primary sources collected directly from archives are merged with published statistical materials covering most of the past century and, finally, modern datasets generated by national statistical agencies. All of these data series are meticulously shaped to ensure consistency over time. Needless to say, utilizing this standardized framework is indispensable when making cross-country or temporal comparisons.[1]

The book concentrates on six Western nations – France, Germany, Spain, Sweden, the UK, and the US – where comprehensive historical data are at hand. While a broader sample would have been ideal, the dearth of historical national balance sheets restricts our scope. Nevertheless, these six countries capture about 75 percent of Western GDP, providing a robust base for insights into private-sector wealth, comprising both households and corporations.[2] In some of the analyses below, I extend the scope to include some other Western countries, but that turns out not to change the overall messages of the core six-country sample.

2.1 THE TRAJECTORY OF REAL PER CAPITA WEALTH

The examination of real per capita wealth reveals the economic pie accessible to the average citizen. The term "real" signifies that wealth values are adjusted for inflation and that they therefore reflect the purchasing power of consumer goods. Note that this average measure is an illustration of aggregate wellbeing. The dispersion of that wealth, or how the pie is divided, is partly a different story that is beyond this section's scope and will instead be discussed in subsequent chapters.

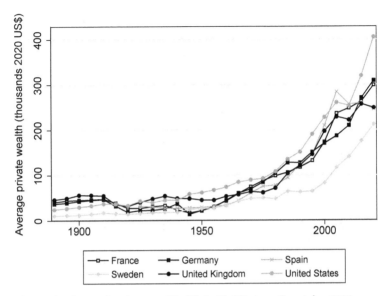

Figure 2.1 Increasing Average Wealth in Six Western Countries, 1890–2020

Note: The figure shows the wealth per adult in constant 2020 US$, reported in five-year averages.

Source: The WID.world database, with consistency checks made using the scholarly works underlying WID.

Figure 2.1 showcases the modest per capita wealth levels during the period 1890 to 1950, which remained roughly around $50,000 in today's prices. During the half-century before 1950, the figure shows that the US doubled its per capita wealth, climbing from a relatively lower standing compared to continental Europe in 1900 to surpass Europe by mid-century. This development aligns with conventional economic narratives of this era, which depict the relative decline of European powers, especially Germany and the UK, in favor of the US.

In general, the evidence suggests that a notable disparity in wealth existed between early industrial powers such as Britain, France, Germany, and the late bloomer, Sweden. Sweden's relatively poor status confirms the country's historiography. Its lack of savings during its early industrialization phase led to reliance on foreign capital for financing the building of a railway network and the industrial expansion in manufacturing and timber industries.[3]

The Postwar Surge

The second half of the twentieth century marked an extraordinary growth in affluence across Western countries, with six- to eightfold increases in per capita wealth. This growth was not merely a recovery from wartime devastation; the data reveal a sustained ascent through the latter half of the twentieth century into the twenty-first. Notably, wealth accumulation picked up pace from the 1980s until the early 2000s, only to slow down after the financial crisis of 2008 and during the 2010s.

The postwar economic miracle in Germany and cooperative international regimes facilitated income and capital growth throughout the West. Yet the momentum extends beyond this initial impetus. The accelerating growth in the 1980s and 1990s may be credited to market deregulation, technological leaps, and enhanced global integration. Since the 2000s, asset price increases have also been fueled by falling interest rates that energised stock and housing markets. The low interest rates reflect both lower overall real interest rates and expansionary monetary policies used in several countries to raise consumer price inflation from historically low levels.

Sweden stood out also during the postwar era as being relatively poor in terms of private wealth among these Western countries. But, in contrast to the prewar period, the Swedish postwar experience reflects instead the impact of its high tax and regulation levels, which effectively hindered private capital accumulation while boosting the country's accumulation of public-sector wealth.[4]

2.2 THE EVOLUTION OF WEALTH–INCOME RATIOS

The wealth–income ratio offers another lens to study economic prosperity in terms of wealth. It compares a nation's total aggregate wealth with its national income.[5] For instance, Germany's private wealth of €18 trillion is approximately 600 percent of its national income, equating to six years of income for the German populace to match their existing wealth stock.

The wealth–income ratio has since long been integral in standard economic growth models, highlighting situations where additional capital investments could lead to income growth.[6] The use of the ratio has also gained traction in recent years, not least in the historical wealth literature, where it has become a standard metric.

Large Variability in Wealth–Income Ratios across Countries

Figure 2.2 provides a historical perspective, charting the evolution of wealth–income ratios in key Western countries from the 1890s to the present. The data underscore both the commonalities and the disparities among these countries.

The first takeaway is the notable divergence across nations. Although the ratios commonly fluctuate around a 400 percent mark, significant variations exist. This demonstrates that a universal wealth–income level, applicable across all countries, is elusive.

France, Germany, and Sweden stand out for their distinct U-shaped curves. These nations saw high ratios in the nineteenth century, a dip in the mid-twentieth, and a resurgence in the twenty-first. That these countries exhibit such a similar time-series pattern is interesting considering their widely diverging experiences during this period. France and Germany were belligerent countries in both of the world wars, but France on the winning side and Germany as the

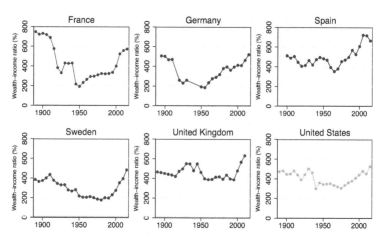

Figure 2.2 Wealth–Income Ratios in the West over 130 Years

Notes: The wealth–income ratio measures the number of years a country needs to earn its wealth stock (in percentages, where 400 percent means four years). All ratios of aggregate private wealth to national income are reported in five-year averages.

Source: Data from Piketty and Zucman (2014) for France and the US; Albers, Bartels and Schularick (2022) for Germany; Artola Blanco, Bauluz and Martínez-Toledano (2021) for Spain; Waldenström (2017) for Sweden; and Madsen (2019) for the UK.

main loser. By contrast, Sweden never participated in any of the great wars.

The ratios of Spain and the UK exhibit a different pattern, remaining relatively constant until the 1990s, after which they began to climb. It is difficult to discern any clear U-shape in these ratios. Spain's ratios were above 700 percent in the early 2000s, the highest recorded level of any country in the modern era. The rise was entirely driven by a widely noted housing and commercial real-estate bubble that started building up in the late 1990s and continued into the early 2000s.[7]

The US offers an interesting case, maintaining a ratio of around 400 percent throughout the 130-year span. While a dip occurred during World War I, the US ratio did not conform to the U-shaped pattern seen in France, Germany, or Sweden. Instead, it remained elevated until the 1940s, declined during the immediate postwar years, and rebounded above 400 percent in the 2000s.

2.3 NINETEENTH-CENTURY CAPITAL: A NEW PICTURE

In the narrative of Thomas Piketty and his coauthors, particularly Gabriel Zucman, capital values were historically high in Europe before World War I, about twice the level of the US, and higher than at almost any point in time afterwards in the Western world. According to this narrative, the ratios fell especially in association with the shocks to capital occurring during the two world wars and then stayed low in the postwar era. After the policy reversals of the 1980s and 1990s, wealth values were resurrected, causing a long-term U-shaped pattern that prompted Piketty and Zucman to declare that "Capital is back!"[8] That claim attracted worldwide attention, not simply because the numbers were dramatic but because, historically, a high wealth–income ratio went hand in hand with elevated levels of wealth inequality, since the vast majority of capital was traditionally owned by the rich. The more capital in a society, the thinking went, the more powerful the wealthiest citizens would be.

Since Piketty's works were published, several new studies have reexamined the historical data on aggregate capital. Some of these have come to revise Piketty's original wealth–income series, while others have presented novel series for previously non-covered countries. In the case of Germany, a group of German economic historians have constructed an updated aggregate balance sheet series going back to 1895. For the UK, a new series that spans almost 800 years has been presented by the growth economist Jakob Madsen. New country series were constructed for Spain back to 1900 by a group of Spanish economic historians, and I myself have constructed a new aggregate series for Sweden going back to 1810.[9]

Examining the UK and Germany is particularly important,

as these are the two major economies for which Piketty and Zucman's original series have been complemented by revised series from other research groups. Investigating the reasons behind the discrepancies and assessing the plausibility of the new series compared to the older ones can provide valuable insights. I will also briefly discuss the new evidence for Spain and Sweden, as these series further our understanding of the wealth–income ratios on the European periphery.[10]

The United Kingdom:
Less Extreme Than Previously Believed

In figure 2.3, the wealth–income ratio of the UK is shown according to Piketty's original series and in the subsequent revision of Madsen. As can be seen from the two series, the revised version brings important qualifications to the UK wealth historiography. Madsen's new time series database covers 800 years of aggregate wealth and income data for

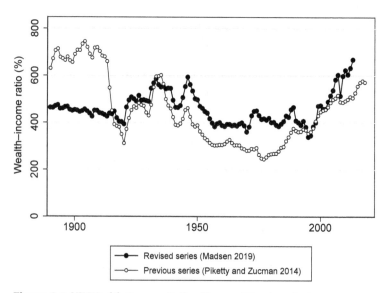

Figure 2.3 UK Wealth–Income Ratios: New and Previous Series
Source: Madsen (2019) and Piketty and Zucman (2014).

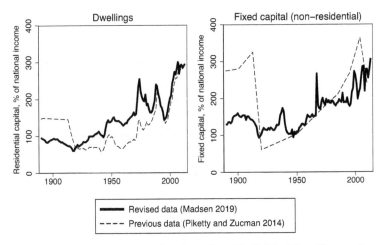

Figure 2.4 The Likely Overestimation of Pre-World War I Dwellings and Fixed Capital in Previous UK Data

Note: "Previous data" refers to Piketty (2014) and Piketty and Zucman (2014). "New data" refers to Madsen (2019).

the UK. While data on the first six centuries are more tentative, Madsen's account of recent centuries is based on a comprehensive analysis of previous economic history research, new source materials, an economic theory-based model, and a thorough revision of the data constructed by Piketty and Zucman.

The key finding from Madsen's research is a significantly lower wealth–income ratio in the decades leading up to World War I compared to Piketty's and Zucman's older series. As illustrated in figure 2.4, this difference of between 250 and 300 percentage points of national income appears in both the estimated residential capital stock (dwellings) and non-residential capital stock series.

Let us now look a bit closer at the instances where the Madsen dataset differs from the Piketty dataset and what the explanations for this difference are according to Madsen's account.

First, Piketty does not use the latest historical national income series (reported by Bank of England scholars in the

2010s). The older national income series results in a higher wealth–income ratio in the eighteenth and nineteenth centuries by on average 77 percentage points. Second, the older estimate for the period 1810 to 1901 includes the wealth of Southern Ireland, but not its national income, which results in a wealth–income ratio that is 90 percentage points too high if one assumes that the assets are evenly distributed across Irish regions. Third, there are some simple data errors in the older series, one being a calculation mistake and another being a double-counting of British and foreign government securities. These errors result in an 80 to 90 percentage point overestimation for the years 1700 to 1913. Fourth, the older series interprets reported "mixed income" and "capital gains" in the historical source as operating profits from business, which can be capitalized into wealth stocks by dividing them by some assumed rate of return.[11] However, Madsen argues that these incomes are in fact labor earnings of family workers in farming, shopkeeping, and wholesale, and therefore not returns to wealth. Redefining these incomes as labor earnings reduces the wealth–income ratio by 90 percentage points.

A specific event in British wealth holdings in the early twentieth century was the sharp decline in net foreign assets following losses in colonial possessions. Madsen's series fully incorporates this decline, from its peak value of around 150 percent of national income in 1900, via a sharp fall of almost 100 percentage points during World War I, and then the gradual decline to almost zero in 1950.

In a final examination, Madsen takes specific issue with the 323-percentage point drop in the wealth–income ratio of the Piketty and Zucman series between 1913 and 1920. Madsen points to several factors that speak against the plausibility of such a large and sudden drop. One is that neither national income growth nor saving rates changed during this period in a way that could account structurally for such a shift.[12] Madsen also suggests a potential, spurious, explanation for the large recorded drop in the Piketty–Zucman series, namely their switch from an older to a newer historical data source in 1920. If this is corrected for, he claims that any remaining differences are mere data artifacts.

Madsen points to the lack of other signs of drastic disturbances to the financial system or to top marginal income taxes that could account for such a large wartime drop in the relative value of capital. This claim has recently received additional support. First, from a couple of recent studies of UK wealth distribution trends, which have collected the probate inventory reports and estate tax returns of all deceased persons with wealth over the past century. Their series suggest no significant change in the average wealth of adults during the 1910s and the 1920s.[13] Second, a study of historical trends in stock market capitalization over the past 140 years finds no evidence of a lasting structural break in the British stock market around World War I. It reports instead stock price-related drops that were offset after the war.[14]

Madsen concludes that an overestimation of pre-World War I wealth–income ratios by Piketty and Zucman remains as the most plausible explanation for all of these inconsistencies.

Germany Revisited; Spain and Sweden Unveil New Insights

German economic historians, who revised the historical wealth series, found a substantial discrepancy in pre-1914 wealth–income ratios compared to the data presented by Piketty and Zucman. Specifically, the new German data presented in figure 2.5 show these ratios to be 100 to 150 percentage points lower than previously thought.[15] A key factor behind this revision is a different approach to valuing land and agricultural assets. Unlike Piketty and Zucman, who relied on estimated capital stocks, the German researchers used tax-assessed records as their primary data source. They argue that these first-hand administrative records offer a more accurate valuation, as there is limited incentive for overestimation. Another contributing factor, albeit a less

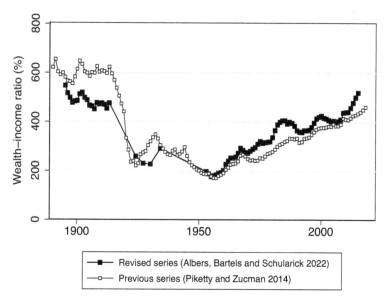

Figure 2.5 Revised German Wealth–Income Ratios, 1890–2017

Source: Albers, Bartels and Schularick (2022) and Piketty and Zucman (2014).

significant one, is the previous overestimation of net foreign assets in the data used by Piketty and Zucman.

Two countries, Spain and Sweden, recently received their first datasets with historical wealth–income ratios, produced by scholars who followed the same research methods and theoretical frameworks as Piketty did. These two country additions offer out-of-sample checks on Piketty's evidence. The figures show that both had more moderate wealth–income ratios like those of the US, rather than the extraordinarily high ratios in France, Germany, and the UK. The revisions made for Germany and the UK, which also showed levels close to the moderate US one, leave France as the remaining outlier.

The historical wealth–income ratios for Spain were constructed by a group of Spanish economic historians, covering the period back to 1900.[16] While their estimated series follow the template set out by Piketty and use many new historical sources, they also draw on previous works on Spanish historical national accounts.[17] In this book, I use as a benchmark their series where corporate assets are valued based on their net assets. An alternative series is one where they have made upward price adjustments of business equity, using either newly created stock market price indexes or capitalized firm profit data. This alternative series generates a higher level in the period 1900 to 1913 by about 100 percent of national income. Although this is in principle a relevant extension, it comes with uncertainties. Early historical stock exchanges were underdeveloped and typically associated with quite small trading volumes, resulting in thin markets and often unrepresentative prices.[18] Finally, the method of capitalizing profits to construct capital values for unincorporated enterprises is a highly uncertain procedure that is sensitive to the definition of profits relative to other incomes, especially to the choice of the capitalization interest rate.

The new Swedish wealth–income ratio was estimated by me, and I followed the standard national accounts definitions and the methodology used by Piketty and Zucman.[19] Sweden's wealth–income ratio before World War I hovered between 250 and 450 percent of national income, with an average of 350 percent and the highest levels recorded around 1910. Thus, Sweden also deviates from the narrative of historically high European pre-World War I ratios. It is closer to the relatively lower levels of Spain, the revised series for Germany and the United Kingdom, and also the levels of the United States.

Home Production: An Income Missing from Historical National Accounts

Comparing incomes today with incomes in economies from the past can be challenging. The modern definition of income focuses on transactions taking place in a market, with buyers and sellers agreeing on a price and payments resulting in incomes. However, in the distant past, especially before the Industrial Revolution, a number of economic activities took place outside of the market. In those situations, exchange took place without money being paid, and therefore people did not earn income in the modern sense.

Home production of industrial goods and services was relatively significant in the nineteenth century. Examples include home-produced foodstuffs, leather works, and metal products. Since this output did not involve market-based transactions, it is excluded from the modern official measures of national income.

How much would national income increase by adding incomes from home production? Would such addition affect the wealth–income ratios studied above? Ideally, we wish to capture true economic activity across different time periods. Economic historians have constructed historical national accounts for this purpose, but they still use only the modern definition of GDP and therefore miss the incomes that stem from the selling of home-produced goods. To my knowledge, there has not been much research done to answer these questions.

One study that tries to incorporate the value of home production examines Sweden in the nineteenth century. It measures the production of foodstuffs, together with leather and metal goods, and adds the value to national income. This results in an increase in national income of 5 to 15 percent. Using this home-production-adjusted national income leads to a lowering of the pre-1914 wealth–income ratio for Sweden by 10 to 50 percentage points.[20]

As for whether national incomes and wealth–income ratios in continental Europe or the US would change by adding income from home production, this remains an open question that requires further study. It is likely, however, that the difference would be smaller than for Sweden, as these countries were more advanced during this early period. Even so, incorporating non-market transactions into historical wealth–income ratios could potentially provide a more accurate representation of economic activity in the past, helping to better inform our understanding of historical capital accumulation trends.

2.4 REASSESSING THE HISTORY OF WEALTH–INCOME RATIOS

New data on wealth–income ratios in Europe before World War I calls for a reexamination of longstanding beliefs about capital accumulation during the era of low taxes and minimal regulation. Was the free-market capitalism of the twentieth century as conducive to extreme inequality as previously thought? Answering this question is not just an academic exercise but also has implications for our understanding of modern economies with low or absent capital taxation and regulation. The task at hand is to diligently review this new evidence and comprehend the variations between the historical sources used.

Updated Insights on Pre-World War I Wealth while Postwar Series Stay Unchanged

The new data significantly alter our understanding of wealth–income ratios before World War I. Compared to Piketty and Zucman's figures, the revised estimates for Germany and the UK are notably lower. Germany's ratio drops from 600 percent to 500 percent, while the UK sees a decline from 700 percent to 450 percent. Newly examined countries, Spain and Sweden, also fall within the 450 to 500 percent range, aligning closely with the revised numbers. For the pre-World War I era, France remains an outlier, with a ratio around 750 percent – much higher than the rest. The US, however, fits well into the revised European pattern, with a ratio of approximately 450 percent.

Looking at the period between and after the world wars, there is less variance between the old and new data series. In general, wealth–income ratios increase across all countries, forming a U-shaped pattern over the long run. This upward trajectory has been attributed to higher levels of saving during the early postwar years and a mix of savings and asset price gains in more recent times.[21]

When considering the precise timing of fluctuations in wealth–income ratios during the twentieth century, the patterns are actually quite varied across countries. Germany experienced significant declines during the world wars, followed by a gradual increase, with the revised series yielding higher levels for recent years that surpass even Piketty's series. The UK series remained more stable, hovering around 450 percent of national income until the 1990s, when it soared to over 600 percent. Spain also maintained stability of around 450 percent until the 1990s, when it escalated to nearly 700 percent. Sweden displayed a gradual decrease from 400 percent in 1910 to 200 percent in 1950, followed by a rapid increase during the 1990s to over 500 percent.[22] Finally, the US series remained stable until the 1940s, when it dropped by approximately 100 percent; it stayed at that level until the 1980s, when it began to rise to prewar levels.

A Vanishing Continental Divide: Europe and the US

With revised data, the historical divide between Europe and the US in wealth–income ratios before World War I diminishes substantially. Using Piketty's original series in the left panel of figure 2.6, prewar Europe, containing series from France, Germany, and the UK, stood at around 700 percent, contrasting sharply with the US level at 450 to 500 percent. The new series, in the right panel of figure 2.6, aligns both continents at around a 500 percent ratio between 1890 and 1914.[23] This convergence suggests that the previously perceived gap was likely an artifact of incomplete data.

The original emergence of the divide between Europe and the US was not completely explained. Piketty and Zucman discussed possible explanations by which Europe's early industrialization allowed more time for wealth accumulation and America's land abundance reduced its value. Both accounts are plausible but face some empirical challenges. The US exhibited high saving rates through much of the nineteenth century, and, alongside income growth, this points to capital

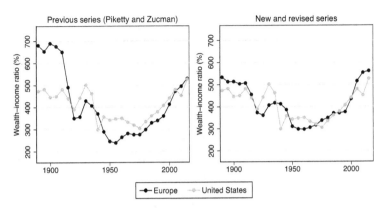

Figure 2.6 The Disappearing Difference between Europe and the US before World War I

Note: The figure shows aggregate private wealth–income ratios in Europe (unweighted average) and the US.

Source: Europe in panel a): France, Germany, the UK (from Piketty and Zucman 2014); Europe in panel b): France (Piketty and Zucman 2014), Germany (Albers, Bartels and Schularick 2022), Spain (Artola Blanco, Bauluz and Martínez-Toledano 2021), Sweden (Waldenström 2016, 2017), and the UK (Madsen 2019).

accumulation rates similar to those of Europe. On the issue of land values, while lower in the US according to the Piketty and Zucman database, they are not significantly so according to the 1985 Goldsmith national wealth database.[24] Comparing Sweden and the US – both with low farmland values and similar wealth–income ratios – I found that American farmland prices per acre were low at the start of the nineteenth century but not a century later.[25]

In sum, updated pre-World War I wealth–income ratios invite a reassessment of capital accumulation in societies with minimal or no capital taxes and regulations. This new understanding could be instructive for both historical and contemporary economic contexts.

2.5 CAPITAL–INCOME RATIOS OFFER MORE STABLE LONG-TERM TRENDS

In the early 1960s, the Hungarian-British economist Nicholas Kaldor formulated a set of "stylized facts" characterizing the macroeconomy. These facts soon came to be established truths among mainstream economists, and one of the starkest of these facts was the stability of the capital–output ratio over long periods of time. That is, the ratio of the capital stock to the gross domestic product can be expected to hover around a stable level in the modern market economy.[26]

However, in the early 2010s, Thomas Piketty challenged this idea by presenting new evidence on long-run trends in wealth–income ratios. His data suggested that these ratios were anything but stable over time, which raised questions about the validity of Kaldor's stylized facts.

Using Capital or Wealth?

Are capital and wealth the same thing, and should we expect them to manifest in the same way over longer passages of time? The short answer to these questions is "no." Capital and wealth are closely related, but they are not identical and they should not be expected to always exhibit the same relationships with other economic variables or patterns over time. Capital refers to assets used in production, such as buildings, infrastructure, machinery, and other corporate assets. Wealth, on the other hand, is a broader concept that includes produced capital assets as well as non-produced property such as land and foreign assets.[27]

Measurement of capital and wealth is also different. The stock of produced capital is typically measured by statistical agencies, by cumulating the value of past capital investments and subtracting the continuous depreciation. Wealth stocks, by contrast, are calculated by multiplying the volume of asset by current market prices. Criticisms of either measure revolve around how well the two stocks capture true market values.[28]

Economists debate whether to use capital or wealth in their modeling and empirical analyses. Most of this debate prevails on a theoretical level, focusing on specific issues such as whether changing values in the housing stock should be interpreted as changes in the capital stock or not.[29] To add some empirical insights to this discussion, I will compare the historical evolution of capital–income ratios, computed from a new historical dataset, with the wealth–income ratios already seen above. Placing these next to each other makes it possible to examine how well they align and whether the conclusions drawn from the analysis of wealth–income ratios can also be applied to capital–output ratios.

Smoother Trends When Using Capital–Income Ratios

Figure 2.7 illustrates the two series from the late nineteenth century to the present, encompassing Europe and the US. The distinctions between these series are striking. The capital–income ratio remains lower and considerably more stable than the wealth–income ratio across both continents and measures. In Europe, the capital–income ratio consistently hovers around 200 percent, whereas the wealth–income ratio fluctuates between 300 and 500 percent. In the US, the capital–income ratio aligns more closely with the wealth–income ratio until World War II, but following the war it remains more stable and eventually falls below 200 percent by the 2010s.

The contrasts between capital–income and wealth–income ratios provide fresh perspectives on economic history and the theories of capital accumulation. Capital's less pronounced relative size in pre-tax, pre-regulation economies challenges the previous narrative about the level and fluctuations of wealth in the nineteenth century.

The resilience of capital–income ratios through the tumultuous periods of the world wars adds further nuance. The stability in these ratios even as we entered the twenty-first

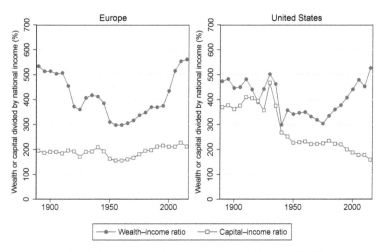

Figure 2.7 Capital–Income Ratios Are Lower and More Stable Than Wealth–Income Ratios

Source: Data on the capital stock and on capital–income ratios come from Madsen, Minitti and Venturini (2021). Data on wealth–income ratios are the same as previously used in figure 2.2.

century suggests that factors such as capital gains, particularly in housing, are important. While these gains are by construction excluded from the measured capital stock, they are captured in the wealth values and seem to contribute significantly to the observed increases in wealth–income ratios. In essence, the evidence presented above corroborates Kaldor's assertion of stable capital–output ratios as a macroeconomic "stylized fact."

When set against this broader backdrop, a revised history of wealth–income ratios in Europe and the US emerges. It paints a picture not of boundlessly escalating wealth stocks in the laissez-faire economies of the nineteenth century but of relatively stable ratios – more in line with our contemporary, regulated systems. The data also offer a picture of smaller economic impacts resulting from the world wars, challenging previous theories about their pivotal role in capital destruction. Naturally, this concerns the long-term effect on aggregate wealth values, and it does not question that the wars both had tremendous short-term impacts, also, on wealth values or on a wide range of other societal outcomes. The deviations we still see in the capital and wealth series, such as France's dramatic wartime losses, become more pronounced against this backdrop of a picture of general stability.

This revised historical reading has implications for how we think about the evolution of wealth inequality. Contrary to previous thought, it seems as if even enormous concentrations of wealth must not be intrinsically tied to skyrocketing rates of capital accumulation. Additionally, changes in wealth inequality do not seem to hinge on massive shocks to capital, such as those thought to have been caused by the world wars. These findings pave the way for more nuanced conversations about the sources and solutions to wealth inequality, topics that will be elaborated on in subsequent chapters.[30]

3

The Changing Nature of Wealth

The age-old adage "money is blind" pertains to the neutrality of means of payment. Regardless of whether your money originates from earnings, unemployment benefits, or a lottery win, it provides the same services and impact on the real economy, which is our ultimate concern.

Wealth, however, is different. Wealth is far from blind; in fact, it is quite the opposite. The reason is that the kind of assets you hold can impact the ways in which you can make use of your wealth or how its value will evolve under different economic circumstances. For example, if the German middle class had invested their savings in housing or gold, rather than depositing them in banks, they might have avoided becoming impoverished overnight during the hyperinflation of 1923, potentially altering the course of history. Had my parents turned down the offers they had to obtain advantageous rental contracts in rent-regulated Stockholm during the early 1990s and instead purchased condominium apartments, my future inheritance would have been substantially larger than it is today given the unprecedented rise in house prices over the past thirty years.

The type of wealth people hold thus has a bearing on what wealth means in real life. Looking at the aggregate level, the makeup of wealth in the population shows the nature of wealth in society. It shows both how wealth may be used to invest or consume and how it develops along with changing economic conditions.

Some may envision wealth as being synonymous with affluence, such as in rich people owning large corporations, opulent mansions, or expansive rural estates. However, wealth can be small-scale. For some people, saving even small amounts out of their low income could mean the opportunity to purchase a car or provide the downpayment for a bigger apartment. In fact, this chapter demonstrates that the view of wealth being something that concerns only the rich is outdated. A hundred years ago, private wealth was indeed linked predominantly to large holdings in the agricultural sector or to industrial and financial corporations. In 1920, three-quarters of all assets were directly associated with these types of wealth, primarily owned by the elite.[1]

Over the past century, however, and especially in the postwar period, the structure of wealth has undergone a significant transformation, driven primarily by the events and reforms of the twentieth century. Political reforms empowered people by expanding suffrage to everyone, increasing educational attainment also among poor people from working-class homes, and amending labor laws to improve working conditions for wage earners. This development led to a more educated, productive, and motivated workforce, resulting in a substantial rise in incomes and soon also in longer lifespans among ordinary people. Coupled with a growing financial system, individuals were able to save and accumulate personal wealth, primarily in housing and retirement savings. Today, these two assets account for three-quarters of all private wealth, a marked increase from one-quarter at the beginning of the previous century.

Wealth today is no longer dominated by the capital holdings of the elite. By contrast, in our time it is comprised primarily of assets that are held by the working and middle classes. In essence, history demonstrates in this way that wealth is not blind. It has changed in nature, and this has implications for how wealth is used and distributed in the population.

In this chapter, I will elucidate the changes in aggregate wealth composition, exploring the historical evidence across various countries and examining the mechanisms behind wealth accumulation that can explain the differing roles of saving and capital gains.

A note of caution is warranted. The quality of historical data on asset composition within individuals' portfolios, and also in the combined portfolio of the whole population, is not always as comprehensive or accurate as we would desire. Information about asset holdings derives from a combination of data sources. Tax authorities sometimes report specific information about certain assets, often the value of dwellings or bank deposits. At other times there is information from household surveys in which people are asked about their asset ownership, but such microdata surveys seldom go far back in time. Researchers have spent much time and effort to construct plausible and consistent estimates of asset holdings for different countries and time periods. The data sources used here have all employed similar methodologies when constructing the final series. Nevertheless, these uncertainties imply that we need to be careful when interpreting finer variations in wealth composition across countries or over time. Similar disclaimers have also been made by some of the pioneers of historical wealth research, such as Raymond Goldsmith and Thomas Piketty.[2]

However, on a positive note, when inspecting and analyzing the data series, a remarkable degree of consistency emerges both in the overall levels and in the trends across the countries studied here, despite the use of diverse series from different sources and scholars. This consistency is reassuring, as all the countries examined were subject to similar economic and political developments.

3.1 WEALTH COMPOSITION A CENTURY AGO: AGRARIAN ESTATES AND CORPORATE SECURITIES

Economic activity in pre-industrial or early industrializing countries revolved around land and its products. Throughout the nineteenth century in Europe and the US, the majority of the population worked in agriculture or services supporting farms and their workers. At least half of a country's national income originated from agricultural output, causing business cycles largely to reflect harvest performance and productivity growth to remain minimal.[3]

Wealth in the Agrarian Era

Wealth ownership during the agrarian era was naturally connected to agriculture. Land ownership was crucial, representing a third of all wealth according to Goldsmith's estimates. Agricultural wealth also encompassed other assets: buildings, livestock, machinery, and inventories possibly accounted for around half of total agricultural assets. Tax records from 1890s Sweden, for example, show that land – encompassing arable areas, forests, and timberland – made up about 40 percent of all agricultural assets, which themselves accounted for nearly two-thirds of the country's total private wealth. Agricultural buildings and structures were thus worth more than the agricultural land, while livestock (mainly horses and cows) amounted to the remaining one-fifth of total agricultural assets.[4]

Figure 3.1 displays a breakdown of household wealth into agricultural land, housing, and other domestic assets, all expressed as a share of national income to relate them to the amount of economic activity at the time. In 1900, agricultural land values were around twice the level, or 200 percent, of national income in France and Spain, 100 percent in the US, and approximately 50 percent in Germany, Sweden, and the UK. The relative importance of agricultural land diminished rapidly throughout the twentieth century, which of course

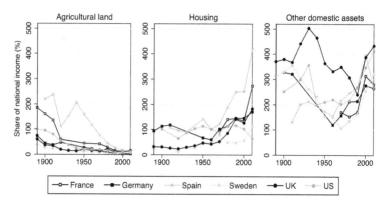

Figure 3.1 Asset Composition Trends: Falling Shares of Agriculture, Rising Share of Housing

Note: The asset categories are defined based largely on data availability for different countries. "Other assets" contain mainly financial assets.

Source: Data from Waldenström (2017) and the sources therein.

reflected the expansion of industry, with late-industrializing Spain as a notable exception. We cannot tell for sure whether this relative decline also holds when including farm buildings and inventories in the estimation, but somewhat more detailed accounts of Swedish household balance sheets suggest that this was indeed the case.

The latter half of the nineteenth century heralded industrial expansion, with the proliferation of railroads signifying the onset of a new economic epoch. By 1900, agriculture's share of GDP had declined to one-third.

Determining when exactly agriculture ceded its economic primacy to industry has engaged economic historians. While there exist discrepancies in exact dating, all Western nations had entered the industrial stage by the time our data series kicks off in 1890. In the six-nation sample of this book, the UK, France, Germany, and the US had been industrial players for quite some time, each following its own timeline. Sweden joined the industrial wave later, in the mid-nineteenth century, while Spain took the slow lane, with its industrialization trickling into the twentieth century.[5]

Industrial Expansion and the Role of Financial Assets

The Industrial Revolution marked one of the most important changes in human life ever seen. It formed the basis for a higher and also constantly improving level of living standards that has spread to the masses around the globe. This great economic development brought both new manufacturing technologies and infrastructural expansion, and it expanded the supply of products and processes in all domains of society.

Financial development became a pivotal component of the industrial transition from the very beginning. The move towards monetized transactions, underpinned by the burgeoning of financial markets, was particularly important. Wages increasingly assumed a cash form instead of such in-kind payments as food or shelter, driving the expansion of banking services. The late nineteenth century saw a surge in bank deposits and an escalating number of banking institutions, setting the stage for a fledgling financial system and an uptick in the value of financial assets.

This new system had a particular bearing on investment strategies and wealth accumulation among high-net-worth individuals. The need for capital to fuel the growth of industrial plants naturally led many corporations to seek loans from banks. Consequently, bank-extended corporate loans skyrocketed during the late 1800s and into the early twentieth century.[6]

Interestingly, John Maynard Keynes, in his reflection on the economic landscape around the time of World War I, discussed the forces enabling the massive capital accumulation and improvements that set this era apart in the nineteenth century. One of the factors he pointed out as key consisted of the successful ventures of industrialists and financiers that paved the way for industrial expansion. Keynes argued that the increased concentration of capital ownership that came with the growing corporate businesses had been crucial. In fact, he saw such inequitable distri-

bution of wealth as one of the cornerstones that justified
capitalism:

> In fact, it was precisely the inequality of the distribution
> of wealth which made possible those vast accumulations
> of fixed wealth and of capital improvements which distin-
> guished that age from all others. Herein lay, in fact, the
> main justification of the Capitalist System.... The immense
> accumulations of fixed capital which, to the great benefit
> of mankind, were built up during the half century before
> the war, could never have come about in a society where
> wealth was divided equitably.[7]

Keynes's assertions about the growth-promoting aspects of
wealth concentration have also rendered support to later
economic researchers. There exist economic models that
underscore the necessity for capital to achieve a specific
level of concentration to function effectively as a foundation for investing in profitable enterprises or extending
credit.[8]

Companies did not just rely on bank loans; they also raised
capital via the issuance of shares and bonds. Initially, on
account of their stable return, bonds and other fixed-income
securities dominated investor portfolios. To make equities
more attractive, firms tweaked dividend payouts to mirror
the consistency of bond coupons.[9] Regulatory changes also
aimed to level the informational playing field, combating
perceptions that equities were riskier investments due to
their unpredictable returns and the potential for corporate
malfeasance. Corporate governance laws took shape across
Western nations: in 1844 in the UK, 1848 in Sweden, 1867
in France, and 1870 in Germany.[10] In the US, similar legislation evolved at the state level throughout the nineteenth
century, laying down the legal groundwork for corporate
governance, including nascent protections for minority
shareholders.

Stock exchanges emerged as vital platforms during this
era, facilitating portfolio adjustments in response to changing investor needs and market opportunities. This led to an

uptick in trading volume in secondary markets, which in turn spurred financial asset valuations and contributed to the growth of corporate capital.

3.2 THE RISE OF POPULAR WEALTH

One of the most outstanding revelations from the previous chapter is the dramatic postwar increase in Western wealth–income ratios. The pace and magnitude of growth over the past 140 years, and since the 1990s in particular, has been unparalleled. To delve deeper into the forces driving this extraordinary development, let us explore two separate pathways. First, we will examine a straightforward model of wealth accumulation, breaking down growth into two fundamental components: new savings (volume channel) and capital gains (price channel). Next, we will divide aggregate wealth into three key asset categories: housing wealth, funded pension wealth, and all other assets.

The Economics of Wealth Growth: Saving and Capital Gains

Let us start with the wealth accumulation model, derived from a standard economics framework. This model describes growth by determining that the wealth of today is equal to that of yesterday after supplementing new savings (the portion of income we do not consume) and asset price fluctuations – that is, capital gains. Even though I call this wealth growth, it is important to note that these changes can all be negative and consist of wealth decreases rather than increases. For example, whenever we need to withdraw capital for consumption, we dissave instead of save. Or, when asset prices decline (a scenario many stock market investors experienced in the Great Depression of the 1930s or homeowners faced during the Great Recession of 2008–9), we experience capital losses rather than capital gains. With this in mind, we can express the wealth growth processes as a simple equation:[11]

Wealth growth = Saved income + Asset price increase

Over extended periods, savings are expected to play a more significant role than capital gains in directing wealth growth. This is because relative price changes that generate capital gains actually signal a relative under- or over-supply of the assets in question. For instance, if housing supply falls short of demand, house prices rise, which generates a capital gain (the second term in the equation above). However, the price increase triggers investment in new housing, causing supply to expand and house prices eventually to drop. In this manner, volume changes stemming from new savings and investment counterbalance the wealth changes brought about by capital gains.

Land provides an interesting exception to this rule. It is a non-reproducible factor of production in fixed supply, which means that new land cannot be produced to meet new demands.[12] Real land prices can increase over time without any forces pulling it down and thus give rise to capital gains.

Decomposing Western Wealth Growth: Saving versus Capital Gains

Table 3.1 provides a glimpse into the historical records of wealth growth, saving rates, and capital gains – that is, relative asset price changes – of France, Sweden, and the US since 1870. Total wealth growth is broken down into the relative contribution from saving, which is observed in the historical national accounts for each country, and from capital gains, which is calculated as a residual component.[13]

The numbers in table 3.1 present several fascinating results. One overarching finding is that building wealth through savings accounts for basically all of the recorded growth in our societies over the long run. To see this, look at the final row in the table, which shows the average annual growth rate over the period 1870 to 2010 in all three countries. The wealth growth and the contributions from saving are almost the same, which signifies that, over such a long time period, we need to invest real resources from our incomes in order to accumulate new wealth.

Within shorter time periods, both saving and capital gains matter. For example, in the late nineteenth century up to 1910, saving mattered the most in France and the US, but in Sweden it was capital gains that stood for almost all wealth growth. In my research, I have examined this era in detail. Although the role of saving should be extensive over such a long period of time, Sweden was too poor a country, and its population had too little income to be able to save. The country was still predominantly agrarian, and most of what people and corporations earned was consumed. The lack of savings and domestic capital boosted Swedish capital prices and soon led to capital imports forming the basis for the country's industrialization.[14] Between the two world wars, capital losses dominated France's negative wealth growth. Despite an average contribution from saving 1.9 percent annually, asset prices fell by on average 3.9 percent per year – of course concentrated in the war years, especially during World War II.

The postwar era saw an accumulation in wealth that was driven entirely by saving in all these countries. The post-1980 period, finally, exhibits a similar pattern. Wealth growth rates were almost the same in all the studied countries, around 3 to 4 percent, and saving accounted for most of this. In one of my studies, I take a closer look at the different components of savings within the private sector, and the data show that corporate saving represents most of the growth, whereas household saving was more modest.[15]

The Democratization of Wealth in the Postwar Era

The post-World War II era marked a transformative period. The 1940s and 1950s were decades that ushered in a remarkable transformation in the landscape of wealth ownership.

As illustrated in figure 3.2, the shares of housing and funded pensions in total private-sector wealth experienced a significant upswing in the West. This is the second fact of historical wealth that was highlighted in the introduction. Table 3.1 showed that, from 1950 to 1980, the growth in wealth was fueled primarily by savings, which in this case refers to building homes for a wider population. The increased labor incomes of wage earners during the high-growth eras in the middle of the twentieth century resulted

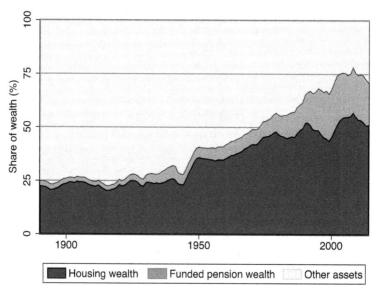

Figure 3.2 The Changing Nature of Wealth in the Twentieth Century

Note: The figure shows average shares of total private-sector wealth from the six countries in our core sample. Housing wealth is the sum of produced assets (buildings) and their associated non-produced assets (land). Funded pension wealth is the sum of funds in occupational pensions and private pensions, together with insurance savings (asset class AF.6 in the national accounts).

Table 3.1 Wealth Growth in France, Sweden, and the US: Savings versus Capital Gains

Annual growth in periods:	France Wealth growth (%)	France Contribution from Saving (%)	France Contribution from Capital gains (%)	Sweden Wealth growth (%)	Sweden Contribution from Saving (%)	Sweden Contribution from Capital gains (%)	United States Wealth growth (%)	United States Contribution from Saving (%)	United States Contribution from Capital gains (%)
1870–1910	1.4	1.5	-0.1	2.7	0.3	2.4	4.0	2.9	1.1
1910–50	-2.2	1.9	-3.9	1.9	1.4	0.5	2.8	2.7	0.1
1950–80	6.6	5.5	1.1	2.4	5.7	-3.1	3.4	3.8	-0.4
1980–2010	3.8	3.0	0.7	4.8	5.3	-0.4	3.2	2.3	0.9
1870–2010	1.4	1.5	-0.1	2.9	2.8	0.1	3.4	2.9	0.5

Note: All numbers in the table refer to average annual growth rates measured in inflation-adjusted currency. Saving rates are measured from the observed income and consumption totals in each country's national accounts. Capital gains, or asset price changes, are estimated on a residual basis.

Source: Data from Waldenström (2017, table 1).

in higher household savings, and most of these savings went into people's housing. We will look deeper into the surge in homeownership and its economic implications in the next chapter. For now, it is worth noting that this housing boom purely impacted the volume of wealth, with house prices becoming a factor only in the 1980s. Furthermore, during the later postwar years, people began saving for retirement in a manner previously unseen. National accounts data reveal funded pension wealth alongside different types of long-term savings, such as life insurance schemes.

We can also break down the average across Western countries in order to examine the developments in the six countries in our core sample separately. Figure 3.3 displays a remarkable synchronicity in the trends of asset owner-ship, although with some notable distinctions. Generally, the share of housing- and pension-based wealth within total private wealth began a significant rise after the 1950s, from a level of around 25 percent in all countries to reach around 75 percent by the year 2000. In Germany and Spain, this growth was delayed, while in Sweden it began earlier.

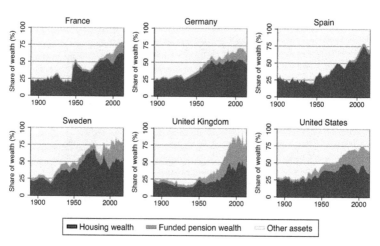

Figure 3.3 The Changing Nature of Wealth in Six Western Countries

Note: The figure shows average shares of total private-sector wealth from the six countries in our core sample.

Noteworthy is the difference in relative importance between housing and pensions across countries. In France, Germany, and Spain, it was the housing sector that primarily fueled wealth growth, overshadowing that in pension savings. In contrast, the US, the UK, and Sweden observed a more balanced growth in both housing and pensions – especially from the 1980s onward. In these latter countries, funded pensions now constitute roughly half of households' financial assets and one-quarter of total wealth.

Since the 1980s, surging asset prices have played an increasingly important role in wealth accumulation. House prices have been a major macroeconomic source of the escalating household wealth observed since 1990. A number of supply-side constraints in the housing market contributed to this. These constraints are of several types, but among the most important have been political regulations at both local and central levels to hinder new construction. Meanwhile, many countries lowered their labor income taxes in the 1980s, and nominal interest rates started falling in the 1990s, which fueled the demand for housing. The supply-side restrictions and elevated demand resulted in a historic boom in house prices seen in all Western economies and a substantial increase in housing wealth.[16]

The role of funded pension wealth should not be overlooked. Political actors and labor market parties agreed to gradually shift the system from pay-as-you-go pensions, where current pensions are financed by fees paid by the working population, to fully funded defined-contribution schemes, where individual or collective pension funds form the basis for payments. This development has been most pronounced in the US, the UK, and Sweden. Since the 1980s, there has also been a general rise in stock prices around the entire Western world, which has made financial asset gains a significant component in the build-up of household wealth.

In their seminal study of British wealth distribution in the twentieth century, Anthony Atkinson and Alan Harrison (1978) described the transformation of assets in household portfolios as the "rise of popular wealth." Through probate inventories, the researchers provided a nuanced view of not just the level but also the composition of assets that UK households held throughout the twentieth century. Housing wealth was central in their storyline, but also the increasing amounts of valuable consumer goods that households started to accumulate over the twentieth century. Let us therefore take a closer look at how important these goods have been in household portfolios over time and in different places.

Cars, Boats, Jewelry: The Role of Consumer Durables and Valuables

Consumer durables are goods that households keep for a long time and that are of notable economic value, such as cars, boats, and electronics. Valuables such as art and jewelry form another category of assets that may be relatively important in people's portfolios. But however relevant these assets may be, they pose several challenges when discussing wealth. In fact, standard practice in the international instructions for computing asset values in the economy usually excludes consumer durables and valuables from household balance sheets and official wealth statistics. The rationale is simple: most goods purchased by households depreciate rapidly, often within the conventional accounting timeframe of a year. Even longer-lasting goods, such as cars or furniture, see their value fall so quickly that they become irrelevant in aggregate accounting. Valuables are excluded simply because they are nearly impossible to observe and record systematically.

However, this strict accounting view tends to clash with reality. Many of these durable goods last much longer than one year. The average American car, for instance, stays with its owner for over eight years, and their values can be of considerable value for many households over this period.[17] How does this matter for the calculation of private wealth totals?

Valuation of these assets is unfortunately far from straight-forward, although it is not impossible. Typical methods begin with the item's purchase price and deduct a certain annual depreciation. A car, for example, loses a third of its value in its first year and another fifth in the second. At the end of five years, it retains only a third of its original value.[18] Valuables such as art and jewelry present another layer of complexity. Though difficult to appraise and often omitted from wealth metrics, they form a negligible part of overall assets.

The datasets underlying the analyses in this book mostly sidestep consumer durables and valuables, following the lead of official statistics. Existing estimates suggest these assets are far from pivotal in overall household wealth; for example, a recent Federal Reserve Board study notes that they make up just 5 percent of total US household assets.[19] Estimates for Sweden are in the same domain, but the share has fluctuated, especially in relation to the increase in car ownership in the postwar era.[20]

However, omitting these items is not without conse-quences. They matter more for households with lesser wealth, meaning their exclusion could underestimate wealth at the bottom and thus distort inequality metrics. Research has illuminated the role these goods play in asset distribu-tion. In the UK, consumer durables have been identified as one of the factors in the century-long trend towards wealth equalization. In modern times, the post-World War II explo-sion in car ownership stands out as a landmark example. A Swedish survey of asset holdings showed that the incidence of car ownership increased more rapidly in low-income pro-fessions than in high-income professions during the middle of the twentieth century, although the overall equalizing role of durables seems to have been modest. A study of the US, however, suggests that the value of durable goods is rel-atively larger in poor households and therefore makes the wealth distribution less unequal.[21]

Yet the bottom line seems to indicate that, despite their importance in individual household economics, consumer durables and valuables do not dramatically alter the land-scape of aggregate wealth or wealth inequality. Given their small share of total assets and the challenges involved in their valuation, their exclusion from most wealth metrics may be defensible but warrants careful consideration, especially when evaluating policies aimed at addressing inequality.

The Asset Composition of Household Portfolios: A Snapshot

How do the results of a rise in housing wealth and pension savings as indicators of people's overall wealth square with individual data on household portfolios? In this section, I present a unique snapshot of the current wealth distribution in Sweden, which exemplifies the extent of this widespread asset ownership.

Figure 3.4 represents the asset portfolios of all adult indi-viduals in Sweden. The picture ranks people from left to right according to the value of their assets. For the households in the bottom half of the distribution, 80 percent of assets comprise dwellings (houses or tenant-owned apartments) or pension savings and similar long-term private savings (pen-sions, insurances, and mutual funds). The remainder consists of bank deposits, which now function as transaction accounts rather than savings vehicles. Elite portfolios within the top percentile are dominated by corporate equity, representing three-quarters of all assets.

In summary, the combined results show that housing and funded pensions became dramatically more important for aggregate wealth, with shares jumping from one-quarter in 1940 to three-quarters in 2000. This shift in the nature of private wealth is recorded for both Europe and the US. The analysis above revealed differences in the relative impor-tance of housing and pension assets between the European countries. Rising housing values are dominant in all coun-tries after 1950, but elevated pension wealth values are also

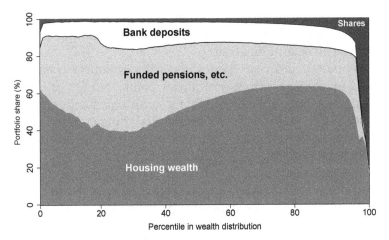

Figure 3.4 The Dominance of Housing and Funded Pensions in People's Wealth

Note: The figure shows the composition of the asset portfolios of Swedish adults in 2007 using data from the country's wealth register. Individuals are ranked from left to right on the x-axis according to the value of their net wealth. "Housing wealth" consists of all property (buildings and land) and also includes value of shares in condominium apartments. "Funded pensions, etc." consists of funded pension savings in occupational defined-contribution pensions and mutual funds. "Bank deposits" are bank deposits and cash. "Shares", finally, contains corporate equity shares in publicly listed and closely held firms.

prominent in Sweden, the UK, and the US, primarily after 1980. Compared to a century ago, the shares of housing and funded pension wealth have thus seen a dramatic increase.

3.3 HOUSEHOLD DEBT OVER THE PAST 130 YEARS

Debt plays an indispensable role in the financial lives of households, facilitating timely investments in housing and entrepreneurship. This book considers wealth in net terms, measuring the sum of asset values minus all outstanding liabilities. This makes it crucial to also explore the trajectory of household debt in Western economies over the past century and more. It is possible that some of the documented wealth changes are the effect of shifts in borrowing behavior rather than in asset accumulation.

Economic historians have studied the evolution of household indebtedness from several viewpoints, but few of these studies examine the role of debt for wealth inequality trends. Instead, the main focus has been on banking credits to the housing sector, investigating how mortgage expansion has affected the stability of the financial system.[22]

Aggregate data over 130 years displayed in figure 3.5 reveal that household debt has grown relative to national income. In the early 1900s, the debt–income ratio ranged from 10 to 20 percent across most nations. Following World War II, this ratio ballooned to between 60 and 120 percent. While comprehensive data from earlier periods are sparse, the broad consensus among researchers points to elevated mortgage borrowing associated with increasing homeownership as the primary driver of debt expansion.[23] Another likely reason for the elevated indebtedness in the modern era is that banks and other financial intermediaries have become better at lending funds and insuring themselves against adverse shocks. Financial industries of today are arguably more efficient in servicing the economy with credit, and this improves the performance of our societies in a great number of ways.

Looking at the specific historical experiences, the figure shows that two nations, Sweden and the UK, display an intriguing deviation – markedly higher debt levels in the early twentieth century. The UK's relative financial maturity and early levels of household borrowing probably reflect the country's general degree of economic and financial development relative to other countries, with London being the world's primary financial center around this time. Sweden's situation calls for a different explanation. Economic historians have pointed to its robust educational and banking reforms in the late nineteenth and early twentieth centuries. These reforms fostered financial literacy and familiarity with credit systems among Swedes. To the extent that we

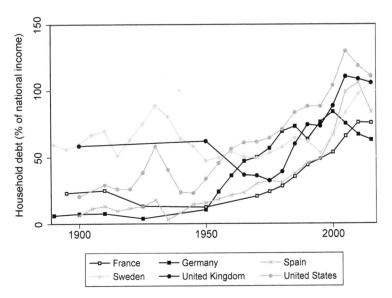

Figure 3.5 Household Indebtedness over 130 Years

Note: The figure shows aggregate amounts of household liabilities, most of it home mortgages, divided by national income, all series in five-year averages.

Source: Data from the same sources as figure 2.2.

can believe in these early data points, it might be that such reforms contributed to setting the stage for a higher level of borrowing among Swedish households.[24]

Some people view debt primarily as a burden on household finances, making people unfree and forced to service lenders at all costs. However, rather than viewing debt as purely detrimental, a more nuanced picture is to see it as a lever used by households during all historical eras to enhance their economic standing. The increased leverage, particularly in housing, enables not just asset accumulation but also social mobility. Taking loans for studying is also highly defendable, enabling people to enhance their educational attainment, so increasing their productivity and lifetime income.

The rising debt to income levels shown in figure 3.5 should therefore be regarded as primarily positive for Western societies and their citizens. Disparity in early twentieth-century debt levels between countries such as Sweden and the UK can be attributed to various historical and institutional factors, underscoring the complexity of the role of debt in the broader context of household wealth.

4

Homes and Pensions: The Pillars of Household Wealth

One morning in 2018, German households were greeted by a harsh news headline: "Wealth Shock: Germans are Poorest in the EU." The news explained bluntly how Germany is out-ranked by all other European countries, except for Portugal, in terms of household wealth. This news may have come as a surprise to many, considering Germany's position as Europe's largest economy.[1]

Unfortunately for the Germans, the numbers are accurate. It has been a recurrent fact in European household wealth surveys over recent years that German citizens rank among the most asset-poor on the continent. The reason behind this gloomy reality for the Germans has a lot to do with home-ownership. In Germany, less than half of the population (49 percent) own their home. This is significantly lower than the percentage in other rich countries such as the US, France, Sweden, and much lower than in Spain, Italy and Portugal, where the figure ranges from 65 percent to 80 percent. Homeownership is one of the pillars of household wealth. Countries with high homeownership rates have a higher average personal wealth compared to countries with lower rates.

In the previous chapter, we learned about the unprece-dented rise in the share of housing and pension wealth in aggregate private wealth in Western countries since the postwar period. In this chapter, we will look deeper into these two pillars of household wealth and explore how they have evolved over time.

The analysis starts by looking at the history of homeownership. How many people owned houses in the past? What led to changes in the rates of homeownership, and what do economists have to say about its importance in household portfolios? Thereafter, we turn to the second major pillar of household wealth: pension savings in funded pension plans. With the average life expectancy having doubled in the past century, people are now living longer in retirement than ever before. At the same time, the financial industry has undergone a revolution, making it easier than ever for households to save in high-return securities at low risk. We will explore how these changes have impacted pension savings in today's society.

4.1 HOMEOWNERSHIP: THE FIRST PILLAR OF HOUSEHOLD WEALTH

In the late 1800s, the majority of people in Europe were tenants. Laborers resided in rented apartments either in the countryside or in the cities. Some of these workers, especially those employed in agriculture, even had housing as part of their contractual income. The owners of this housing ranged from landed nobility to factory owners and wealthy businessmen in the cities. There existed also homeowning households, not least since the enclosure movement that created a new group of self-employed farmers. Many soldiers were also given small land lots and houses after having served in the military.

The idea of homeownership for ordinary people began to take hold among Western populations in the first half of the twentieth century. This concept was imbued with ideals of the "yeoman" farmer and the notion of independent urban workers and middle-class families. Organized movements advocated for an extension of homeownership to new groups in society. In Sweden, a so-called own home (*egnahem*) movement emerged around 1900, encouraging poorer people

– initially mainly agricultural workers, small farmers and low-level civil servants – to acquire their own or improved housing. Later in the century, governments started subsidizing new housing projects and even offered discounted mortgages to low-income families.[2]

Owning a home is perhaps the most prominent cornerstone of the American Dream, and this sentiment has been echoed in Western popular culture for decades. In the film *The Wizard of Oz*, Judy Garland's character, Dorothy, famously declares, "There's no place like home!" Little did moviegoers know that her statement would coincide with the beginning of the largest rise in homeownership in modern US history. In just two decades, from 1940 to 1960, the percentage of American households owning their homes increased from 44 percent to 62 percent.

The US may have led the way, but the postwar era saw rising homeownership rates across Western countries. We can see this in figure 4.1, which uses newly collected historical data, some from as far back as the early 1900s, to document changes over time.

As figure 4.1 shows, all countries in the West have experienced an increase in the percentage of households that own their own homes. In the first half of the twentieth century, the rates were relatively low, hovering around 25 percent in countries such as Germany, the UK, France, and the Netherlands. Meanwhile, in the US, Italy, Sweden, and Spain, the rate was somewhat higher, around 40 percent.

The Historical Rise in Homeownership Rates

In the postwar era, something happened with homeownership in the West. Rates skyrocketed, with most countries experiencing sharp increases during several decades. By the turn of the twenty-first century, the picture had changed dramatically, seeing rates between 60 and 80 percent. Germany is an interesting exception, remaining at a level just below 50 percent.

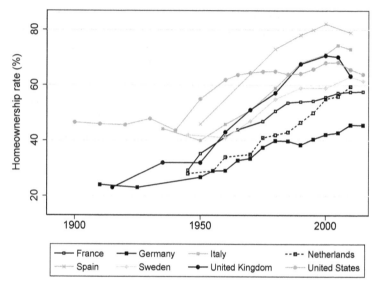

Figure 4.1 Rising Homeownership Rates in the West

Source: Data from Kohl (2017) and later updates on Sebastian Kohl's website (www.sebastiankohl.com).

When zooming in on different countries, it becomes clear that the speed and magnitude of the rise in homeownership was not exactly the same in all countries. In the US, the change happened relatively quickly, taking place over just twenty years in the 1940s and 1950s. Meanwhile, in European countries, the rise in homeownership began later, in the 1950s, and was a more gradual process that lasted for several decades up until the 2000s.

This dramatic increase in homeownership in Western countries has intrigued economists and historians alike. What could explain the developments and also the differences observed among countries? While few cross-country comparisons have been made, several individual case studies have been conducted. In the US, rising real incomes, new suburban living spaces, favorable tax laws, and the GI Bill of 1944, which granted low-interest loans to homecoming veterans and farmers, are among the factors that have been proposed as drivers of the increase in homeownership.[3]

The role of public policy in the historical expansion of homeownership has attracted a lot of scholarly attention. As mentioned, the home loan benefits that were granted in the US during World War II and the Korean War, in particular the GI Bills, have been credited with a central role. But the impact of this policy should not be overestimated, as it coincided with other contemporaneous changes in society that also spurred homeownership, such as the rise of car ownership and road infrastructure that stimulated the construction of new suburban areas.[4] In other countries, different sorts of policies were important. Reforms in Franco's Spain promoted private ownership by introducing tax subsidies to homeowners, subsidizing the construction of affordable housing directed towards low-income families, and imposing strict rent controls that made owning rental apartment buildings unprofitable. The UK policy called "Right to Buy" has had a similar emphasis, offering tenants in so-called council homes the opportunity to purchase their property at a discount.

Some government policies have had the opposite effect, preventing the spread of homeownership to ordinary people. In Germany, the tax code has never been favorable to those needing mortgages to purchase a home. The Swedish Social Democratic government's massive public spending programs in the 1960s and 1970s aimed to boost the construction of publicly owned rental apartment buildings within the so-called million program. This policy effectively crowded out the popular movement of owning one's home, which had its roots in the late nineteenth century.[5]

Homes as Profitable Investments

Owning a home is not only a source of pride but also a financial investment. Indeed, property is typically a homeowner's most valuable asset, central to their financial stature. This investment aspect has long been recognized by politicians and leaders, such as Franklin D. Roosevelt, to whom the following statement has been attributed: "Real estate cannot be lost or stolen, nor can it be carried away. Purchased with common sense, paid for in full, and managed with reasonable care, it is about the safest investment in the world."[6]

But how has housing performed as an investment compared to other investments? A recent research project by American and European economic historians attempted to answer this question by creating a new database with housing and stock market returns in sixteen Western countries over the past 130 years. The findings were remarkable. Residential real estate, not equity, has been the best long-run investment over the past century. While the returns to housing and equity were similar, at around 7 to 8 percent annually, the standard deviation in returns was more than twice as large for equity than for housing. This means that investing in a home has given the same expected return as a stock investment at half the risk. Figure 4.2 depicts this result.

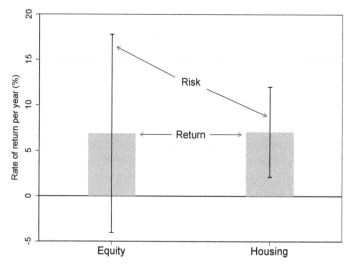

Figure 4.2 Return and Risk in Equity and Housing Investment over the Past 130 Years

Note: Equity denotes publicly listed corporate shares. Housing denotes owned and rented housing. "Risk" is measured as the average real rate of return over the postwar period; it is the standard deviation of real rates of return over the same period.

Source: Data from Jordà et al. (2019).

Owned Homes Depreciate Slower Than Rented Homes

When discussing the economic aspects of homeownership, private property rights play a crucial role. Research has looked into whether homeowners take better care of their homes than renters. As Roosevelt emphasized in the quotation above, taking care of one's property is important. The research literature has specifically asked whether economic depreciation is slower in owned properties than in rented properties. This comes down to assessing the rate of "wear and tear" through which the structure loses value. Measurement problems are of course considerable, since scholars need to infer the quality of housing at two comparable points in time between which the depreciation is measured. One of the most important challenges facing researchers is how to design a convincing identification strategy that meets the empirical standards of today's academic research. Here the biggest difficulty is selection – that is, that people may themselves choose to live in different types of housing. Individuals who know that they will not take good care of their homes may elect to become renters rather than homeowners, and vice versa. In such circumstances, it is difficult to distinguish between the homeowning effect on caretaking and the effect from people being homeowners taking better care of their homes regardless of its kind.

Notwithstanding these challenges, the majority of the findings in these studies suggest that depreciation rates are substantially higher in renter-occupied homes than in owner-occupied homes.[7] Simply put, homeowners do seem to take better care of their homes than renters do.

One of the most convincing recent studies of the effects of homeownership is an investigation looking into an unusual policy experiment in Stockholm during the 2000s. In this case, there was a sudden change in the composition of the Swedish government, which gave rise to a law that abruptly halted the selling of government-owned rental apartment buildings to their tenants. As a consequence of the quick implementation of the new law, some large apartment complexes came to consist both of tenant-owned and rental apartments. This meant that almost identical housing units, and households, were separated from one another based only on whether tenants had been given the opportunity to purchase their home or not. Such a near-experimental situation with both a treated and a control group offers excellent opportunities for causal analysis.

By comparing subsequent outcomes the researchers made several interesting findings. First, housing collateral allows households to borrow against their housing wealth and to smooth consumption in the face of an adverse income shock. Second, homeownership promotes geographic mobility. Moving rates of young households increase substantially after privatization. Some of these households use their accumulated housing wealth to climb the property ladder by making a down payment on a home in a better neighborhood. Third, homeownership interacts with portfolio choice. Older households increase the risky share of assets, consistent with the rise in home equity they experience. The concomitant increase in borrowing capacity effectively makes them less risk-averse.[8]

Overall, a large body of research suggests that owning a home not only provides a sense of security and stability but also serves as a valuable asset that usually appreciates over time. In light of the historical expansion of homeownership around the Western world, where today a majority of households own their homes, these results may also have distributional implications. We will return to this issue in the analysis of wealth inequality below.

4.2 PENSION SAVINGS: THE SECOND PILLAR OF HOUSEHOLD WEALTH

Funded pension savings serve as a largely underestimated cornerstone of household wealth. Contrary to popular belief, many individuals hold significant amounts in pension wealth of which they are now always aware. In these cases, they significantly undervalue their true financial worth because they disregard this form of deferred income as an asset. Recent data also bear out this point; for instance, a survey found that 75 percent of adults in the UK were unaware of the actual status of their pension accounts.[9]

The neglect concerning the importance of pension funds to one's financial standing is not limited to the general public; it also manifests in scholarly work on wealth inequality. In studies such as my own on Sweden's private wealth accumulation and distribution through history, the role of funded pensions received scant attention.[10] Atkinson and Harrison's influential 1978 study also sidestepped the issue, possibly due to data constraints. In their defense, pension funds did not start to bulk up household portfolios until after the 1970s, when financial markets were unregulated and years of economic growth could be fully capitalized in asset prices.[11]

How Funded Pension Savings Took Off after 1980

The widespread lack of awareness of the role of pension savings in household portfolios is actually quite remarkable given the amounts that wage earners have stored in these funds. Chapter 3 showed that the expansion of capitalized pensions began in the postwar era and took off in the 1980s. Figure 4.3 shows this development in concrete numbers. In 1980, the total value of pension funds in OECD countries was $0.8 trillion (in 2021 US$). Forty-one years later, in 2021, the amount had grown to $39 trillion.[12]

To see the full scope of the growth in funded pension assets in recent decades, we can relate it to other outcomes. Looking at the total size of household balance sheets, pension funds today account for between one-tenth and one-third of all household wealth in Western countries and up to half of all financial assets owned by households. Since 1980, the figure above shows that pension funds increased fiftyfold

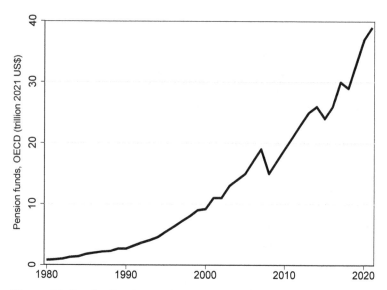

Figure 4.3 Pension Fund Assets in OECD Countries, 1980–2021 (2021 US$ trillion)

Note: The figure shows the total value of pension fund assets in OECD countries. Pension funds are defined as assets bought with the contributions to a pension plan for the exclusive purpose of financing benefits. Country coverage is poor in the 1980s and increases over time, but this should not affect the overall trend too much.

Source: Data from OECD (2021) and from OECD's pension funds' assets (doi: 10.1787/d66f4f9f-en).

in constant US$. But the rest of the economy also grew, and we should perhaps therefore relate the development to the overall size of the economy. Figure 4.4 shows that, when dividing pension savings growth by GDP, there is still a sixfold increase, which is substantial. Funded pension savings have become a key asset, the second "pillar," in household wealth of the populations in Western countries.

What were the causes of the large increases in pension savings during the postwar era? In this section I will empha-size three factors that stand out: longer life expectancy, securitization of pension systems, and overall increases in financial asset prices.

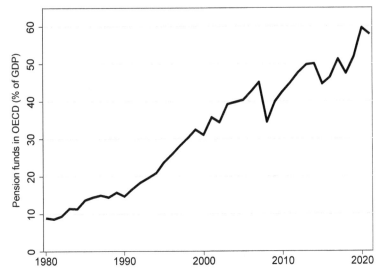

Figure 4.4 Pension Fund Assets as a Share of GDP, OECD, 1980–2021

Note: The figure shows the total value of pension fund assets divided by GDP in OECD countries.

Source: Data from OECD (2021) and from OECD's pension funds' assets (doi: 10.1787/d66f4f9f-en).

Higher Life Expectancy

We can see in figure 4.5 that lifespans have been increasing since the 1920s. When this is compared to the statutory retirement age, which in Western countries varied around sixty to sixty-five years during the twentieth century, it becomes clear that people are living longer after retirement.[13] This demographic trend has led to an increased willingness among people to save for their later years. Although some of the increase in life expectancy can be attributed to reduced infant mortality, the fact that people are living longer and healthier lives due to improved healthcare and elderly care has also played a significant role in the need for pension savings. The longer the lifespan, the greater the need for financial security during retirement.[14]

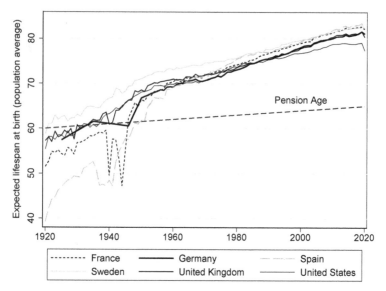

Figure 4.5 Rising Life Expectancy in the Twentieth Century

Note: The figure shows life expectancy at birth, reported in five-year averages. The dashed line "Pension Age" going from sixty to sixty-five years approximates the level and upward in Western countries (see OECD, 2011, chapter 1).

Source: Data from https://ourworldindata.org/life-expectancy.

Securitization of Pensions

A second factor behind the increasing importance of funded pension savings is the organizational transition in many countries from traditional pay-as-you-go systems to funded pensions with securitized pension rights. In the US, this transition began in the 1970s with the Employee Retirement Income Security Act of 1974, while the other Western countries started shifting to funded systems in the 1980s and 1990s. Under the traditional pension system, current workers finance pensions for retirees. In contrast, under the funded pension scheme, workers accumulate pension wealth through contributions made during their working lives which later make up their future income.

There were several motivations for making the transition to funded pensions. One key weakness of the traditional pay-as-you-go system was its financial sustainability. As populations age, fewer workers support more retirees, creating financial strain, while a fully funded system is more financially sustainable since each individual's pension is financed by their own contributions over time. Shifting to a funded system might also present a solution to the current demographic crisis. This approach substitutes declining human capital with real capital and aids in evenly distributing tax burdens and child-rearing expenses across different generations.[15]

Another weakness with the unfunded system is its dependence on the policyholder's financial status. During financial crises, the value of pensions could be debased by the overall size of the system becoming reduced, which would shrink the income stream for retirees.

A Financial Market Boom since 1980 Has Raised the Value of Pension Funds

A third contributing factor to the rise of funded pensions has been booming asset prices in Western financial markets since 1980. In a fully funded system, contributions are invested and often yield higher returns than the pay-as-you-go system could provide through taxation. This means that shifting from the traditional defined-benefit pensions to defined-contribution pensions potentially leads to larger payouts. Mutual funds have also accelerated the securitization of pension systems. The mutual fund is a financial innovation that democratizes finance, offering ordinary ill-informed savers the potential for high returns with low risk. Because of this, mutual funds quickly spread throughout the Western world in the 1980s and later, and today they form the standard vehicle for household financial savings.

Some Critical Remarks about the Transition to Funded Pensions

Naturally, the funded pension system is not flawless. Some critics point to the increased exposure to risk on account of stock market volatility. In some cases, this criticism can be valid, especially when workers' pension funds are placed in the stock of single companies. For example, the scandalous episodes of the Enron and WorldCom pension crises saw these companies go bankrupt in the early 2000s, which nullified the pensions of thousands of retired workers as the funds had been placed mainly in Enron and WorldCom shares. However, in most cases, pension funds are placed in well-diversified mutual funds that are constructed to distribute risk across many securities while maintaining high average returns.

Another critique against pension securitization argues that transitioning from pay-as-you-go to funded pensions may appear costly if funds have not been built up sufficiently. However, many countries have gradually made this shift over several years. Most pay-as-you-go systems have actually been more costly on the whole, which has motivated some countries to move away from them. Furthermore, the unfunded pay-as-you-go systems are not risk-free, as their funding weakens during economic downturns when unemployment rises and pension fees decline.

Some people have expressed skepticism towards an increased role for pension fund companies in managing these institutionalized household savings, which has made them major stakeholders in many corporations. This phenomenon has been referred to as "funded capitalism," in which the institutional owners hold large corporate ownership stakes around the Western world.[16] A concern is that pension fund institutions are perhaps less active or more shortsighted than smaller private owners. Some research studies have tried to examine whether this is the case, but it is fair to say that no consensus has yet been reached on this issue.[17]

Funded Pensions: A Success Story

Taking stock, it is safe to say that the historical shift to capitalized pensions, invested in the world's securities markets, that has taken place in many countries, at least in part, has been a resounding success. Funded pensions offer a sustainable, transparent high-return, low-risk system. Since the 1980s, stock market capitalization has increased tenfold in all developed countries because of market deregulation, tax reforms, and technological developments. Capital account liberalization has enabled pension funds to be invested around the world, lowering risk and raising returns for the average pension saver. The timing of the pension securitization reforms in the 1990s was almost perfect, coming at a time when the market was ripe for investment.

Part II
Wealth Inequality

5

The Great Wealth Equalization of the Twentieth Century

Wealth and power are often the subjects of envy, admiration, and suspicion. The media is well aware of this, and it happily showcases the extreme fortunes of the world's wealthiest individuals. Seeing the pictures of their lifestyles, with mansions, yachts, private jets, and even space travels, could give the impression that wealth inequality today has reached unprecedented levels.[1] However, as I will show in this chapter, this is not the case. Wealth was far more uneven in the distant past, and, in most Western countries, inequality has not increased much over the recent years.

Before we dive in, let's be clear: there are people today who are immensely rich, even by historical standards. Gaps in wealth between the richest and the poorest are enormous, and this is true also with respect to average middle-class families. When discussing inequality, however, we also need to consider the wealth of the non-rich. That is, we look at differences in wealth between the rich, the poor, and everyone in between. This means assessing the wealth holdings of the entire population, not just the top.

Wealth inequality is a complex but fascinating societal phenomenon. It is undeniable that wealth concentration is high today. The wealthiest 10 percent of Western societies own around 60 percent of all marketable wealth. By comparison, the same fraction of the income distribution earns only circa 30 percent of all income, revealing that wealth inequality is twice as high as income inequality (measured by the Gini coefficient, which is about 0.75 for wealth and 0.35 for disposable income).

However, our interpretation of this high wealth concentration depends on several parameters, and the same goes for how we think about trends in wealth inequality. For example, how people become rich matters for how we judge their position. Self-made entrepreneurs who have spent years of hard work to establish a business that offers new products or services to willing customers, hire people who earn an income, and pay taxes to government are often regarded as deserving their wealth. People who become wealthy because of luck, perhaps from windfall gains through unexpected stock market or house price increases, might be a more difficult call for some. As for changes in wealth inequality, this also calls for a closer look before any quick judgements can be made. A decrease in wealth inequality could arise from a reduction in wealth among the rich, or it could be the result of an increase in wealth among poor or middle-class households without changing that of the richest at all. The complexity of wealth inequality therefore calls for informed analysis in order to make balanced judgements.

In this chapter, we will explore wealth inequality in the Western world by analyzing the latest available historical wealth inequality series. Focus will be on top wealth shares, which is the primary inequality metric available far back in history. The chapter will take us back to the past 130 years, examining how wealth concentration has changed over this long period of time. The main results show that wealth concentration has actually plummeted in the entire Western world over the past century. Wealth inequality a century ago was about three times larger than it is today, with Europe seeing a starker equalization than the US. While it has not changed much in Europe since the 1980s, it has increased in the US. We also zoom in on the super-rich, exploring whether the same economic rules that govern the economy as a whole also apply to this exclusive elite.

Finally, the chapter takes a look at the lower end of the distribution. I first ask how concerned we should be about large groups of people who lack personal wealth. It turns out that many of the wealthless people are not in bad economic shape but are simply young or people living in a welfare state where not only taxes are high, but so are public spending on welfare services such as schools, healthcare and elderly care. The actual wealth status of those who lack personal wealth may be different when accounting for the capitalized value of future incomes coming from pensions and other social insurance transfers, an issue which I will revisit in chapter 8. The chapter ends with a brief discussion about racial and gender disparities in wealth. These types of inequality are not studied anywhere near as much as differences in household wealth, mainly because of a general lacuna in the information about the background characteristics of wealth holders. I review some of the main findings about race and gender in the Western wealth distributions and their developments over time.

5.1 THE EVOLUTION OF WEALTH INEQUALITY OVER THE PAST 130 YEARS

Top wealth shares are the main measures of inequality utilized by scholars in the historical wealth literature. A top wealth share shows how large a fraction of total wealth in the economy is owned by a small proportion of the richest households. Although it may be interesting to study the elite groups themselves, a practical reason for examining their relative position is that they are the most homogeneously observed group in most countries' historical data. Early tax systems focused on the wealthiest groups, since that is where the money was, and therefore collected their wealth in a consistent fashion over long periods of time. Relating the wealth of the richest to estimates of the total wealth in the economy, which can be computed in part from other sources, thus allows scholars to measure the top wealth shares consistently over time, and this can also be done for several Western countries offering similar administrative source materials.[2]

Falling Top Wealth Shares Over the Twentieth Century

Figure 5.1 provides a first glimpse into the long-run evolution of wealth distribution by depicting the wealth shares of the richest 10 percent in France, Sweden, the UK, and the US. Perhaps some people think that one-tenth of the population seems too small a fraction to be representative of the entire population. But taking a look at the numbers on the vertical axis of figure 5.1 is revealing. In the early twentieth century, this elite group held around 90 percent of all private wealth in each of the Western economies. That is, a tenth of house-

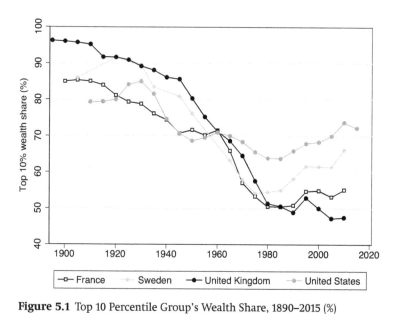

Figure 5.1 Top 10 Percentile Group's Wealth Share, 1890–2015 (%)

Note: The figure shows the share of total private wealth held by the richest tenth, or the top decile group, of each country's adult population. All series are in five-year averages.

Sources: See the list in figure 5.2.

holds owned nine-tenths of all wealth. Today, this elite group has lost a sizeable share of its position. The figure shows a stark equalization in all countries over the past century but, despite this, the top tenth still owns well above half of all private wealth in the country. In other words, tracking the richest decile group thus gives us a fairly representative picture of the overall distribution of wealth over time.

Looking more closely at the numbers, the figure shows that the top decile share started falling in the 1920s in France and the UK and in the 1940s in Sweden and the US. Then wealth inequality fell steadily until the 1980s, when this trend stopped. In 1980, the top decile group's wealth shares were between 50 and 65 percent in these Western economies, which can be compared with shares between 80 and 95 percent in 1910. Since 1980, the shares have remained historically low. In Sweden, the share has increased somewhat, but it has been stable in the other European countries and also in the United States.

Let us now turn to an even more exclusive group in the wealth elite: the top percentile group and their share of total wealth. This is by far the most studied top group in the past inequality literature concerning both income and wealth distribution. Figure 5.2 presents top percentile wealth shares since 1890 for the core country sample used in the above analyses: France, Germany, Spain, Sweden, the UK, and the US.[3] This is one of the key illustrations of the book, demonstrating the dramatic fall in wealth concentration over the past century. This is the third fact of historical wealth I talked about in the introduction.

Around the outbreak of World War I, wealth ownership was extremely unequal throughout the Western world. The richest percentiles in Europe owned between 50 and 70 percent of all wealth. In the US, the top percentile's wealth share was lower, around 45 percent. From a wealth perspective, Europe was thus a more unequal continent than North America at the beginning of the twentieth century. From the 1920s to the 1970s, however, the situation changed dramatically. During this period, all these countries experienced large

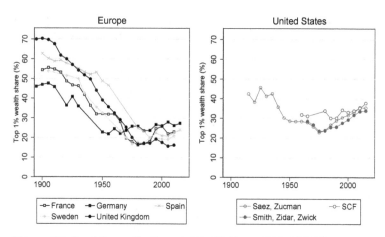

Figure 5.2 Top 1 Percentile Group's Wealth Share, 1895–2015 (%)

Note: The figure shows the share of total private wealth held by the richest one-hundredth (top percentile group) in the adult population. All series are in five-year averages.

Sources: France: Garbinti, Goupille-Lebret and Piketty (2021), Piketty, Postel-Vinay and Rosenthal (2006); Germany: Albers, Bartels and Schularick (2022); Spain: Alvaredo and Artola Blanco (2023) for 1901–58, Martínez-Toledano (2020) for 1984–2015; Sweden: Roine and Waldenström (2009), Lundberg and Waldenström (2018); UK: Alvaredo et al. (2018); US: "Saez, Zucman" is Saez and Zucman (2016, 2020), "Smith, Zidar, Zwick" is Smith, Zidar and Zwick (2023), "SCF" (Survey of Consumer Finances) is Wolff and Marley (1989), Sabelhaus and Volz (2020).

declines in wealth concentration. The UK saw the most dramatic fall, from a staggering 73 percent in 1901 to 16 percent in 1984 – a collapse in the top percentile's wealth by more than four-fifths. Similarly, France's top percentile dropped from 57 percent in 1905 to 16 percent in 1984, Spain's from 65 percent in 1901 to 19 percent in 1993, Sweden's from 54 percent in 1908 to 17 percent in 1995, and Germany's from 48 percent in 1908 to 21 percent in 1969. The US experienced a wealth equalization similar to that of Europe, with the top share dropping from 45 percent in 1913 to between 20 and 23 percent in 1978.[4]

Despite some differences between the countries, such as the timing of the equalization, a common trend is evident: all countries have moved from extremely high levels of wealth inequality a century ago to significantly lower levels today. In France, the top decile share began declining in the 1920s, while in Sweden and the UK the decline started after World War II. The US, however, saw its largest fall in the early 1930s, during the Great Depression. Although the Depression had an impact on European economies as well, their elites were apparently able to avoid the same level of damage.

In the postwar era, European top shares fell sharply until the 1980s, after which they remained at historically low levels. The US also experienced a slight fall in top wealth shares in the early postwar period, but not to the same extent as Europe. By around 1980, the US top decile share was 65 percent, compared to 50 percent in Europe.

Wealth Inequality since 1980

From the 1980s onward, the top percentile wealth shares in Europe and the US have followed different patterns. While they have remained relatively stable in the European countries, with top shares ranging from 15 to 25 percent of total wealth, the US has experienced a significant increase in wealth concentration. From the early 1980s to the most recent observations in the late 2010s, France's top share increased from 17 to 18 percent, Germany's increased from 26 to 27 percent, Spain's decreased from 25 to 24 percent, Sweden's increased from 18 to 21 percent, and the UK's decreased from 17 to 16 percent.[5] This almost four-decade-long stability is remarkable and challenges the common belief that there have been "growing wealth gaps" in Europe in recent years.

One of the key findings is thus that the years since 1980 have been characterized by stable and historically low wealth concentration levels in Western countries. Figure 5.3 examines this latter period more closely, displaying annual data points instead of the five-year averages used in most of the book's figures. The conclusion remains the same. Some countries have experienced increases in top wealth shares:

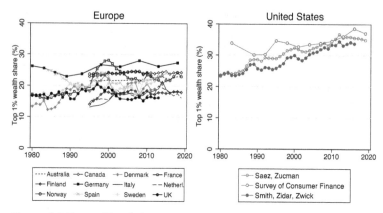

Figure 5.3 Recent Trends in Top 1 Percent Wealth Shares in Europe and the US

Source: See figures 5.2 and 5.4.

Canada, for example, went from 24 percent in 1984 to 29 percent in 2012, and Italy went from 16 percent in 1995 to 23 percent in 2015.[6] Although these changes are not insignificant within this relatively short time period, they are relatively small when considering the extensive historical equalization or when comparing them with the US levels and trends.

Widespread Historical Wealth Equalization in the Western World

How well do the six countries studied above represent the Western world as a whole? While they are the only ones for which I have been able to collect all the essential historical series required for the analyses in this book, it is crucial that the evidence demonstrates external validity, reflecting patterns in other parts of the West as well. To achieve this, I have collected additional evidence of top percentile wealth shares for eight other countries. The data for these countries are more scattered in terms of sources and methods used, and they cover shorter time spans.[7] For each of these new countries, I also present two series. One, called "Observed,"

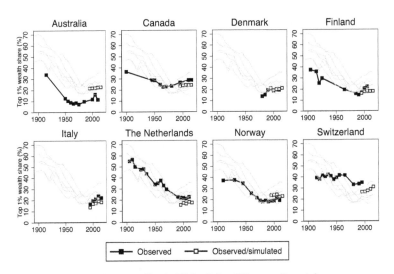

Figure 5.4 Wealth Inequality in Eight Other Western Countries

Note: The series show the top 1 percentile share of total private wealth, with some differences in definitions of wealth and populations.

Sources: Observed and simulated data series from World Inequality Database (www.wid.world) are available from 1995, displayed as hollow squares. Observed series for Australia, Finland, the Netherlands, Norway, and Switzerland are available from Roine and Waldenström (2015) (see specific country sources therein), for Canada from Davies and Di Matteo (2020), for Denmark from Jakobsen et al. (2020), and for Italy from Acciari, Alvaredo, and Morelli (2024).

is based on historical source materials in the form of tabulated distributional evidence, often covering some years in the first half of the past century. The other, "Observed/simulated," comes from a specific international database that contains series with a later start date, in 1995, but offers more comparable and meticulously researched estimates.[8]

Figure 5.4 presents the eight new countries in separate panels, plotted against the five European countries from figure 5.2, which are depicted as gray lines. Overall, these additional countries display a remarkable consistency in long-run wealth inequality trends with those reported earlier. In Australia, Canada, Finland, the Netherlands, and Norway, the long-run equalization trend is clearly evident. The exact magnitude of the decline varies slightly, which could reflect either genuine differences or simply measurement errors. Switzerland stands out by exhibiting a much weaker trend, although it seems to have experienced a reduction in wealth gaps in recent years.

It is fascinating to observe that the European countries demonstrate such a strong common trend in wealth equalization, even during a historical period of such extremely diverse political developments and economic outcomes. This of course raises questions about the role of wars in wealth equalization, which some scholars emphasize as the central element in any lasting wealth equalization. How they can do so becomes even more puzzling when considering that, in the wars of the twentieth century, some countries were winners, one was a big loser, and two did not even participate, and yet they all followed a common pattern. I will delve into this issue and other potential driving factors of wealth inequality in chapter 6.

In summary, the main takeaway from broadening the database to include a larger sample of Western countries and focusing on the post-1980 period reinforces the main empirical results. The Great Wealth Equalization of the twentieth century and the subsequent low inequality since 1980 seem indeed to be general patterns across the Western world, maybe with the partial exception of the US, which emerges as an outlier.

Why Was Wealth Inequality So High in 1900?

Among all the facts shown so far, one of the most striking features to me has been the degree of inequality in the Western countries at the turn of the twentieth century. Data show that the richest percentile owned more than half of all wealth, and in the UK they held over two-thirds. What could explain such extreme levels of inequality?

The historical wealth literature offers some potential accounts. Industrial expansion had a direct impact on a unique build-up of new large financial fortunes. Studies of French wealth elites using estate tax returns data from the late nineteenth century showcase a rapid accumulation of industrialist and financier fortunes during this escalating industrialization era, adding to the already existing affluence of the landed elites of the aristocracy.[9] The role of technology and demography offers another explanation. One study shows that inequality, using the ratio between land rents and real wages, was driven up by technological progress and population growth in several European countries.[10] Since land was concentrated among the wealthy, this likely contributed to a markedly high inequality of wealth before the fertility transition began and low-income groups started to have fewer children.[11]

These explanations imply that wealth inequality may not always have been rampant before 1900 but, rather, that the extreme level around that time is a snapshot of inequality when it was approximately at its highest level. Although it is fair to say that, on account of the lack of reliable sources, consensus is not reached regarding pre-industrial wealth inequality, there is some recent evidence pointing in this direction. Several new research studies present evidence from different European countries and subregions, and most of the series suggest that inequality was increasing during the eighteenth and nineteenth centuries to reach a peak level around 1900.[12]

A Debate about Trends in Top Wealth Shares in the US

In contrast to Europe, the concentration of wealth in the US has been on the rise, although the extent of this increase is currently a matter of debate among researchers. The debate revolves around both data and methodology, with the benchmark data on US wealth inequality trends coming until recently from the triannual Survey of Consumer Finances (SCF) run by the Federal Reserve Board.[13] According to the SCF, the top percentile wealth share remained relatively stable at between 30 and 35 percent between 1963 and 2010. After that, it increased slightly to between 35 and 38 percent until 2020. The only other available series was based on estate tax records associated with a small group of super-rich Americans, which showed low and stable inequality throughout the post-1980 period.

In 2016, Emmanuel Saez and Gabriel Zucman, both of the University of California, reintroduced an old method, the capitalization approach, to estimate top wealth shares. The method involves dividing capital income tax records by an assumed rate of return to get the wealth stock.[14] This approach has a lot of advantages, including being able to use annual data on taxed capital income and aggregate household wealth. Saez and Zucman's results showed a drastic increase in wealth inequality, from 23 percent in 1978 to 42 percent in 2012.

But it is well known that the capitalization approach is sensitive to the assumptions made about rates of return. Several studies have shown that returns can vary considerably across assets and wealth holders, and that this could influence estimates both of amounts and of inequality.[15] A replication study that used the same capitalization method and data but varied the assumed rates of return, especially for fixed-interest securities, found lower top wealth holdings and a slower increase in wealth concentration since 1990. Its new estimate for the top percentile wealth share in 2012 was 32 percent, which was 10 percentage points lower than that of Saez and Zucman.[16]

Despite the ongoing academic discussion concerning the exact trajectories of recent wealth inequality in America, it remains indisputable that this was lower than European wealth inequality a century ago and that it has increased in recent decades, landing at substantially higher levels than in Europe.

Wealth Shares in the Bottom, Middle and Top

To better understand the evolution of inequality over time, researchers have combined the evidence for the top decile and the top percentile to construct estimates covering the entire population. In figure 5.5, such data are shown for France, Sweden, the UK, and the US, depicting wealth shares of three broad groups in society: the rich in the top percentile ("Top 1%"), the upper middle class in the top decile's lower nine percentiles ("Next 9%"), and the rest in the bottom 90 percentiles ("Lowest 90%").

The figure does not add any new information, but it clarifies the wealth inequality patterns in two specific respects. The first is that the bottom nine decile groups of the wealth distribution have seen a remarkable surge in their share. In the UK, for example, this went from 5 percent in 1900 to 50 percent in 1990. In France and Sweden, it rose from somewhat higher levels in the early era and reached 50 percent around 1980. In the US, the bottom 90 percentiles realized

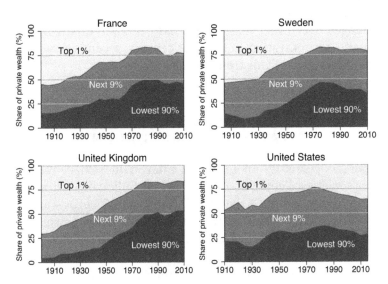

Figure 5.5 Long-Run Trends in the Wealth Distribution in Four Countries

Source: Data are based on figures 5.1 and 5.2.

their highest level in the 1910s, above 20 percent, but never reached 50 percent, and barely attained 40 percent over the entire postwar era.

The second interesting finding from the combined data is that the group gaining during the interwar period consisted of intermediate rich people in the lower part of the top decile, the upper middle class. In order to better understand this group of wealth holders, a study of Swedish wealth inequality trends during this time exploited a specific feature of the tax administration data. What made it unique was that it allowed for a matching of incomes and wealth holdings across different groups, thereby shedding light on the role of income for wealth accumulation in the upper middle class. The results showed that the intermediate rich exhibiting relative wealth growth were in fact professionals, whose pay improved so that they started accumulating wealth. By contrast, the richest percentile did not acquire new wealth at the same speed and therefore lost shares to those immediately below.[17]

Overall, by looking at the trends for the top decile and the top percentile, we can see how wealth distribution has changed over time. While there has been a dramatic fall in wealth concentration in the past century, recent years have seen a reversal of this trend in the US.

5.2 DID THE SUPER-RICH ESCAPE THE GREAT WEALTH EQUALIZATION?

There is currently an immense interest in rich people in our societies. People at the top of the billionaire listings – Elon Musk, Bernard Arnault, Bill Gates, or Jeff Bezos – are as famous as the superstars in the movie or pop businesses and far better known to the common man than almost any president, author or, for that matter, researcher. In the context of understanding trends in wealth concentration, this section asks whether the super-rich managed to escape the profound wealth equalization over the twentieth century or if they too saw their relative positions decline over time.[18] A lingering question concerns the type of equalization the economy truly requires. Does the downfall of a billionaire, perhaps due to an external shock to their business or a regulatory action severely impacting their operations, benefit society at large? Or is a more advantageous form of equalization achieved through the dynamic mechanisms of the market economy, where others, through intense yet fair competition, catch up and possibly surpass those at the top?

How Wealthy Are the Richest Today in Historical Perspective?

Before examining the historical trends, let us first ask how the wealthiest people today compare to the richest in history. The economist Branko Milanović made an intriguing observation by comparing the wealth of Microsoft owner Bill Gates to that of the wealthiest individuals in history. In 2005, Gates's $50 billion fortune would have generated an annual expected return equivalent to the annual earnings of 75,000 workers. That would put him ahead of the Roman triumvir Marcus Crassus in 50 BCE, whose wealth generated an income equal to the annual earnings of 32,000 workers, and Andrew Carnegie, whose wealth could have purchased the labor of 48,000 workers. However, Gates still came in second place to the Gilded Age tycoon John D. Rockefeller, whose wealth could have purchased the labor of 116,000 workers.[19]

Let us also take a look at the wealthiest Swede today and a century ago. In a unique survey of the country's wealth tax register in 1914, the listings showed that Emil Possehl, a German-Swedish iron merchant and Lubeck senator, was recorded as the richest man, with a taxable wealth of 42 million Swedish kronor. Assuming an annual nominal return of 7 percent, that would yield an annual income equivalent to the earnings of almost 4,000 workers. Fast forward to today, and the owner of H&M, Stefan Persson, is probably (we cannot tell for sure) the richest Swede, commanding a fortune worth around 150 billion Swedish kronor ($15 billion), a fortune that could yield an average annual return of 5 percent, which is around 12,500 times the earnings of each worker.[20] Measured in numbers of laborers' incomes, today's richest Swede is thus three times richer than the richest Swede a century ago. In addition, the lower Swedish multiples compared to the American ones square well with our understanding of the role of market size for returns to market leadership.

It is thus clear that the wealth of the super-rich today is of historic proportions. Even compared to the wealthiest individuals in history, today's super-rich have a commanding presence over labor that in some respects dwarfs that of their predecessors.

Who Are the Super-Rich and How Do We Measure Their Fortunes?

Measuring the wealth of the most affluent individuals poses numerous challenges. Many household surveys run by governments fail to capture the richest people, leading to an underestimation of wealth inequality. If even a few of those who are most well-to-do are included in the sample, the top wealth shares will increase significantly. Recent academic research has highlighted the sensitivity of top fortune estimations to sampling, with a few families potentially having a significant impact on top wealth trends.[21]

Some studies have turned to journalistic rich lists to expand the coverage of the very top of the distribution. These sources have become increasingly reliable over the past four decades, with annual publications of data on global wealth stocks and distributional outcomes. For example, the *Global Wealth Report* merges available household survey data with the estimated fortunes of US$ billionaires listed by *Forbes* magazine for all countries in the world.[22] Ultimately, despite challenges in accurately measuring the wealth of the super-rich, it is clear that their fortunes are of historic proportions.

It is difficult to estimate the wealth of the super-rich accurately, and even the rich lists have their limitations. The magazines in which they appear do not offer systematic methods and reliable data for estimating wealth, and they view their data as proprietary value added, which makes it difficult to ensure the quality of their estimates. One problem is that the named listed individuals could represent a whole family or even a clan consisting of dozens of family members. One study that tried to look into this issue found that the number of wealth holders would have to be at least doubled for each listed fortune when attaching it to administrative population or wealth data. The effect is more diluted wealth in the top and smaller top wealth shares.[23]

One of the biggest challenges is to estimate the value of corporate equity correctly in closely held companies that are not listed on stock exchanges and whose shares are being traded regularly. Owners who cannot easily sell the shares of these companies will discount their value. However, the discounts used by magazines tend to be too small, and that leads them to overestimate asset values.[24]

Debts are typically less openly disclosed in public sources and therefore unknown to journalists and other outside observers. This can be an important problem in determining overall wealth. For instance, Robert Maxwell, the British media tycoon, was listed as one of the richest men in the world in rich lists, but after his death it was revealed that he was actually almost bankrupt on account of hidden debts. Another challenge is determining the extent to which the most affluent have portions of their wealth hidden in offshore havens. The issue of offshore wealth will be discussed in more detail in chapter 7.

To overcome some of these difficulties and operationalize the analysis of the super-rich, researchers have often come to define this group based on distributional data. A common approach is to classify the super-rich as those whose wealth is extensive enough to qualify for the richest ten-thousandth in the adult population – the top 0.01 percentile group. This group is the elite within the elite within the elite, or the richest percentile of the richest percentile. Naturally, there are other ways to define this group, but studies have shown that most variants deliver by and large the same overall patterns.[25]

The dynamics of entry and exit at the pinnacle of the wealth distribution are often overlooked but are crucial in understanding the super-rich and their relative standing. Tracking the super-rich over time might suggest a stable, homogeneous group, yet in reality the composition of this elite fluctuates significantly, as individuals and families ascend into or drop out of this category. For instance, a study of Sweden's wealthiest families revealed that only thirteen of the 147 billionaire families listed in 2014 were also on the list in 1964 – a mere 9 percent. Similarly, a comparison of billionaires listed in 2021 with those in 1991 showed that only thirty-two of the 542 listed in 2021 were also listed two decades earlier, representing 6 percent.[26] Another vital aspect of mobility within the elite is the proportion of self-made entrepreneurs versus those who have inherited their wealth. This topic, particularly the role of inheritance in shaping long-term wealth inequality trends, will be further explored in chapter 9.

No, the Super-Rich Did Not Escape the Great Equalization

Given the documented historical trend of wealth equalization in the West, a pertinent question arises: have the super-rich managed to evade the phenomenon? If so, does it suggest that the decline in wealth inequality was due largely to the financial woes of the intermediate rich rather than the relative decline of the super-rich? Research on financial crises indicates this to be the case. The study found that those with relatively less wealth among the affluent had larger debts, leaving them more exposed to financial turmoil. On the other hand, the wealthiest had greater capacity to bear losses and still maintain a positive net position, making them less vulnerable.[27]

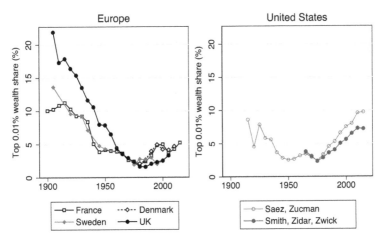

Figure 5.6 The Wealth Share of the Super-Rich Over 130 Years

Source: The wealth shares of the richest ten-thousandth (top 0.01 percent) use the same data as in figure 5.2 and Jakobsen et al. (2020) for Denmark.

Figure 5.6 showcases the top 0.01 percentile wealth shares in five countries over the past century, revealing an interesting trend. Despite their immense wealth and influence, the super-rich were not immune to the effects of wealth equalization, particularly in Europe. For example, in the UK, they saw their wealth share drop from a staggering 20 percent in 1910 to less than 2 percent in the early 1980s, representing an implosion of their relative position. Similarly, in France and Sweden, the wealth share of the super-rich fell from 10 percent to 2 percent over the same time period, highlighting a pronounced compression in their wealth. In fact, this compression was even more significant than that observed for the top percentile.

In contrast, the top 0.01 percentile in the US exhibited a clear U-shape over time. In the 1910s, their wealth share stood at 7 to 10 percent and then gradually fell around mid-century to 2 to 3 percent, only to rise in the 2010s back to 7 to 10 percent.

Figure 5.7 offers a closer look at the post-1980 developments in the wealth share of the super-rich in Western countries, allowing for a comparison between Europe and the US. The findings indicate that, unlike the top percentile, the super-rich

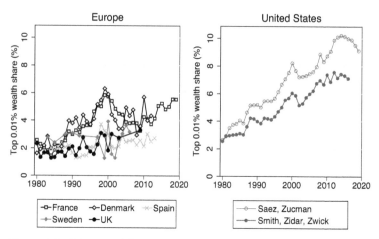

Figure 5.7 A Return of the Super-Rich Since 1980?

Source: The wealth shares of the richest ten-thousandth (top 0.01 percent) use the same data as in figure 5.2 and Jakobsen et al. (2018) for Denmark.

in all Western countries have experienced a significant positive trend in wealth share since 1980. The increase was particularly pronounced in the US, with a rise from around 3 percent in 1980 to between 7 and 10 percent around 2015, representing a doubling or tripling of their wealth share over the past four decades, depending on which series is used.

In Europe, the wealth share of the super-rich has also grown since 1980, but the increase has been smaller than that in the US. All countries had shares around 2 percentage points in 1980, but, by the 2010s, France and Germany saw their wealth share double to 4 to 5 percent, while Sweden and the UK had a slightly lower increase, and Spain had a gain of nearly 3 percent. Evidence from the lower part of the top percentile, the top 1 percent minus the top 0.01 percent, confirms that their wealth shares were fairly stable in Europe, but increasing in the US.

So, did the super-rich manage to escape the Great Wealth Equalization of the twentieth century? The answer is not quite. The European super-rich saw their wealth share plummet more in relative terms than the top percentile. The American super-rich experienced falling wealth shares until the postwar era, but since 1980 they have managed to regain their relative position and reach the same level as in the 1910s. This analysis highlights that the super-rich are far from immune to wealth equalization, and their fortunes can be subject to significant fluctuations over time. Once again, it should be noted that data are highly uncertain. In addition, we are not talking about the same individuals or families in this exclusive group. As already mentioned, there has been a large turnover of people and businesses among the super-rich in all Western countries over the past decades. This is important, since it signals that, even though the super-rich as a group retain or even strengthen their position relative to the rest of the population, the dynamics of the market economy ensures (at least on the whole) that it is the most successful and profitable entrepreneurs who are in the top positions at each point in time.

5.3 WHO ARE AT THE BOTTOM?

So far, our analysis of wealth inequality has centered around the top of the distribution. There are several grounds for this focus, in particular because the most affluent own the majority of all wealth and the historical sources are such that only the rich are observed consecutively over long periods of time. Still, it is a relevant question to ask why there is not more attention paid to the bottom of the distribution. Shouldn't we talk more about the asset-poor when examining wealth inequality?

Asset poverty is a special phenomenon. It deviates from the standard poverty measures that are based on income, and it behaves differently in a number of respects. Looking at the shape of wealth distribution, a recurrent feature is that people in the bottom half own very little wealth, having a share of total wealth typically around 0 percent, or at most not much more. It is a striking fact that this low share recurs in almost any country or historical era, from Sweden and the US today to these and other countries a hundred years ago.

However, as it turns out, asset poverty is not so highly cor-related with other kinds of material deprivation. This section discusses the issue of asset poverty and why wealth inequality scholars actually do the right thing when turning their attention to the top of the distribution rather than to the bottom when trying to understand the nature of wealth inequality and its trend over time.

Many Asset-Poor Are Not Income-Poor

The traditional economic analysis of poverty focuses on income poverty, which is a measurement approach that captures the extremely low consumption opportunities, or socio-economic status, of certain groups. However, some scholars have broadened the poverty analysis by integrating wealth ownership, aiming to capture the fact that certain low-income individuals may have substantial wealth that can be used for consumption or other purposes if needed. The reasoning also holds in the other direction, namely that some of the people without wealth, the asset-poor, may have some income to live off.

Although the academic literature on asset poverty is fairly small, there are some studies that have been made for a number of countries. One survey of the asset-poor in the US in the early 2000s defined as asset-poor those having a net wealth that was less than one-quarter of the poverty line income. The study found about 15 percent of households were asset-poor, but only half of these were both asset-poor and income-poor, since most of them were in employment. An analysis of administrative microdata on the income and wealth of Swedes during the same period shows that the individuals in the bottom half of the wealth distribution owned 0 percent of total wealth but earned 23 percent of total disposable income. These patterns of many asset-poor individuals not being income-poor has also been found in a larger sample of several Western economies.[28]

Some of the Asset-Poor Are Simply Young

The Nobel Prize in Economics in 1985 was awarded to the Italian-American economist Franco Modigliani "for his pioneering analyses of saving." In essence, this referred to his contributions to our understanding of people's savings behavior over the life cycle. His research described and explained why people build wealth during their working life and dissave during retirement. As a result, the age–wealth profile of the average person should be hump-shaped. Young adults are typically penniless, as they have not had much time to accumulate wealth since graduating from school. As they start working, they can begin saving and building personal wealth. This accumulation continues until retirement, when they stop earning an income and instead consume using their savings. Upon death, their net wealth would be zero if they timed their consumption and death perfectly.[29]

Many economists undertake empirical studies on how the age–wealth profile looks in the population. The findings suggest that it appears to fit with most real-world settings. Figure 5.8 illustrates the age–wealth profile in Sweden during the 2000s, which closely resembles the expected hump-shaped life-cycle pattern. People accumulate wealth up to retirement and thereafter start spending it. Interestingly, wealth is not on average at zero at age ninety, which could indicate either that people are unaware of when they will die, and therefore hold on to their wealth even at very advanced age, or that they wish to leave some of their assets to their children. I will discuss the role of inheritance for wealth inequality in chapter 9.

Figure 5.8 shows that the young are overrepresented among the low-wealth groups. The study mentioned above of the asset-poor in the United States found that more than two-thirds of adults aged below the age of twenty-five were asset-poor, as were almost half of those aged between twenty-five and thirty-four.

One way to see the impact of age on wealth distribution is to remove this almost mechanical life-cycle effect. The

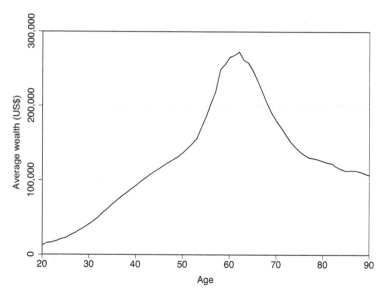

Figure 5.8 The Age–Wealth Profile Over the Life Cycle

Source: The figure presents the average wealth among Swedish adults within yearly age cohorts, observed in 2007 using administrative wealth register data from Statistics Sweden.

most famous attempt to do so was made in a study from 1975 by the economist Morton Paglin. His research showed that, when accounting for the age effect by removing the average wealth differences across age cohorts, the Gini coefficient for wealth among US households in 1962 dropped by one-third, from 0.76 to 0.50. This finding has been replicated in numerous studies across different countries.[30]

Other Reasons for Not Worrying Too Much about Asset Poverty

There are additional reasons for why asset poverty alone may not signal socio-economic vulnerability or deprivation. One is that there are some who freely choose to live without accumulating assets or debts. These individuals may have a job and live a good life, choosing to spend their income every month. In the economics research literature, such people are sometimes referred to as "hand-to-mouth" households, who may have a good quality of life despite having no net wealth. Although it is difficult to determine exactly how many of the wealth-poor fall into this category, an income and wealth survey in the US found that even those in the bottom quintile (the 20 percent with the lowest net wealth) earned between 5 and 10 percent of all incomes.[31]

Yet another group of asset-poor individuals consists of those who have saved in public social insurance systems rather than privately in bank accounts or property. This group appears poor because we use the standard measure of marketable net wealth, which doesn't include the value of drawing rights on future pensions or other forms of social security income that people receive when they are unemployed, sick, or elderly. It is debatable whether the net present value of these drawing rights should be considered wealth equivalent to money in the bank. However, without tax-financed welfare systems, people would need to save privately to access such services. Estimates show that adding the estimated value of these future income streams significantly increases the wealth of the marketable wealth-poor, raising the share of the bottom half of the wealth distribution from 0 to 10 percent. I will revisit the main analysis by examining the role of social security wealth in chapter 8.

Some assets that poor people own are also not fully recorded in the distributional data. For example, vehicles are exempt from most register-based series in the Nordic countries. As some household surveys show that vehicles may account for a sizeable share, perhaps even one-third, of total assets among the asset-poor, ignoring vehicles means underestimating wealth of those at the bottom.[32] Boats or unincorporated businesses are other examples of such tangible assets that are sometimes exempt.

The human capital that people possess never forms part of wealth inequality analyses. Even if human capital, measured as the present value of future labor income, is not recorded in balance sheets, it often generates a liability in the form of student loans, which can make young adults appear poor. The issue of human capital and its role for wealth inequality is not well understood and needs further attention.

In summary, there are several compelling reasons not to assume that all people with no wealth according to official statistics are completely destitute. In this sense, it is reasonable for wealth inequality researchers to zoom in primarily on the top of the wealth distribution when analyzing the main distributional questions. That being said, there are many individuals who lack both assets and income, and who may live partly outside the social insurance system or in a country with a relatively small public safety net. In these contexts, the issue of poverty undoubtedly becomes a real welfare concern, raising questions that scholars should study seriously.

5.4 GENDER AND RACIAL DISPARITIES IN WEALTH HOLDINGS

Wealth inequality has many layers, yet two aspects that have historically been underexplored are the gender and racial disparities. The scarcity of in-depth academic analysis, particularly in tracing historical trajectories, is a significant gap in our understanding of the complex landscape of wealth distribution in the Western world.

Several factors contribute to this oversight. A primary one is the immense challenge of mapping and analyzing overall distributional patterns and their historical shifts, which has consumed a substantial amount of research energy. Additionally, there is a fundamental lack of detailed data revealing the demographic profiles of wealth holders. Most tax systems treat individuals or families uniformly, minimizing the motivation to collect data on the diverse socioeconomic backgrounds of taxpayers.

In this section, I examine some of the critical findings and debates that research has brought to light regarding disparities in wealth based on race and gender. While the focus is predominantly on contemporary data, some studies also shed light on historical patterns, offering some insights into the evolution of these disparities.

Racial Disparities in Wealth

The most extensive body of research on racial disparities in wealth, particularly the divide between black and white populations in the US, spans the period from 1860 to the present day. A significant study employing historical census data and surveys has traced the trajectory of this wealth gap. Initially, in the nineteenth century, the average net wealth of white adults was between twenty to sixty times that of black adults. This disparity decreased to approximately tenfold in the first half of the twentieth century and further diminished to around five times by the 1980s. However, since then, the gap has seen a moderate increase. Much of this reduction is attributed to the growing economic integration of the black population into the formal US economy, enhancing their labor incomes and the opportunity for homeownership and savings.[33]

A significant contributing factor to this persistent wealth gap is the disparity in homeownership rates. While nearly 75 percent of white Americans own their homes, the rate among black Americans is only about 50 percent.[34] One study monitored black and white renters over time to understand the racial differences in applying for mortgages and the success rates of these applications. It discovered that black applicants are nearly twice as likely to be denied finance as their comparable white counterparts, even after accounting for credit history and household wealth. Furthermore, black individuals are also less likely to apply for mortgages in the first place. The primary reasons for this include differences in income, family structure, and the ability or willingness of parents to assist with downpayments.

Gender Disparities in Wealth

Delving into the nuances of gender-based wealth disparities presents unique challenges, particularly in discerning the ownership of assets within households. For single individuals, gender-linked wealth status can be clearly observed through microdata. The waters become muddy, however, when examining cohabitating couples, as it is often unclear how to accurately distribute ownership of shared or individually held assets and debts. While administrative data may link assets or debts to individuals, discerning whether this reflects true ownership or simply practical arrangements is complex. The common approach is to divide all assets and debts evenly between spouses, aligning with many marital laws. However, this becomes more intricate with unmarried couples, leading researchers to make educated but uncertain assumptions about individual wealth within these partnerships.

Historically, our understanding of gender wealth disparities is limited. One of the rare studies exploring this in earlier periods discovered that, in late eighteenth-century America, the estates of women were generally less than half the size of those of their male counterparts, with women owning a mere 4.2 percent of total physical wealth in their names. Though many women undoubtedly benefited from their families' wealth, very few possessed substantial independent wealth.[35]

An innovative study exploring women's wealth ownership throughout the twentieth century utilized estate tax returns to chart the proportion of those among the US's wealthiest. A notable discovery was that women's representation peaked in the late 1960s at nearly half and subsequently fell to about one-third. This trend may indicate shifts in the role of inherited wealth, inferred from the percentage of wealthy women, as they are more often heirs rather than self-made entrepreneurs.[36]

In Europe, recent access to new household survey data has enabled closer scrutiny of gender disparities in wealth. A particular study in Germany examined wealth distribution within couples, both married and cohabiting. The findings revealed that men's wealth constituted nearly two-thirds of the couple's total assets. Interestingly, the research also investigated how financial decisions within partnerships influence wealth distribution. It observed a significantly narrower wealth gap in scenarios where it was predominantly the female partner who handled financial decisions.[37]

6

Exploring the Great Wealth Equalization

Unraveling the causes and effects between different societal outcomes has long been a preoccupation for social scientists, not least economists. The building blocks of inequality change is an excellent example of this, forming a complex structure of factors that range from longstanding institutional influences to shorter-run outcomes in the economic and political spheres.

This chapter explores some of the most plausible explanations for the wealth inequality trends documented in the chapters above. As it happens, the previous research literature already offers some suggestions for the main driving forces behind changes in wealth inequality. One of these emphasizes the difference between the rate of change in the returns to capital and the growth of labor earnings, which correspond with the classical division between capital, mainly owned by the rich, and labor, owned by the rest. Other models emphasize differences in savings propensities, inheritance, and capital returns, while other approaches focus on the distribution of labor income as the root cause of disparities in wealth accumulation and, ultimately, of wealth itself.[1]

For the explanatory models to be interesting, they must be able to account for the book's two key findings presented in the earlier chapters: the significant wealth growth experienced by Western countries during the past century and the substantial decrease in wealth concentration from extreme levels hundred years ago to significantly lower levels today.

Naturally, there are no simple and straightforward answers when searching for the causes of these phenomena. Wealth is an intricate socio-economic outcome influenced by numerous factors, such as individual abilities and behaviors, labor and capital market choices, life-cycle realities, family ties, luck, policy impacts, and macroeconomic effects. No single theory can comprehensively explain all the factors driving wealth inequality trends in such a multifaceted landscape.

We will begin by examining wealth accumulation across the top and bottom of the distribution to identify the winners and losers in both absolute and relative terms over the past century. Next, the specific role of "popular wealth" – the widespread housing and pension assets accumulated by low- and middle-wealth households is discussed. Then the impact of wars and progressive taxes is reviewed concerning their function as shocks to the capital of the wealthy, which according to some scholars has been a pivotal and indispensable driver for equalizing wealth. Finally, the chapter discusses the impact of early twentieth-century political reforms that profoundly changed the rules of the game in Western capitalist economies. Democratic rights, broader educational attainment, and labor rights all aimed to include larger groups in the productive market economy. How did these fundamental institutional changes influence personal wealth-building and the reduction of wealth inequality over the past century?

6.1 COMPARING THE WEALTH GROWTH OF THE RICH AND THE POOR

One approach towards understanding trends in wealth inequality is to compare changes in the wealth holdings at the top and the bottom of the distribution. This provides insight into the absolute changes in wealth status, which is important for analyzing long-term trends. Even if inequality is inherently a relative phenomenon, many models of inequality focus on changes in absolute wealth in different groups. This is particularly true for studies of long-term trends such as the one presented here.

In the first part of this book, we saw how aggregate wealth trends and the composition of wealth across assets have changed over time. In this second part, we show how wealth inequality has decreased significantly over the past century. I will now present a simple accounting framework to reconcile these two developments, in which the absolute wealth growth of both the bottom and the top groups is estimated and compared with respect to their role in changes in inequality.

A Simple Growth Decomposition

To gain some structure for the understanding of the forces at play, I will introduce some simple math. Doing this is often useful for researchers to fix ideas, but it is not necessary to follow the details in order to understand the key mechanisms.

We know from the analysis above that top wealth, W_{TOP1}, consists mainly of agricultural property and corporate stock. Furthermore, we know that the wealth of the rest of the population in the lower 99 percentile groups, W_{LOW99}, is dominated by housing and pension assets. We can express the top percentile wealth share $WS_{TOP1} = W_{TOP1}/W_{ALL}$ as the ratio of wealth in the top percentile, W_{TOP1}, to all wealth, $W_{All} = W_{LOW99} + W_{TOP1}$. The ratio and its relationship to the different assets held by different groups in the wealth distribution can be written as follows:

$$WS_{TOP1} = \frac{W_{TOP1}}{W_{LOW99} + W_{TOP1}} = \frac{Agrarian\ estates + Corporate\ equity}{Dwellings + Pension\ savings + W_{TOP1}}$$

The formula helps us to understand the historical pattern of wealth changes, including both absolute changes in bottom and top wealth and changes in top wealth shares. For example, an increase in the value of dwellings, while all other assets remain unchanged, would lead to an increase in the denominator of the ratio, while the numerator remains constant, causing the top percentage share to fall. Naturally, attributing all agrarian assets and corporate equity to the elites and all housing and pension wealth to the rest of the population is a bold simplification. But it serves the purpose to convey the broad links between aggregate asset composition and wealth distribution.

Still, how far from reality is this simple characterization of asset holdings across the rich and the rest? As for the nineteenth century, we unfortunately do not know that much. Microdata are scarce, and economic historians seeking to identify past wealth holders have to rely on assembling various pieces in a puzzle. Tax archives, containing primarily probate inventories and estate tax returns, serve as a key source. One study of wealth ownership in England calculated the average holdings of people in different occupations. The findings for the late nineteenth century showed that the two occupation groups that held the largest amounts were titled aristocrats and merchants. The wealth of the nobility was predominantly agrarian, while the merchants held more urban assets. Their wealth was a hundred times greater than that of the average laborer, twenty times more than that held by small farmers, and ten times larger than the wealth of the professional classes.[2]

The history of French wealth ownership has been studied on several occasions.[3] In a comprehensive study, tens of thousands of estate tax returns were analyzed after having been manually collected from the tax archives of the city of Paris between 1807 and 1994. The data showed that aristocrats owned half of all the wealth held by the top 0.1 percentile around 1850, suggesting that agricultural estates played a significant role in high-end wealth. Later in that century, industrialists and financiers partly replaced aristocrats as the largest wealth-holding groups, indicating the increasing aggregate importance of corporate assets. A couple of studies of nineteenth-century Sweden showed that the nobility was highly overrepresented among the wealthiest groups, holding predominantly rural assets. However, Sweden experienced comprehensive land reforms, the enclosures, during the century, creating a new category of middle-class tenant farmers. As a consequence, the share of rural land held by the wealthiest decile of landowners declined from 60 percent in 1800 to 48 percent a century later.[4]

Looking finally at twentieth- and twenty-first-century asset ownership patterns, the picture of homes and pensions being the primary asset of ordinary households and the top owning predominantly corporate shares is widely corroborated by available data, as also shown in several places in this book.

Western Wealth is Equalized through Lifting the Bottom, Not Lowering the Top

Figures 6.1 and 6.2 use the equation above to decompose changes in the top percentile's wealth share into the growth of average wealth of the lower 99 percentiles (grey bars) and the top 1 percent (black bars). Admittedly, referring to the lower 99 percent as a joint bottom group is bold, given that it contains pretty much everybody, including some very rich people. Below I also study inflation-adjusted per adult wealth changes in the bottom 90 percent or even the bottom 50 percent, all depending on the granularity of the available data. The changes in average wealth are calculated for three episodes, 1910–1950, 1950–1980, and 1980–2010.[5]

The results show that, during the period of Great Wealth Equalization from 1910 to 1980, most of the country episodes were associated with positive wealth growth for the bottom 99 percent rather than decreasing wealth for the top 1 percent. The grey bars, representing growth at the bottom, were mostly positive, while the black bars, representing top growth, were mostly around zero or positive.

In the period 1910 to 1950, average wealth holdings increased for both the top and the bottom, but since bottom wealth grew faster, top wealth shares fell. For example, in the UK, the top percentile wealth share fell by an average

um, the real wealth growth data suggest that the histor-
ealth equalization was driven primarily by the expand-
ealth of ordinary people rather than the decline of elite
es.

he Trajectories of Wealth among Lower and Upper Groups

introductory section, I delineated three key facts char-
zing the historical evolution of wealth in Western coun-
The first and third facts underlined the increase in the
of overall wealth and the rise in wealth equality. How
ese two facts intersect, especially in how they shape
ealth dynamics of society's top and bottom echelons?
6.3 attempts to tackle this by presenting the total
h in current US$ owned by the top 1 percent and the
m 90 percent. The scope is limited to France, Sweden,
K, and the US, which offer a long record of top decile
data.

iscuss what the figure shows, let's begin with the sit-
h in 1910. At this juncture, the top 1 percent of the US
ation had amassed $2.4 billion – more than double the
tive wealth of the bottom 90 percent. To cast this in
dual terms, the average affluent American was about
imes wealthier than his middle-class counterpart.
European nations the disparities were even starker.
nce and Sweden, the wealthiest percentile held four
the collective wealth of the bottom 90 percent, while
UK it was a staggering twelve times. When expressed
ltiples of average middle-class wealth, the gap was 190
US, above 300 in France and Sweden, and 1,100 in the

ng forward to 2010, the gap had narrowed decidedly. In
S, the top 1 percent held $40 billion in wealth, versus
llion for the bottom 90 percent – a difference that had
ed down to 1.3 times. In Europe, a dramatic reversal
red: the bottom group in France and the UK accumu-

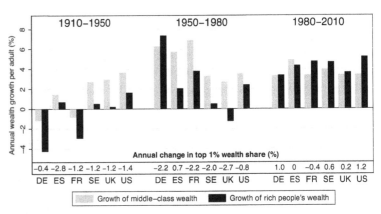

Figure 6.1 Wealth Growth among the Middle Class and the Rich in the Twentieth Century

Note: The figure shows annual average compounded growth rates for "rich people," here measured as the top 1 percent in the wealth distribution (black bars), and for the "middle class," the bottom 99 percent (grey bars), and their respective wealth shares. For data availability reasons the start year for the United States is 1913. Country labels: DE = Germany, ES = Spain, FR = France, SE = Sweden, UK = United Kingdom, US = United States.

Source: Data are based on aggregate wealth and top wealth shares reported in chapters 2 and 5.

of 1.2 percent each year, but behind this fall was a wealth increase in both the top percentile, by 0.4 percent per year, and the bottom 99 percentiles, by 3.1 percent per year. The same pattern, with falling top wealth shares that reflected positive growth everywhere in the distribution, but with faster growth in the bottom than in the top, is also found in Spain, Sweden, and the US. Only in France and Germany did the falling top wealth shares reflect negative growth in the entire population, and where wealth fell faster at the top than at the bottom.

After 1950, the trend of falling top wealth shares while real per capita wealth grew, mainly among bottom groups, continued, and it was even more pronounced than during the first half of the century. This pattern is observed in all countries. Between 1950 and 1980, the bottom 99 percentiles experienced average annual growth rates ranging from 2.4 percent in the UK to 7.5 percent in France. Meanwhile, the top percentile experienced positive wealth growth ranging from 0.4 percent per year in Sweden to 7.6 percent per year in Germany. The UK's top percentile is the only exception, experiencing negative real per capita growth during this era, at an annual rate of −1.6 percent. Looking at the aggregate wealth and top wealth shares, it seems that the stagnation of top wealth occurred mainly during the 1970s.

These are crucial findings. They reveal that the wealth equalization of the twentieth century was not a result of capital destruction among the rich. On the contrary, the wealthy elites experienced positive wealth growth in most countries and during most periods from 1910 to 1980. The driving force behind this equalization was the widespread asset accumulation among ordinary people, who built personal wealth primarily through homeownership and pension savings. Both the top and bottom segments experienced positive growth during the century, but wealth expanded more rapidly among the less affluent than the already rich.

After 1980, Western societies underwent significant transformation. Markets were liberalized, taxes were reduced, and technological advancements ushered in a new era of globalization. As we have seen in previous chapters, macroeconomic growth surged during this period (chapter 2). Notably, while wealth concentration remained relatively stable in Europe, it increased in the US (chapter 5).

Does the real wealth growth among top and bottom groups align with these aggregate and distributional developments? Figure 6.1 clearly demonstrates that the answer is "yes." The post-1980 era witnessed the most rapid and extensive increases in wealth in the past century, and likely throughout modern history. Top percentile wealth grew by around 4 percent annually in Europe, while in the US it grew even faster, at an average annual rate exceeding 5 percent.

The rapid growth in wealth of the US top percentile has attracted specific attention among researchers. One study decomposing asset growth points to the relatively large

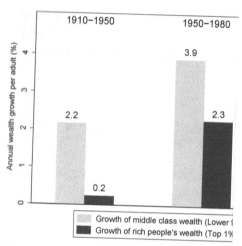

Figure 6.2 Western Wealth Growth Averages People, 1910–2010

Note: The figure shows annual average compou rates per adult of "rich people," here measured the wealth distribution (black bars), and of the 99 percent (grey bars). Five-year wealth-weight different years are used to avoid unrepresentat

Source: Data are based on aggregate wealth and in chapters 2 and 5.

build-up of corporate equity values b portfolios of the wealthy.[6] But the we percent also expanded – by about 3 both Europe and the United States. T the top and bottom European group wealth growth, the top US group sig bottom group.

Figure 6.2 summarizes the results b wealth growth in all Western countri The wealth of Western middle classes year up to 1950 and by 3.9 percent b The top growth was around zero, 0.2 p 2.3 percent between 1950 and 1980. S has grown in the entire population, l the top.

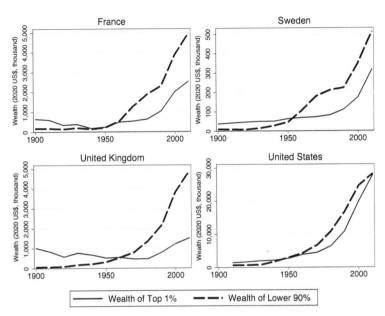

Figure 6.3 Wealth Amounts Held by the Top 1 Percent and Bottom 90 Percent

Note: The data series show aggregate wealth amounts (in constant US$) held by the bottom 90 percentiles and the top percentile in each country's wealth distribution.

Source: Data sources are the same as in figures 2.1, 5.1 and 5.2.

lated twice as much wealth as the top echelon, and similar trends were observed in Sweden.

The sheer scale of this bottom-up accumulation is shown in figure 6.4, which elucidates how many times the wealth holdings for each group multiplied from 1910 to 2010. The picture it paints is illuminating. Wealth for the bottom 90 percent surged by between 25 times in France and the US, to 54 times in Sweden and 80 times in the UK. This uptick encapsulates both an accelerated accumulation of wealth among the middle class and increased wealth-building participation among the less affluent. By contrast, the multiples for the top 1 percent were far more modest – ranging between one and eight in Europe and 16 in the US. The average annual

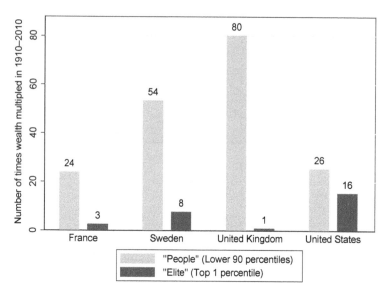

Figure 6.4 The Number of Times Wealth Has Multiplied during 1910–2010: the Elite and the Rest

Note: Labels show the number of times the amount of wealth in 1910 multiplied over the following century. Multiples are computed by dividing the amount in 2010 by the amount in 1910 (less one), all in constant US$.

Source: Data used are the same as in figure 6.3.

increases stood at between 3 and 4 percent for the bottom and 1 to 2 percent for the top.

The scrutinized data on absolute wealth growth buttress the key thesis of this and the preceding chapter – that a significant convergence in wealth distribution has unfolded across Western economies. This convergence is what translates into the redistributional shift, and it also points towards an intriguing pattern showing when and where all of this took place over the past century.

6.2 HOW HOMEOWNERSHIP AFFECTS WEALTH INEQUALITY

Homeownership is today a widespread phenomenon in all Western countries. The previous chapters showed that it gradually became more extensive during the past century, taking off in particular in the 1940s and thereafter. Among homeowners, the dwelling usually represents the dominant asset in a household's portfolio. In this section, I will discuss what implications homeownership may have for wealth inequality.

Homes in Middle-Class Portfolios

In their groundbreaking analysis of British wealth inequality in 1978, Anthony Atkinson and Alan Harrison were among the first to emphasize just how important homeownership had become for wealth inequality in the modern era. Similar observations have since then been made by other researchers for several countries, especially Spain, Sweden, and the US.[7]

Figure 6.5 shows the importance of housing wealth in the household portfolios over the US wealth distribution today. As can be seen, the value of the primary residence represents two-thirds of household wealth for those in the lower 80 percent in the wealth distribution. By contrast, it represents less than 10 percent of the wealth in the richest percentile group.

Tracking the historical importance of how housing has mattered for individual household portfolios is unfortunately difficult because of a general lack of adequate historical microdata. But some attempts have been made. In a recent study, researchers found unique archival materials dating from the late 1940s of the forerunner of the Federal Reserve Board's Survey of Consumer Finances, today's primary data source for US wealth inequality.[8] The new evidence showed that primary residence has been the main asset in household portfolios for American families in the low- and

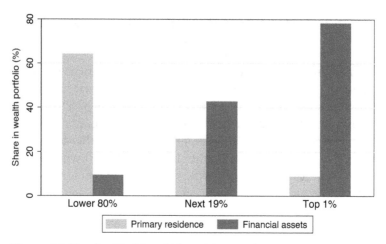

Figure 6.5 Housing Wealth and Financial Assets across the US Wealth Distribution

Source: The three wealth holder groups "Top 1%," "Next 19%," and "Lower 80%" are defined based on their percentiles in the US household wealth distribution as reported in Wolff (2021).

medium-wealth groups ever since the 1950s – that is, basically having the same role as it has today. This finding came as a surprise to some because the expansion in US homeownership rates had just begun in the 1940s – right before the first measurement waves of the wealth survey.

What the scholars could also show with their new data was how important house price changes were to build new wealth over time, especially in comparison to financial asset price changes or new saving. Figure 6.6 shows the relative importance of increasing house prices, increasing share prices, and saving out of the labor income in the wealth growth of the lower half, the next four decile groups, and the top wealth decile groups.

The results in the figure reveal a fascinating wedge between the upper and lower halves in accumulation behavior. In the lower half, house price increases account for almost all (four-fifths) of wealth growth, which fits well with the fact that housing wealth makes up almost all of their ownership. By contrast, for the more affluent groups in the upper half,

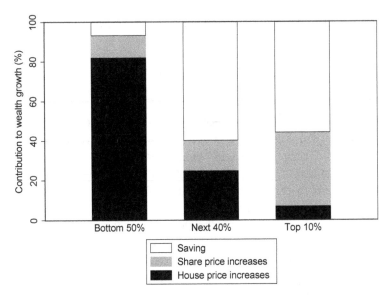

Figure 6.6 Contributions from Asset Prices and Savings to Wealth Growth across the US Wealth Distribution

Note: The figure singles out the impact of asset price changes and new saving for total wealth growth during 1971–2007 in the lowest half of the US household wealth distribution ("Bottom 50%"), the wealth holders between the 50th and 90th percentiles ("Next 40%"), and the top wealth decile ("Top 10%").

Source: Data from Kuhn, Schularick and Steins (2020, figure 18).

saving was the primary source of wealth accumulation. This finding underscores the fact that wealth is closely intertwined with other socio-economic outcomes, particularly labor earnings. The higher saving among the upper wealth groups was made possible by their greater labor incomes. Finally, note that there is a difference in the type of asset price changes that contribute to wealth growth in the upper half. Among the next four deciles, the increase in house prices is the most important, but, in the top decile group, financial asset price increases are the most important. Of course, this also mirrors the compositional structure, with corporate shares being the most important asset for the wealthiest echelons.[9]

The Negative Correlation between Homeownership and Wealth Inequality

Is there a systematic relationship between the share of a country's citizens owning their home and the level of wealth inequality? The question is intriguing as it asks about a link between two of the most commonly discussed outcomes in both policymaking and academic research. A priori, we know from analyzing household wealth data that the value of dwellings is relatively more important to middle-class households than to the wealthiest households. This suggests that countries with a comparatively high share of households owning their own homes should have proportionately low wealth inequality. What do the data say about this relationship? This section intends to answer that question.

Figure 6.7 plots countries according to their homeownership rates and wealth inequality as measured by the Gini coefficient based on recent wealth and homeownership surveys. The results are broadly affirmative with respect to the presumed link: countries with higher levels of homeownership have lower wealth inequality. The straight line in the figure is a simple line fit which aims to capture the general tendency in the data. Its message is that, if the homeownership rate increases by ten points – say, from 50 to 60 – then the Gini coefficient for household net wealth will decrease by 0.04 Gini points.[10]

To understand the economic significance of these numbers, let us consider the case of Germany. The results in figure 6.4 suggest that, if Germany were to increase homeownership levels towards those of France, which would be to move from 44 percent to 58 percent, then Germany should expect a Gini reduction by almost 0.06 points, an 8 percent inequality decrease. If Germany were instead to extend the homeownership rate to that of Norway, which stands at 80 percent, German wealth inequality would fall by 0.14 points, or a 20 percent inequality reduction. Such swings in wealth inequality are quite large, and it may be unrealistic to expect them over a short period of time, but the simple model helps shed

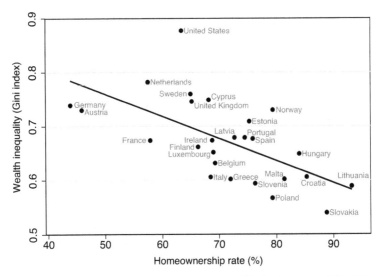

Figure 6.7 Homeownership and Wealth Inequality in Europe and the US

Note: The regression equation, shown as a straight line, reflects a slope coefficient of −0.41 with a standard error of 0.11, which suggests a statistically significantly negative correlation between the homeownership rate and wealth inequality.

Source: Data from the 2017 wave of the Eurozone countries' wealth survey *Household Finance and Consumption Survey* (ECB 2020, tables B3, J4). Data for the US wealth inequality from Wolff (2021) and US homeownership rates from the OECD.

light on the order of magnitude that is at play when discussing the role of household asset ownership and a country's wealth distribution.

Altogether, the lessons from history, and in particular from today's sizeable variation across countries in housing ownership arrangements, suggest that spreading private homeownership in the population can be crucial for attaining a more equal distribution of wealth. This finding has also been encountered in country-specific case studies, indicating that it is a quite robust pattern.[11]

6.3 WARS AS SHOCKS TO CAPITAL

When discussing the trends in wealth inequality over the twentieth century, it is impossible to escape a special look at the role of the two world wars. These geopolitical events reshaped Western societies and thoroughly impacted economic life.

One strand in the historical wealth literature places wars at center stage when explaining the wealth equalization of the twentieth century. Thomas Piketty, for example, argues that they slashed the capital of the rich, either directly through war-related destruction or indirectly via wartime regulations and special tax hikes.[12] Walter Scheidel, in his book *The Great Leveler* (2017), makes a vast and informative examination of economic inequality patterns over the past thousand years. One of his main arguments is that wars have been a "necessary condition" for sustained inequality decline, working through the capital-destroying and regulating political mechanisms that reduce the capital holdings of the wealthy. Other accounts of the history of inequality place wars in a less high-profile position. For example, Branko Milanović points to their overall importance but considers their influence to be less decisive than that of many other economic and political factors. Guido Alfani draws similar conclusions from chartering European pre-industrial inequality trends.[13]

In this section, I will reexamine how the twentieth-century wars influenced wealth inequality in the West. I begin by showing how the top 1 percent wealth share has changed and then decompose the top adjustments in wealth share into changes in the absolute wealth holdings of the top and the rest of the population.

Before launching the investigation, a general disclaimer is required. Understanding the pathways through which wars influence wealth inequality is far from trivial, and my discussion will be agnostic at best. No one, to the best of my knowledge, has tried to identify the exact impact that wars have on wealth inequality. Despite being great shocks, wars do not occur in isolation, and their influence works through intricate structures of causal effects and feedback loops. My aim here therefore will be to shed light on the order of magnitude of their effects rather than to question the effects' existence.

The World Wars Did Not Universally Lower Top Wealth Shares

From a theoretical standpoint, it is not clear how war-related capital destruction would affect capital values. The value of capital, or wealth, is a combination of asset volumes and asset prices. If asset volumes shrink on account of bombing, capital values will initially decrease. However, the resulting capital shortage generates price increases in the remaining assets when the demand for capital services exceeds their supply. These positive price effects will offset the negative volume effect. The exact extent of this offsetting effect is not clear beforehand, but it will determine whether the ultimate value of capital falls as a result of bombing. Researchers have long studied the interplay between volumes and assets when characterizing the evolution of the capital stock and its aggregate value. There is, however, no consensus on the degree of these offsetting forces.[14]

There are a number of attempts to estimate the values forgone in wartime capital destruction. One study found that France and Germany both experienced a significant depression in capital values during the wars, while the UK suffered much less widespread capital destruction. Another study, on Spain, found that around 5 percent of the total net capital stock was destroyed during the civil war in the 1930s, mainly transport equipment and machinery. However, it is challenging to determine the precise impact of war-related capital destruction on capital values. The value of capital depends on both asset volumes and prices in a sophisticated interplay. While researchers have studied this extensively, it is fair to say that consensus has not been reached concerning the net effects of the offsetting forces.[15]

Table 6.1 Top 1 Percent Wealth Shares during the World Wars

| | Percent change in top percentile wealth share | | | | | |
| | Belligerent | | | | Non-belligerent | |
	France	Germany	UK	US	Spain	Sweden
World War I						
War (1914–18)	−4.7		−6.1	−11.5	3.9	−4.2
Postwar (1918–24)	−8.8		−4.9	−6.4	−12.2	
War + postwar (1914–24)	−13.5	−19.6	−11.0	−17.9	−8.3	
Spanish Civil War						
War (1936–9)					−0.3	
World War II						
War (1939–45)	−11.4		−14.8	−19.2	0.8	−11.8
Postwar (1945–51)	−6.9		−9.2	−11.7	−9.3	−14.7
War + postwar (1939–51)	−18.3	−31.8	−24.0	−30.9	−8.5	−26.5

Source: Data are the same as for figure 5.2.

The figures in table 6.1 confirm that the wealth distribution became more compressed during the war years, as top wealth shares fell by an average of 7 percent during World War I and 15 percent during World War II in the belligerent countries (France, Germany, the UK, and the US). Of the two non-belligerent countries, Sweden's top wealth shares fell by almost as much as in the belligerent countries, while Spain's top wealth shares did not fall at all.

However, the evidence presented in the data is too aggregated and covers too few countries to draw a clear causal relationship between war damage and wealth inequality. A recent study examining the geography of bombing in England during World War II provides more insight. The authors found no significant impact on wealth inequality at the country level. However, when examining northern and southern England separately, a different pattern emerged. In the southern parts of the country, where there was relatively light bombing activity, wealth inequality did not change much. In contrast, in the northern parts of the country, where bombing was heavier, researchers found a significant impact on wealth inequality, as it decreased as a result of the destruction of housing and other structures.[16]

Table 6.1 also shows that top wealth shares fell both during and after the wars, with postwar declines almost as large as those recorded during the war years. Interestingly, while this pattern is seen in both belligerent and non-belligerent countries, it is perhaps most evident in the latter group. The available estimates of the top percentile's wealth share suggest that it did not change at all in Spain around the time of the Spanish Civil War (1936–9), being 53.3 percent in 1935 and 53.2 percent in 1941.

Absolute Wealth Holdings during the World Wars

The investigation continues by asking how the real amounts of wealth holdings among top wealth groups and the rest of the population evolved during the world wars. This is a similar analysis to that above, but I now decompose the changes in top wealth shares in the wartime years into the amounts held by the top and the rest. A specific twist is to split the episode into two periods: the actual war years, when bombings and other war activities could inflict physical damage on the capital stock in addition to any other wartime changes in policy or market outcomes, and the immediate postwar years, when other factors than physical damages were at play.

Figure 6.8 shows the changes in real average wealth in the top 1 percent and the bottom 99 percentiles during the two wars.[17] Looking first at the World War I episode, wealth decreased in all countries during these years, and both the rich and the rest of the population saw their wealth deteriorate. The French took a particularly hard blow, with a recorded wealth drop of around one-third. Going from bad to worse, they also experienced a continuation of decreases in wealth in the immediate aftermath of the war, recording negative changes in postwar years. Of course, it should be noted that this result is in part a function of the extraordinarily

high levels of pre-World War I wealth in France highlighted
in chapter 2.

The years right after the war led to rather different experiences in other Western countries. That period was characterized by an unusual degree of political and economic
turmoil. There were war reparations, the emergence of
democracy, and an immense amount of financial turbulence.
For instance, Germany printed money to finance its repara-
tion debts, resulting in hyperinflation and financial distress.
Sweden returned to the gold standard at prewar exchange
rates, causing deflation, a downturn, and a severe banking
crisis. Despite this, the return of peace and market operations meant that wealth levels could bounce back in most
Western countries during the early 1920s. The figure shows
that both the richest percentile and the rest of the population
saw their wealth appreciate; the lower group experienced the
largest gains and, as a consequence, wealth inequality fell.

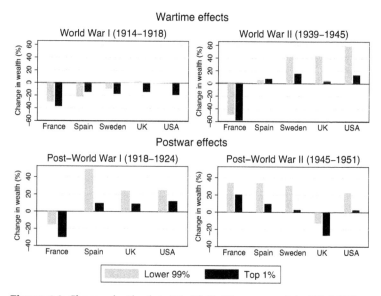

Figure 6.8 Changes in Absolute Wealth Holdings around the World Wars

Source: The figure shows average annual compounded changes in real
wealth per capita in both the bottom 99 percent and the top 1 percent
groups using the same data as in figure 6.1.

World War II brought slightly different experiences as to how wars can affect the wealth distribution. Recall that table 6.1 showed how top wealth shares fell in all countries during the war and its immediate aftermath. Looking at figure 6.8, we see that the falling wealth concentration was not a function of reduced capital holdings among the rich, which several scholarly accounts have suggested. Instead, wealth appreciated among all groups, the rich and the rest, and this happened both during the years 1939–45 and in the postwar period up to 1951. The explanation for the falling top wealth shares was that the prosperity of the people increased more than the affluence of the elite. This development occurred throughout the West. Wartime developments in the labor market, with women entering the labor force and workers' pay increasing faster than that among the higher paid strata, enabled people to start saving. Post-World War II policies also imposed market regulations and tax hikes that hindered wealth accumulation among business owners.

A conclusion from this evidence is that there is no such thing as a specific "war effect" on wealth. World War I resulted in substantial losses for the rich, while World War II rendered them better off. The wealth of the bottom 99 percentiles either decreased or stayed unchanged during the first war but increased during the second. France and Germany are the only two countries where both wars were associated with capital losses in all classes. However, for the majority of countries, the overall results suggest that not everyone loses out during wartime in terms of wealth ownership. Finally, the wars seem to have had similar effects on wealth in belligerent and non-belligerent countries. This is a striking result and reinforces the overall result that wars do not have any specific, one-directional effects on the wealth in society.

Wars Are Not Necessary for Wealth Inequality to Decline

Are wars a necessary condition for sustained inequality decline, as argued in the past research? Despite this widely held belief, the data suggest otherwise. Take Sweden, for example. While many other Western countries participated in both wars, Sweden remained neutral. Yet Sweden still experienced a similar trend in wealth equalization to other Western countries throughout the twentieth century. It is important to note that Sweden was not completely unaffected by the surrounding turmoil. It introduced conscription and implemented regulations and taxes as a result of the wars.[18] However, the country did not experience direct involvement in fighting or war-related capital destruction.

Spain offers another example. The country experienced large reductions in the top wealth share during both world wars despite not participating in either. By contrast, during its civil war, the top wealth share did not experience a great fall, although admittedly the historical data are less certain around these years.

Examples of inequality reduction in incomes may also be found where there is no influence from war. A compelling case is that of Southeast Asian economies, where Malaysia, South Korea, and Thailand fueled high-growth outcomes during peacetime while reducing poverty and income inequality. These countries achieved equalization through their impressive economic growth, expanding opportunities and incomes for broad segments of the population. This demonstrates how a larger pie can lead to a larger slice for everyone.[19]

In summary, the studied changes in top wealth shares and in the absolute holdings of the top and the rest of the population suggest that wealth did indeed become more equal during the world wars. However, equalization was in many cases larger in the immediate aftermath than during the actual wartime years. Effects were similar across countries, which is notable since not all countries were participants. Altogether, the findings of wealth inequality during wartime

EXPLORING THE GREAT WEALTH EQUALIZATION   145

episodes question claims that war is necessary for wealth equalization, and even that wars are the main events during which wealth inequality declined over the past century.

6.4 TAXATION AND THE SHAPING OF WEALTH INEQUALITY

The impact of taxation on the observed trend of wealth equalization throughout the twentieth century remains uncertain. There is a substantial body of research examining the effects of taxes on income disparity, yet our understanding of how taxes influence the accumulation and distribution of wealth is notably less developed.

The question of how taxes affect wealth and its distribution is debated among scholars and decision-makers. Simplified, taxes on wealth or its return can be useful tools for funding public expenditure and redistribution between groups. This is especially true since high-income earners often have additional income from investments, suggesting a positive correlation between income and wealth ownership. However, the efficiency of capital taxes can vary depending on how they are designed. If they obstruct entrepreneurship and the growth of successful businesses, their net effect on both economic activity and tax revenue might even be negative.[20]

Wealth Tax versus Capital Income Taxation: A Discursive Divide

Taxation theory admits the need for some kind of tax on capital, but the tricky part is deciding on the best kind. Taxes on capital income, which is essentially a tax on the capital stock multiplied by some rate of return, are generally preferred by many economists for their wider scope. However, capital income taxes miss a key point: you cannot tax wealth that has not yet been converted into income. Here is where a wealth tax could come in. Yet it soon turns out that life is not that simple. Wealth taxes can be tough to implement, especially when you have to value assets that are not traded or worry about their liquidity. In fact, almost all countries that did have a wealth tax removed it a long time ago, precisely because of the problems it caused for businesses without rendering almost any substantive revenues.[21]

Inheritance taxation is a variant of wealth taxation that focuses on the wealth of the deceased. While inheritance taxes are suggested by several theoretical works, the same practical and conceptual problems as for wealth taxation apply to inheritance taxes.[22] I return to the issue of inheritance in chapter 9.

A Retrospective on Historical Tax Impacts

Understanding the historical impact of taxes on wealth and wealth inequality is an important topic as it concerns one of the key policies that directly addresses wealth. Yet exactly how to go about the analysis of this relationship is not always straightforward. As for so many other variables, one imminent challenge is that we do not access proper historical data on capital taxation for most countries and historical eras. There are historical datasets reporting on the highest marginal income tax rates, since they are relatively easy to observe in tax tables. However, we do not know how many individuals actually paid those rates, and information is also scarce about the historical variation in all the specific clauses that determine effective capital tax rates, such as tax base definitions or the size of deductions. All of this makes it hard to gauge the real impact on the rich from capital taxation.[23]

Over the last century, governments have generally increased taxes, with the burden falling mostly on workers rather than on owners of capital. The tax to GDP ratios increased in Western countries from around 10 percent to 40 percent, and most of this was in the form of higher direct and indirect taxes on labor earnings. Capital taxes also increased over this period, affecting both capital income and on property, wealth, and inheritance.

In his analysis of how capital taxation has influenced wealth inequality over the past century, Thomas Piketty suggested that the gradual rise in capital taxes reduced effective post-tax wealth returns in a way that reinforced the equalization trend, especially preventing top wealth accumulation after World War II.[24] This storyline has a bearing on the observed outcomes, but its simplistic analysis also has limitations. The multiplicity of capital taxes and asset returns implies that there is not a single net of tax return to wealth over the past century, and research shows that both the different returns and the different capital tax rates have evolved in different directions over time, making it difficult to fully reconcile them with the trend in wealth inequality. The storyline also disregards the role of labor taxes. Admittedly, this issue is complicated and the links could work in different directions. Increasing postwar taxes on labor prevented the poor and middle classes from saving privately, which obstructed wealth equalization by slowing growth from below. But the tax-driven growth of government also gave people access to publicly subsidized welfare services such as education and healthcare, and the analysis in chapter 8 demonstrates that incorporating the social security wealth reflecting the values to households in these systems has a significant equalizing effect on wealth distribution. It is also possible, as one study argues, that lower income taxes for high-income earners contribute to the accumulation of large fortunes, potentially increasing wealth inequality.[25]

Understanding the relationship between capital taxation and wealth inequality is further complicated by the political dynamics that shape tax policies. Political backing is essential for the introduction or increase of a capital tax. Such support tends to grow during periods of high wealth inequality, especially if the tax is seen as effective in redistributing wealth.[26] The history of capital taxation reflects these fluctuations in political will, often hingeing on perceptions of the tax's efficacy in wealth redistribution. The political scientists Kenneth Scheve and David Stasavage highlight the role of war in gaining support for higher capital taxes. They argue that mass mobilization for war generates public demand for taxing the wealthy more heavily to share the financial burden of the conflict.[27] Studies focused on Sweden's postwar era further illustrate this point, linking the decline of high capital tax rates after the 1970s to perceived inefficiencies. These taxes were found to discourage productive investment while poorly targeting tax bases, ultimately resulting in regressive taxation.[28]

In the mid-twentieth century, the design of tax and industrial policies in Sweden by the ruling Social Democracy fueled a development that discouraged private wealth accumulation. Elevated levels of personal wealth and inheritance taxation led affluent family business owners to move their assets into foundations. This circumvention tactic preserved operational control while forgoing legal ownership – a manifestation of social democracy advocating for "affluent firms without affluent firm owners."[29]

An interesting question is why the US has both high wealth concentration and low taxes, while Europe has the opposite. One theory suggests that this reflects a deliberate difference in societal focus. The US has organized an economy based on a low-tax, high-inequality model that fosters innovation and long-term growth. By contrast, Europe has focused on inclusive welfare states rather than innovation and growth and has benefited by free-riding on the innovations coming from the US without having to adopt the same harsh policy approaches.[30] While this explanation might be debatable, for example by pointing to the growth-enhancing role of public spending on infrastructure or education, the fact that the US has generated most of the world's technological development and economic growth in the postwar era, resulting also in some of the world's largest fortunes, provides food for thought.[31]

In sum, the relationship between taxes and wealth inequality is a topic often discussed but not fully understood, especially when considering long-term trends. This gap in our understanding calls for continued research to shed light on how different types of taxes have historically affected the balance of wealth.

6.5 INSTITUTIONAL CHANGE AND WEALTH INEQUALITY TRENDS

Understanding the root causes behind such societal shifts as changes in wealth inequality is a complex yet critical endeavor. This book posits that declining wealth inequality has coincided with a rise in middle-class wealth accumulation. However, the question arises: is it the act of personal saving among workers that has leveled the wealth playing field, or could it be institutional changes, such as educational and labor market reforms, that have uplifted skill levels and earnings, enabling greater degrees of saving? Adding another layer of complexity, educational reforms may not be self-originating but could be the outcome of more fundamental societal shifts, such as the expansion of democratic rights in the early twentieth century, which paved the way for improved educational policies.

This quest for underlying causes brings us to what economists define as institutions – those sets of rules and norms that govern economic behavior and interactions. Take, for example, democracy and property rights; these fundamental "rules of the game" guide economic choices.

The Political Process and Economic Outcomes: An Institutional Feedback Loop

The iterative relationship between political structures and economic outcomes has long fascinated social scientists. Policy decisions shape the economy and its distributional aspects. Conversely, the economy also affects the political landscape. This two-way relationship creates an intricate feedback loop, with each influencing the other in myriad ways.[32]

Douglass North, a Nobel laureate and noted economic historian, was a pioneer in emphasizing the vital role of institutions in the economy. In his investigations into the origins of industrialization, he designated institutions as the "fundamental causes" of economic growth. According to North, what we often consider the drivers of growth – such as innovation, education, capital accumulation, and economies of scale – are actually the manifestations rather than the originators of growth. He termed these elements "proximate" causes, concluding that they do not generate growth; rather, they are its expression.[33]

When discussing the blend of economic and political power, certain figures – such as Italy's Silvio Berlusconi and America's Donald Trump – emerge as iconic. These individuals, both economic magnates and political leaders at different points in time, encapsulate the intense interplay between economic clout and political authority. History contains numerous situations when periods of economic development have not automatically benefited the majority but instead advantaged primarily small, well-organized elites.[34] In the United States, for instance, research by political scientists has posited that the uptick in inequality since the 1980s could be traced back to a "capture" of the political system by extremely wealthy individuals during the 1970s and 1980s.[35] But this is not just a modern phenomenon; historical accounts are replete with instances where economic elites transitioned into political roles, and vice versa.[36]

Educational Reforms and the Diffusion of Knowledge

The rise of welfare states throughout the twentieth century marks another way in which political systems have influenced economic outcomes in Western economic history. As social spending grew as a share of GDP, its integral role in economic development became increasingly apparent.[37]

Among the various facets of social spending, the widespread improvement in educational attainment stands out as a milestone. Education not only equips individuals with skills that enhance their productivity but also raises their earning potential. Claudia Goldin and Lawrence Katz's seminal work on the US education system reveals that educational expansion benefited even marginalized groups. Their findings illustrate a two-sided effect: while education and technological advances heightened productivity and increased labor demand, they also exerted pressure on wages as a result of a swelling pool of skilled labor.[38]

Broader perspectives on knowledge creation and their role in inequality has been discussed recently. The latter half of the twentieth century, according to some scholars, marks a pivotal change in growth strategies among advanced economies. Earlier growth was largely tethered to fixed capital – machinery, infrastructure, and the like. However, a transition has occurred to a more post-industrial paradigm where knowledge accumulation is paramount. This is not merely incidental; economic historians such as Joel Mokyr and Deirdre McCloskey posit that this focus on intellectual investment is deeply rooted in culture.[39]

The evolution towards research and innovation-driven intangible investments has multiple and complex implications. It is presupposed to be a hidden catalyst for various economic phenomena, including income inequality and stagnant productivity growth.[40] Investment in research and development could affect wealth inequality although the pathways are diverse. It could exacerbate inequality by inflating the corporate wealth–income ratio, but innovation could lead to broad-based income growth that benefits workers and facilitates the emergence of new firms. However, despite its growing influence, this area remains underexamined in the literature.[41]

Labor Policies and the Rise of Professionals

The emergence of political rights in the early twentieth century also brought change in labor laws and union rights. While the role of these legal frameworks for wealth inequality is not fully understood, to the extent that they bolstered wage levels it is possible that they also fueled productivity gains by enhancing worker morale and working conditions. Collective bargaining rights further empowered workers, granting them a more influential voice in workplace affairs, thereby fostering a more equitable income distribution. Such labor market reforms were not confined to any one country but were a general phenomenon across the Western world, enabling such standard-setting measures as minimum wage laws and limits on working hours.[42]

To further explore the relationship between professional education and wealth distribution, let's turn to interwar Sweden as a case study. During this era, a burgeoning class of well-educated, well-compensated professionals flourished, contributing significantly to wealth accumulation. Unique tax records from 1911 to 1948 offer insights into both income and wealth among adult Swedes. Alongside democratic reforms and the rise of progressive political ideologies, tax structures became more liberal, encompassing both labor income and wealth.[43]

Figure 6.9 maps the shifting fortunes of two distinct wealth-holder groups in the upper echelons of wealth distribution: "rentiers," whose income stemmed primarily from returns on their assets, and "high-paid employees," whose earnings were largely labor-derived. Data show that, between 1911 and 1941, high-paid employees saw their wealth share surge from 14 percent to 31 percent. In contrast, rentiers experienced a decline in their wealth share, from 34 percent to 26 percent. This trend aligns with the broader transformation of economic elites, especially the rise of industrial moguls and high-ranking executives, further underscoring the pivotal role of educational and labor market institutions in shaping wealth distribution.[44]

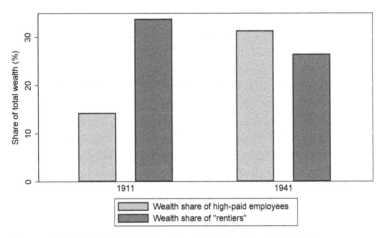

Figure 6.9 A New Wealth Elite: From "Rentiers" to "High-Paid Employees" in Sweden

Note: The figure shows the shares of total household wealth held by wealthy "rentiers" (defined as individuals obtaining most of their income from capital) and "high-paid employees" (those receiving most of their income from labor earnings).

Source: For data and discussion of the definitions, see Roine and Waldenstrom (2009, table 1).

How Financial Development Helped Workers Accumulate Wealth

The expansion of financial institutions and markets – collectively referred to as financial development – has been instrumental in elevating the financial wellbeing of ordinary citizens. This development has notably facilitated homeownership and pension fund growth, significant indicators of household wealth.

Empirical studies underscore the role of financial development in broadening homeownership opportunities. A developed financial system enhances access to credit, lowers borrowing costs, and democratizes mortgage financing. Consequently, nations with robust financial systems exhibit higher homeownership rates, which is a pattern that has received empirical support in the research literature.[45]

However, when borrowing constraints become less restrictive they increase the opportunities for productive entrepreneurship. That could both generate capital accumulation and expand the pool of successful entrepreneurs, which could either lower or raise wealth inequality depending on how much wealth these entrepreneurs generate.[46]

Moreover, financial development has engendered the securitization of pension savings, a topic elaborated on earlier in this book. The maturation of financial markets has allowed pension funds to diversify their asset holdings, extending beyond traditional savings into securities such as stocks and bonds. This diversification not only boosts the potential for higher returns but also grants individuals easier access to their pension reserves.

Summing up, institutions matter for long-term wealth trends in a number of ways. A comprehensive understanding of wealth ownership among the lower and middle classes in the Western world mandates an exploration of the underlying institutional factors. While this book has delved into several such elements, future research should aim to disentangle the importance of institutional reforms for education, labor markets, and the financial sector, as all these turn out to be crucial for both the accumulation and distribution of wealth in society.

7

Hidden Offshore Wealth

Offshore wealth has long been a hot topic in the Western world. Money that flows to other jurisdictions often remains shrouded in mystery. It is hard to pin down just how much wealth Western citizens stash away in offshore locations, partly because there is no clear-cut definition of what offshore wealth actually is. According to a recent estimate, there is about $12 trillion in financial assets that can be classified in this way. This is a very large amount, although it is only about 2 percent of the $500 trillion of assets that the world's citizens own.[1]

In this chapter, we look deeply into history and explore the relationship between offshore wealth and wealth inequality. While cross-border capital flows have been around for ages, their impact on the economy has grown significantly with the rise in recent decades of financial globalization. The chapter sheds light on the most recent research findings about the amounts of hidden wealth Western residents keep in other jurisdictions.[2]

The big question is: did the existing estimates of offshore wealth and its distribution among the Western population affect the level and trends in wealth inequality throughout the twentieth century? Could it be that mainly tax-driven capital flight has been happening behind the scenes, secretly driving up Western wealth inequality?

7.1 DEFINING OFFSHORE WEALTH

Offshore wealth refers to assets held in foreign jurisdictions. While some people place their assets offshore to dodge taxes in their home country, others might do so for more legitimate and fully legal reasons, such as better investment opportunities or risk diversification. To measure offshore wealth accurately, we need to clarify a few definitions and distinctions. One important distinction is between legal and illegal tax-driven wealth transfers. Legal transfers, which in the tax literature are often labeled tax avoidance, mean that investors use legal means to minimize their tax liabilities. On the other hand, illegal transfers, or tax evasion, involve investors breaking the law by not disclosing assets and other required information. The line between legal and illegal practices is not always clear-cut, and sometimes this has to be settled in court. For example, a recent report of global offshore assets estimates that about one-quarter of these transfers can be deemed as evasion, with thus three-quarters being legal in all concerned jurisdictions.[3]

I will focus on the assets of individuals and leave corporations aside, the reason being that my analysis of wealth inequality concerns differences among individuals in the Western home countries. It can be difficult to determine fully the legal status of who owns offshore wealth and, to the extent that it is possible, I include only holdings linked to individuals or families.[4]

Note that attention here is entirely on individuals who remain in their Western countries of origin. In some well-known cases, it is not only the fortunes of the rich that have moved abroad but also the rich themselves. Several of France's billionaires have moved their money and themselves out of the country because of the high taxation – for example, the owner of the Nicolas wine stores, Pierre Castel, and Chanel's owner Gérard Wertheimer both officially reside in Switzerland. Sweden can also offer several stark examples of tax-driven emigration, many of them dating back to the 1970s, when the country's elevated wealth and inheritance taxes pushed some of its most prominent entrepreneurs out of the country: IKEA founder Ingvar Kamprad, H&M founder Erling Persson, and Tetra Pak heirs Hans and Gad Rausing. However, for the purposes of wealth inequality estimation, it is important to note that, by leaving their high-tax country of origin, these individuals also left the tax population which forms the basis of analysis when studying the wealth distribution.

Offshore Wealth Is More Than Just Tax Evasion

A common misconception is that offshore wealth and cross-border capital flows are solely about wealthy individuals and corporations evading taxes in their home countries. This is the form of offshore wealth that hits the headlines. But in reality there are capital flows from high-tax to low-tax jurisdictions that are legitimate and economically sound. The reasons why investors choose to place their funds abroad vary. One is international diversification of portfolios, which can reduce the volatility of one's asset holdings while maintaining the expected level of returns. Another obvious reason is that overseas ventures can be promising and, if they eventually turn profitable, become part of corporate growth and global market expansion.

Moreover, not even all tax-driven capital flows are about evading taxes in a legally dubious manner. Countries naturally compete with one another for corporate presence and investor capital, and offering competitive tax rates is one way to attract these resources. A low corporate tax, average dividend taxes, and low or no personal taxes on wealth and inheritance can mean a lot financially to wealthy private business owners. However, low tax rates alone are not enough to entice foreign investments. Factors such as strong property rights, political stability, and modern infrastructure are also crucial. Not all countries having low capital taxes receive capital inflows, with examples being Brazil and most sub-Saharan countries. In other words, connecting offshore wealth exclusively with tax avoidance is an oversimplification that misses several important aspects of cross-border capital flows.

The Overused "Tax Haven" Label

A "tax haven" is a jurisdiction or country that provides minimal tax liabilities and disclosure requirements for foreign investments.[5] The stereotypical image is a tropical island with palm trees, white sands, and a small office building where banks and law firms manage their foreign clients' accounts. Well-known examples include the Cayman Islands, the Bahamas, and the less remote Channel Islands of Guernsey and Jersey. However, there is no formal definition for tax havens, and this label is therefore used widely in both policy debates and academic research when discussing international dimensions of tax policy and cross-border capital flows. Such use can be misleading.

Interestingly, some organizations and researchers classify a number of larger and far less remote countries as tax havens. Switzerland, Luxembourg, Singapore, and Ireland, for example, have all been labeled as such. These countries attract capital inflows by offering lower taxes on corporate profits and wealth returns, coupled with institutional stability and high-quality infrastructure. Switzerland alone may host up to one-third of the world's offshore wealth.[6] Ireland changed policy in the early 2000s when the country drastically reduced its corporate tax rate from 36 percent to 12.5 percent. This move sparked complaints from other Western countries, as their tax differentials with Ireland skyrocketed. Subsequently, companies such as Facebook and Google flocked to the island, accompanied by a wave of skilled workers from around the world.

Labeling countries as tax havens based solely on their low corporate tax rates is a contentious practice. If low corporate tax rates were the sole criterion, then Hungary and Lithuania, with some of the OECD's lowest rates, at 9 and 15 percent, would also be classified as tax havens. When considering the taxation of corporate income alongside personal income taxes on distributed profits, countries such as Estonia, Latvia, Hungary, Greece, and the Slovak Republic would emerge as the ones with the lowest rates, ranging between 20 and 25 percent. This is in stark contrast to the higher rates in Switzerland and Luxembourg, at 38 and 41 percent respectively.[7] Yet these low-tax nations aren't typically labeled by leading researchers as tax havens, indicating a degree of arbitrariness and potential overuse in how the term "tax haven" is applied to various countries.

7.2 ASSESSING OFFSHORE WEALTH AND ITS OWNERS

Determining the amount of offshore wealth and identifying its owners is crucial to understanding how the growth of offshore wealth in recent years may have influenced wealth inequality.

Estimating Global Offshore Wealth

No one knows the exact amount of wealth Westerners hold in foreign jurisdictions, as there is no official statistical source for such assets. Researchers must rely on a range of sources and methods to estimate it, with varying degrees of credibility.

Some studies use macroeconomic data to assess offshore wealth. One common approach involves cross-checking national balance sheets, which list each country's reported assets and liabilities for domestic and foreign investors. Mismatches between reported assets and liabilities, such as when low-tax countries report larger liabilities to high-tax countries than those high-tax countries report as assets, are interpreted as signaling hidden offshore wealth.[8]

Another method uses flow data from national accounts and balance of payments. If savings in the national account (income minus consumption) do not match savings in the financial accounts (growth in reported bank deposits and securities funds), the resulting discrepancy is considered hidden wealth. Similarly, imbalances in the balance of payments, where foreign sales of goods and services are not matched by inflows of payments from other countries, suggest hidden offshore wealth.[9]

Estimates of offshore wealth vary depending on the methods and datasets used. A 2007 estimate suggested $5 trillion, representing 2.5 percent of global wealth that year.[10] A more recent report from the OECD found that total offshore assets reached $11 trillion in 2019, and another recent assessment by the EU Tax Observatory came up with a similar number. While this figure is undeniably significant, it represents only around 2 to 3 percent of total global wealth, estimated according to the *Global Wealth Report* at $454 trillion in 2019.[11]

It is important to note that macro-statistical errors can significantly impact these estimates. Timing errors, exchange rate variations, and traditional summing-up errors can all contribute to large accumulated errors, although error bands are rarely calculated. For example, an update in Swedish national accounting standards in the 2000s drastically changed national income estimates, reducing the level of savings and causing offshore wealth estimates to fall to almost zero.[12] While the actual amount of offshore holdings was likely positive and substantial, this example highlights the sensitivity of macro-based estimates.

Identifying the Owners of Offshore Wealth

Linking offshore assets to individuals in wealthy Western countries is a challenging task. Many countries hosting such assets have bank secrecy laws and reporting standards that make it difficult to obtain information. Generally, investors in offshore assets are assumed to be relatively wealthy, given the costs of establishing connections with foreign banks in tax havens and the progressive nature of capital taxes in Western countries.

Several studies have assumed that offshore wealth is held by the richest individuals in their countries of residence. However, this assumption might not apply to some of the wealthiest individuals, particularly successful entrepreneurs who have their wealth tied to their businesses. Intermediate wealthy individuals might be more interested in the tax incentives offered by low-tax jurisdictions.

Recent research has utilized leaked documents from offshore banks and law firms, such as the "Swiss Leaks," "Panama Papers," "Paradise Papers," and "Pandora Papers," to gather information about individual holdings. One study examined lists of named individuals in Nordic countries who appeared in leaked documents or who voluntarily reported their holdings to tax authorities after an amnesty for international tax evaders: 1,422 Norwegians and 6,811 Swedes were named. These were matched with administrative tax records in their home countries to determine their positions within the domestic distribution of wealth. The study found that 77 percent of these individuals were in the top 0.1 wealth percentile, and 52 percent were in the top 0.01 percentile.[13] Although the analysis could not definitively establish the effect on estimates of wealth inequality, the existence of hidden offshore assets potentially distorts official statistics on personal wealth and its distribution in Western countries.

Microdata evidence suggests that most offshore wealth owners are at the top of the wealth distribution in their home countries. The following analysis assumes that all offshore wealth can be attributed to the top percentile of Western countries' domestic wealth distributions. However, this assumption may overestimate the impact on inequality, as even microdata show that some less wealthy households hold assets abroad.

The Revenue Effects of Capital Tax Evasion

A central aspect in the political discussion about offshore wealth is how tax revenues are affected in Europe and the US. Since tax differentials comprise one important motivation for investing offshore, it is interesting to think about counterfactual outcomes in tax revenues without cross-border capital flows.

Estimating the level of forgone capital taxes in rich countries as a result of offshore tax evasion is quite difficult. The global minimum tax of 15 percent that was introduced in 2024 has been said to increase total corporate tax revenues in OECD countries by one-tenth.[14] Similar calculations for individually owned wealth and capital income taxes are not available, but their impact on revenues in Western countries is probably marginal because of the small number of individuals concerned and the relatively small amounts held.

A sound level of skepticism towards the estimates of forgone capital taxes is required. The methodological challenges relied on are large. The most important problem is that small or no behavioral responses are assumed on behalf of the rich individuals, or corporations, who have moved their assets to lower-taxing jurisdictions. Calculations are made by multiplying the estimated evaded capital income by the tax differential on capital income in high- and low-tax countries. But had the rich individuals and corporations kept their assets in their high-tax home countries, it is not certain that capital incomes would have been as extensive. As a matter of fact, studies have shown that people's responsiveness to capital income taxes are perhaps three times greater than their responsiveness to labor income taxes, and rich people have been highly responsive to wealth taxes, leading ultimately to lower than expected tax receipts in high-tax countries.[15]

7.3 HOW OFFSHORE WEALTH AFFECTS WEALTH INEQUALITY

How does accounting for offshore wealth impact wealth inequality in Western countries? And, if the effect is significant, does it influence the long-run trends in wealth inequality examined in this book?

Offshore Wealth and Top Wealth Shares

An initial investigation uses data points on estimated offshore wealth in 2007 for several countries, with most of the observations coming from asset holdings in Switzerland, the largest single host country for offshore assets. The basic method in the analysis involves adding the estimated offshore wealth to the wealth of the domestic top percentile (and to the total wealth).

The results show two key findings. First, offshore wealth does indeed make domestic wealth distribution more unequal. All the countries in figure 7.1 experience higher top percentile wealth shares when offshore wealth is added. Second, and perhaps more interestingly, the impact on inequality from adding offshore wealth is relatively small. The largest effect is found in the UK, where the top percentile share increases from 20 percent to 22.5 percent, a rise of 13 percent or one-eighth. The average effect on top percentile shares from adding offshore wealth is 7 percent, with the lowest effect found in Denmark, where the top share increases from 21 percent to just 21.5 percent, a rise of just 3 percent.

Offshore Wealth and Long-Run Trends in Wealth Inequality

In a second analysis, the time series pattern of offshore wealth is examined. Unfortunately, we lack data for most

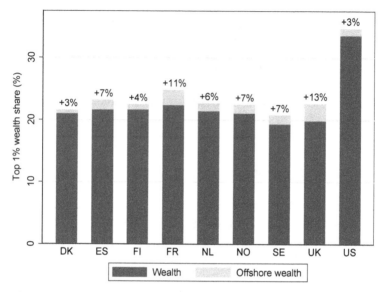

Figure 7.1 How Adding Offshore Assets Changes the Top 1 Percent Wealth Shares

Note: Country labels: DK = Denmark, ES = Spain, FI = Finland, FR = France, NL = the Netherlands, NO = Norway, SE = Sweden.

Source: Data on top wealth shares from chapter 5 and offshore wealth estimates in Alstadsæter, Johannesen and Zucman (2018).

countries in the longitudinal sense. Comparable data spanning the period from the 1970s to the 2010s is available for only two countries: Spain and Sweden.[16] The Spanish series is based on data from the Swiss National Bank and asset composition evidence in Spanish wealth survey data. The findings for Sweden are based on the cumulated net errors and emissions in the balance of payments, which are assumed to correlate with tax-driven capital flows. Note that all of these estimates are highly uncertain and should be treated with caution.

Figure 7.2 presents trends in offshore wealth holdings and the effects on inequality when adding offshore wealth. The left panel displays the macroeconomic role of offshore wealth by showing its impact on aggregate wealth–income ratios. In both Spain and Sweden, the impact is relatively small: offshore wealth accounts for at most 5 percent of the total, with some variation over time. The right panel shows how top percentile wealth shares are affected when offshore assets are allocated to the wealthiest individuals. The impact here is more notable than at the aggregate level. In Spain, the top wealth share increases by between one-tenth and one-quarter, from 20 to 25 percent without offshore assets to 25 to 30 percent with offshore assets. In Sweden, the top share increases almost as much in relative terms, from 18 to 22 percent to 22 to 26 percent when allocating offshore wealth.

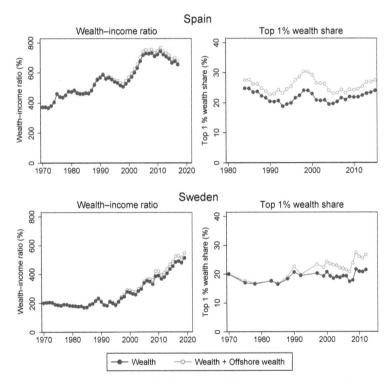

Figure 7.2 The Evolution of Offshore Wealth in Spain and Sweden since 1970

Note: Left panels show aggregate wealth–income ratios with or without added total offshore wealth amounts. Right panel shows how the top 1 percent wealth shares change when the estimated offshore wealth is added to the observed domestic wealth of the top 1 percentile group.

From a historical perspective, adding offshore wealth appears to play a small role. The top percentile's wealth share in Spain fell from 60 percent in 1910 to around 25 percent in the 1980s. The few percentage points increase resulting from adding offshore assets to the wealthiest Spaniards does not alter the long-term equalization result. The same can be said for Sweden, where the top percentile group owned more than 50 percent of all wealth in 1910 but only 20 to 25 percent after the 1970s. Adding offshore wealth to the group does not change this.

The findings for Sweden are particularly interesting as they can be further qualified. As mentioned earlier, many Swedes have considered tax-driven capital flight to be a significant phenomenon in this high-tax country. Swedish taxes on capital, especially wealth and inheritance taxes, reached historically high levels in the 1970s and met heavy criticism. Some of the richest entrepreneurs protested by moving out of the country, taking their capital with them. This raises the issue of whether to include residents or citizens in the calculations. When including the super-rich migrants residing in other countries, should we not also include all Swedes living and working abroad? In the Swedish study, we found that adding the wealth of the IKEA owner Ingvar Kamprad alone more than doubled the wealth share of the top 0.1 percentile, indicating that his fortune was twice as large as those of the 5,000 richest Swedes living in Sweden. An additional aspect of adding Kamprad's fortune is that he gave away all his IKEA shares to a family-controlled foundation in the Netherlands. This decision cannot be undone, and it effectively implies that no individual will ever own IKEA. Despite this, Kamprad continued to be listed as the owner by *Forbes* magazine and Swedish magazines publishing similar rich lists.[17]

In conclusion, this chapter's results suggest that allocating estimated offshore wealth to wealthy individuals makes wealth distributions more unequal. Official inequality estimates may therefore be downward biased in many Western countries, since they typically do not account for offshore holdings.

But the quantitative importance of offshore assets on wealth inequality is limited. Top wealth shares increase by less than a tenth, and in the US by much less than that. Gini coefficients hardly increase at all. Long-run historical trends are also not affected much. The historically low wealth inequality observed in European countries since the 1980s remains after adding offshore assets, and US wealth inequality trends hardly change at all.

8

Public-Sector Wealth

Consider a world devoid of taxes, public pensions, or welfare services, where citizens must depend solely on private savings for a secure retirement. Fortunately, this is not our reality. Most nations provide a publicly funded safety net of pensions and welfare services offering at least basic services to the elderly. However, the redirection of resources from the private sector to the public sector through the tax system has implications for how much wealth is ultimately held by households and how much is being controlled by the government.

The prevailing understanding of wealth focuses on marketable net assets, comprising items such as property, cash, shares, and funded pension savings, all appraised at current market prices. What this wealth definition excludes, however, is a substantial asset possessed by many: entitlements in unfunded pay-as-you-go pension systems and social security. These entitlements can be expressed in asset value terms as they promise a stream of future incomes from pensions and social insurance payments to all individuals who are part of the system.

Post-World War II Western economies witnessed the rise of the welfare state, financed largely through taxes. But public provision can lead individuals to reduce private savings for retirement, a phenomenon economists term "crowding out." Pioneering work by Harvard's Martin Feldstein illustrated that tax-funded social security could reduce private savings by up to 50 percent over four decades. Subsequent studies have confirmed this effect, albeit with variations across countries.[1] Feldstein's innovation lay in treating future pension and social insurance entitlements as assets. To quantify this, he introduced a method that converts future income streams into a net present discounted value, termed "social security wealth." The slice of this wealth linked specifically to future pensions is known as "pension wealth" or "retirement wealth."[2]

The sheer scale of the unfunded transfer wealth is striking. In the US, social security wealth approximates $30 trillion, equivalent to 150 percent of GDP, or half of all household net financial assets. For European countries, estimates of public pension entitlements range between 150 percent to 400 percent of GDP.[3]

The distribution of the unfunded assets in the population holds vital implications for wealth inequality. The dispersion of social security wealth, given that it derives from workers' earnings, likely mirrors that of earnings. Income, as we have seen, is more equally distributed than marketable wealth, making it plausible that pension and social security wealth follow a similar pattern.

This chapter navigates the influence of public-sector assets on long-term wealth accumulation and inequality trends. First, I augment the conventional wealth concept by incorporating unfunded pension and social security wealth. I present cross-country evidence on the current landscape and a limited historical overview. Second, I examine governmental wealth, often overlooked in inequality analyses. I estimate its total size and allocate it across the population, amalgamating it with private wealth to offer a holistic view of national wealth inequality.

8.1 SOCIAL SECURITY WEALTH AND ITS IMPACT ON WEALTH INEQUALITY

In the past, old age often spelled impoverishment. Around the turn of the twentieth century, one-third of English individuals aged sixty-five and over were recipients of poor relief, and a public investigation in Sweden classified the majority of elderly who did not have a paid job as living in poverty.[4] Rudimentary schemes such as occupational pensions and thrift savings plans barely sufficed for a dignified life in retirement. As a remedy, nations began designing public solutions for the "old age problem," with Sweden leading the movement by introducing the world's first universal pension system in 1913. Yet these early pension systems were very basic, leaning more towards poor relief than being robust retirement packages. The postwar era saw the roll-out of more comprehensive systems such as the US's Medicare in the 1960s.

Many of these emerging welfare systems were financed through taxes. In return for tax payments, workers accrued entitlements to future pensions, known as pay-as-you-go pensions. This is in contrast to fully funded pension plans, where the pension is funded by the employer rather than by its future beneficiaries.[5]

Computing Social Security Wealth

The task of calculating the wealth value from unfunded pensions and social security benefits, so-called social security wealth, involves transforming the anticipated future pension and social insurance incomes of individuals into an asset value, which equals the present discounted value of these future incomes. Introduced in the 1970s, this methodology has since been applied across countries.[6] The algorithm hinges on several variables. Statutory rules dictate pension entitlements for different categories of worker. Demographic data provide longevity estimates, and a discount rate adjusts for the time value of money. This last variable is a subject of academic debate but usually falls within a 2 to 3 percent range. These elements combine to assign a wealth value for each individual in a population.

Before delving into outcomes, let me address two recurrent critiques of incorporating unfunded assets into personal wealth analysis. First, the claim that discounted future incomes cannot equate to marketable wealth. This is a well-taken point, indicating that money in the hand today is worth more than money in the future. However, the application of a discount rate partly counters this criticism, as it means that we give future incomes less weight than today's incomes. The ideal rate of discounting remains a contentious issue.[7] Second, unfunded pension assets lack corresponding liability for the policyholder, relying instead on governmental promises of future payments.[8] This is also a valid point, but its significance hinges on one's view of government expenditure utility. If you consider these services would cost the same if procured privately, then including unfunded pensions in wealth measures gains credibility. Having said this, while unfunded pension assets increase the aggregate stock of household wealth, their equivalent unfunded liabilities reduce the aggregate wealth of the public sector (which is the main policyholder), leaving national wealth unaffected.

It is also crucial to remember that the social security wealth of households corresponds to liabilities for the government and private policyholders. When future pensions and social insurance incomes are tallied into a social security wealth value for individuals, an equal liability is accrued by local and central governments and private companies responsible for these future payments. While this factor does not influence the analysis of household wealth inequality, it is significant on a broader scale. It means that, despite rising private wealth values, the nation's overall wealth remains unchanged because these increases are counterbalanced by corresponding liabilities.

The Distributional Effects of Social Security Wealth

To fully grasp the implications of adding unfunded pension and social security wealth to the standard concept of marketable wealth, we need to tackle a pivotal question: what impact does this have on wealth inequality? This question will be answered in two parts. The first delves into the immediate repercussions of adding unfunded pension wealth to current wealth inequality measurements in Western countries. The second analyzes the long-term influence of unfunded pension and social security wealth on inequality, focusing on the scant but valuable data from Sweden and the United States.

Figure 8.1 highlights the distribution of both marketable and augmented wealth – where augmented includes unfunded pensions – based on household wealth surveys from Europe and the US. The Gini index serves as our inequality yardstick. A noticeable dip emerges, from an average Gini of 0.6 based solely on marketable wealth to 0.44 when factor-

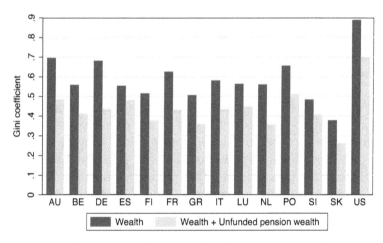

Figure 8.1 The Equalizing Effect of Adding Unfunded Pension Wealth

Note: Country labels: AU = Australia, BE = Belgium, ES = Spain, FI = Finland, FR = France, GR = Greece, IT = Italy, LU = Luxembourg, NL = the Netherlands, PO = Portugal, SI = Slovenia, SK = Slovakia, US = United States.

Source: Sierminska and Wroński (2022).

ing in unfunded pensions – a decline of roughly 25 percent. This reduction varies by country; for instance, in Spain, the decline is a mere 13 percent, while in the Netherlands it reaches 36 percent. The upshot? Adding the present value of unfunded pensions significantly levels the wealth playing field in Western nations today.

Historical Perspectives on Social Security Wealth

We now turn to the long-term trends using the historical data series available for Sweden and the United States. While Sweden's data focus solely on unfunded pensions, US data encompass social security wealth, a broader category that also includes defined-benefit pensions.[9]

Figure 8.2 offers a telling story. Inclusion of social security wealth influences aggregate wealth–income ratios and top percentile wealth shares markedly in both nations. After Sweden initiated its universal pension system in 1948, the wealth–income ratio surged by 100 to 150 percent and has remained steady since. Concurrently, the top percentile of wealth fell precipitously. In the US, the trajectory is similar: the aggregate wealth–income ratio has shot up by 200 percent or more since the 1960s, and the top percentile plummeted nearly 50 percent when accounting for social security wealth.

The repercussions are seismic when we account for the full scope of governmental growth in Western countries in our wealth inequality metrics. The Gini index falls by approximately one-quarter, and the top percentile of wealth drops nearly in half upon adding unfunded pensions or social security wealth. This outcome is consistent across numerous studies and is anticipated, as social security incomes are often tied to labor earnings and have a broader, sometimes universal, base of beneficiaries. The most striking result? Post-1980 top wealth shares in the United States, which are considerably less than those calculated with marketable wealth alone and display a smaller upward trend when social security wealth is factored in.

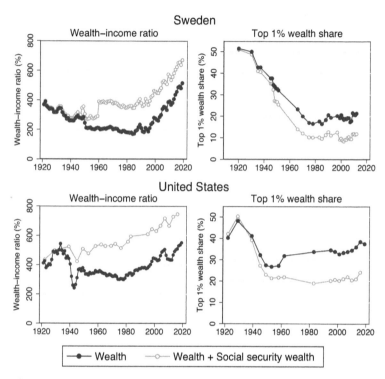

Figure 8.2 Adding Social Security Wealth: Wealth–Income Ratios and Top Wealth Shares

Note: Figures show how private wealth–income ratios and top percentile wealth shares change when unfunded pension wealth (Sweden) or social security wealth (US) are added to the standard private wealth of individuals.

Source: Swedish aggregate wealth–income ratios from Waldenström (2017) and top wealth shares from Roine and Waldenström (2009) and Lundberg and Waldenström (2018). US aggregate wealth–income ratios from Piketty and Zucman (2014), Wolff and Marley (1989), and Sabelhaus and Volz (2020) and top wealth shares from the latter two references.

8.2 ALLOCATING GOVERNMENT WEALTH

The question of who owns the assets commanded by government, and how that wealth relates to private wealth, is complex and has not been extensively studied in the previous research literature. One reason why scholars shy away from this topic is that valuing government assets is difficult. Public infrastructure, government buildings, parks, and water are largely not traded on markets, which makes putting a price on them almost impossible. Another challenge is how to assign government wealth to individual citizens. While the most reasonable rule for democratic states is equal sharing among citizens, this may not be appropriate in other contexts where command over public-sector resources is consequential.

Recently, some researchers have attempted to allocate national income using distributional assumptions. They estimate a household distribution of national income, treating citizens as the ultimate claimants not only on their personal income but also on the incomes of corporations and the government.[10]

In this section, I allocate the entire national wealth to households, following a similar program that has been carried out previously for national income, namely by summing government and private wealth and distributing it to all citizens. This estimation of the distribution of national wealth is rarely done, but it is possible by making bold assumptions about the valuation of government assets and the weighting of citizens' drawing rights on the public sector. Note that I do not include the unfunded pension assets or social security wealth more broadly in this part of the analysis since they net out when both assets, held by households, and liabilities, held by the policyholders, being the government and various public and private employers, are included.

Government Net Wealth Is Close to Zero

To begin with, we need to determine the value of government net wealth in various Western countries. This should include the central government, which holds assets but most importantly all the liabilities related to the sovereign debt, as well as all local governments that also command assets and can be borrowers on the bond market. We can see from figure 8.3

that government wealth is significantly lower than private wealth in all six countries. Government wealth divided by national income results in a ratio that hovers around zero percent, with occasional spikes up to 100 percent and down to minus 200 percent during extraordinary periods of government borrowing.

Increases in government debt have occurred primarily during wartime episodes, but the Covid pandemic in the early 2020s also resulted in a sharp increase in public-sector indebtedness. In contrast to government wealth levels, recall that the private wealth–income ratios analyzed in the first part of the book are much higher, often reaching 400 to 500

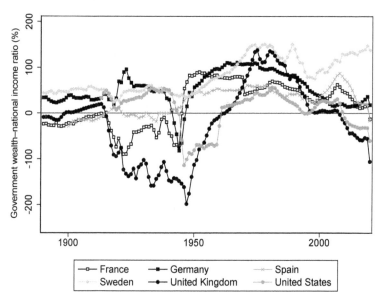

Figure 8.3 Government Wealth–Income Ratios in Six Western Countries (%)

Note: The figure shows the ratio of net government wealth to national income.

Source: Data for France and the US from Piketty and Zucman (2014); for Germany from Albers, Bartels and Schularick (2022); for Spain from Artola Blanco, Bauluz and Martínez-Toledano (2021); for Sweden from Waldenström (2017); and for the UK from Madsen (2019). Updates available at WID (https://wid.world).

percent or more. This means that, regardless of how government wealth is allocated, it will have a relatively small impact on the overall distribution of national wealth.

Distributing National Wealth

Taking the discussion a step further, we turn to the allocation of government wealth – or, rather, national wealth – among citizens. The following analysis operates on an egalitarian premise: that each adult individual receives an equal share. While this notion is controversial, particularly in authoritarian settings, Western countries with universal suffrage provide a relevant context for such a distribution. Since government wealth in these nations has been marginal for most of the past century, the impact of such a distribution on long-term wealth inequality metrics is minimal.

Figure 8.4 traces the trajectory of top percentile national wealth shares from the late nineteenth century to the present day. The overall pattern that emerges from these series is that not much happens to wealth inequality when government wealth is distributed to citizens. Wealth concentration falls over the twentieth century and remains at historically low levels after the 1980s. But there are some exceptions. A marked deviation emerges during wartime, when governments lean heavily on borrowing. This surge in debt drives up top national wealth shares above top private wealth shares, since the increased public debt makes everyone poorer, and the equal amounts of debt distributed to everyone have a relatively larger impact on the wealth standings of poor and middle-class households. These wartime debt effects are most notable in the UK, France, and the US. Germany was an outlier, opting to fund its wars through printing money or direct taxation, thereby sidestepping a wartime debt spike. These disparate financial strategies during war periods had tangible economic repercussions – hyperinflation in Germany and debt overhang in France and the UK.[11]

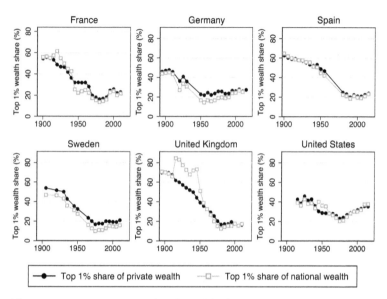

Figure 8.4 Top 1 Percent National Wealth Shares

Note: The figure shows the top percentile group's share of national wealth, using private wealth shares from chapter 5 and allocating government wealth per capita in the adult population.

Source: As for figures 5.2 and 8.3.

In the post-World War II era, Western nations, typified by Sweden, Germany, and the UK, introduced comprehensive pension systems funded through public buffer funds. These funds were born out of forced saving schemes and have the potential for equalizing wealth when redistributed to households.[12] Consequently, top national wealth shares during this period were consistently below that of their private counterparts. In the UK, national wealth shares were roughly a tenth lower; in Germany, a fifth lower; and, in Sweden, a third lower. Despite the appearance of progress, these differences have not left a lasting imprint on wealth inequality.

Government Wealth: A Limited Instrument

While the idea of government wealth acting as a counterbalance to private wealth is appealing, history offers cautionary tales. In times of economic downturn or warfare, governments have resorted to heavy borrowing, which not only fails to alleviate inequality but sometimes exacerbates it. Given that government wealth has been historically inconsequential in shaping overall wealth inequality in Western countries, there is scant justification for expecting transformative change from enlarging government balance sheets.

To sum up, while various government initiatives have episodically nudged wealth inequality downward, their enduring impact has been modest at best. Government assets are rarely substantial enough to effect meaningful change, and fluctuating levels of government debt can introduce new economic complexities. Recognizing these limitations is vital when considering the potential of government wealth accumulation as a means towards addressing enduring wealth inequality.

9

Inheritance and Wealth Inequality

As we strive to understand the underlying factors that contribute to wealth disparities, one topic that consistently draws attention is the role of inheritance. Throughout history, family fortunes have been passed down through generations, shaping dynasties and determining social status. In this chapter, I explore the complex relationship between inheritance and wealth inequality, examining the historical significance, current implications, and future trends of this phenomenon.

At the heart of wealth accumulation are two distinct paths: the self-made route, where individuals save and invest their own income, and the inherited route, where wealth is received as gifts or bequests from others. Public sentiment tends to favor the self-made approach, with individuals who build their own fortunes garnering greater respect and admiration than those who inherit their wealth. This distinction is essential when discussing tax policy, as it influences public opinion on the fairness of wealth redistribution. To better understand the role of inheritance in shaping wealth and inequality, we can look to the past. By examining historical data, generated by previous research in this area, it is possible to assess how the importance of inherited wealth has evolved over time and the implications this has on contemporary society.

This chapter examines four central dimensions. First, what is the share of inheritances in relation to national income or overall wealth? Data stretching from the late nineteenth century to the present provide a macroeconomic perspective on the role of inheritance in a country's financial ecosystem. Second, does inheritance exacerbate or ameliorate wealth disparities? Although this question is not new, advances in datasets now permit more conclusive answers. The chapter synthesizes current research to elucidate the factors shaping this relationship. Third, addressing a different set of questions, what are the effects on social generational mobility? Beyond assessing outcomes, the chapter looks at inequality of opportunity. Do inheritances cement or erode socioeconomic mobility across generations? The discussion incorporates evidence on the correlation between parental and offspring wealth and the modifying role of inheritance. Finally, are the fortunes of the super-rich self-made or inherited, and how has this dynamic evolved? Employing a unique categorization of the world's wealthiest, the chapter scrutinizes trends in wealth accumulation among this exclusive segment within Western economies.

9.1 A MACROSCOPIC VIEW OF INHERITED WEALTH

Let us begin by examining the big-picture role of inheritance in society. This section uses the power of aggregate economic data to charter inheritance flows over the past century. The analysis employs a statistical model that blends together total private wealth, population mortality, and the average wealth of those who have died in relation to those who are still alive. Our result comes together in two sets: first, we explore the proportion of annual inheritance flows relative to national income and total private wealth and, second, we will calculate the share of inherited wealth in total aggregate wealth.

A Model to Compute a Country's Total
Inheritance Flows

Researchers have struggled to measure the aggregate amounts of bequests and gifts within a year. Capturing the full extent of transfers from parents to their children either at death or during the entire lifespan is of course impossible. However, one useful source of information consists of probate inventory records, which report the balance sheets of diseased individuals. A problem with such an approach is only that a very large number of persons die every year, and collecting all the required data would be extremely costly. Another, more tractable, method to estimate aggregate inheritance levels is to employ available macro-series that contain information about the key dimensions in the demographic and economic wealth-holding trends at the country level. In the following, I will show how this can be done and what the resulting evidence has to say on these outcomes.

Estimating the annual flow of bequests and gifts, designated as B, and comparing it to national income, Y, offers a relevant statistic for the importance of inheritance in the macroeconomy. It can be constructed using a structural formula with only three variables.[1] The first variable is the aggregate wealth–income ratio W/Y, which we examined in detail earlier in the book. This ratio shows the amount of wealth available for transfer; if there is no private wealth ownership and wealth equals zero, then there will be no inheritances to transfer.

The second variable of interest is the average wealth of the deceased relative to the living, represented as μ. This ratio quantifies the wealth set to be transferred upon death compared to the wealth of those still living. The higher the ratio, the more total wealth is held by the deceased, and the more that will thus be passed over to heirs. To ascertain this variable, data from estate tax returns and wealth surveys have been synthesized to generate age–wealth profiles, outlining the wealth dynamics across different age cohorts. Importantly, lifetime gifts also need to be accounted for. A low μ value, indicating that the deceased are relatively less wealthy, might be because they have given away most of their wealth before passing away. To correct for this, data on gift tax revenues or gift surveys is used, although these sources are often scarce and incomplete.

Finally, the third variable is the mortality rate, m, which reflects how quickly people pass away. If no one dies and m is zero, then the flow of inheritances will also be zero. Combining these components allows for the calculation of the share of yearly inheritance flows over national income using the following equation:

$$\frac{B}{Y} = \frac{W}{Y} \cdot \mu \cdot m$$

Though simple, this equation encapsulates the core dynamics influencing aggregate inheritance flows in a nation. The annual inheritance flow is a function of the amount of wealth it is possible to inherit, the share of all wealth that is held by those who die, and the rate at which people die. Relating the inheritance flow to the stock of total wealth, B/W, is also an interesting measure showing how important bequests and gifts are in relation to already existing wealth.

Historical Trends in Inheritance Flows: A Secular Decline

Figure 9.1 delineates the magnitude of inheritance flows throughout the twentieth century in France, the UK, and Sweden – three Western nations with reliable historical data. Before World War I, France exhibited inheritance flows amounting to 20 to 25 percent of its national income, the highest such rate in any of the sampled nations or periods. The UK also showed elevated levels during this early era, although the data are somewhat less reliable due to subsequent revisions in wealth–income ratios (as discussed in chapter 2). This lack of clarity is indicated by a dashed line pattern in the UK series before 1920. Sweden, by contrast, recorded lower flows of inheritance, being around 10 percent. When dissecting the underlying causes, research attributes these rates primarily to wealth–income ratios, while mortality rates and wealth disparities between the living and deceased play a less pivotal role.[2]

In the interwar and postwar periods, the proportion of inheritance flows to national income diminished across all examined countries. This decline was partially attributable to a decrease in mortality rates, coupled with declining wealth–income ratios. However, this descending trend arrested in the 1980s, when inheritance flows as a proportion of national income began to rebound, fueled primarily by ascending wealth–income ratios.

By the 2000s, French inheritance flows had surged dramatically, nearly doubling within a few short years – a phenomenon that has garnered substantial scholarly and policy attention. In contrast, neither Sweden nor the UK witnessed

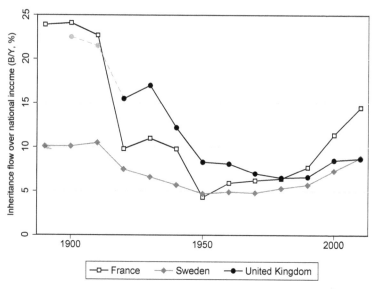

Figure 9.1 Aggregate Inheritance Flows as a Share of National Income, 1890–2010 (%)

Source: Data from Piketty (2011) and Ohlsson, Roine and Waldenström (2020).

such sharp ascents, showing modest increases, if any. While the root cause of France's exceptional rise remains somewhat enigmatic, closer scrutiny suggests it is driven mainly by a spike in gifts, which coincided with the introduction of new tax laws. These laws incentivised affluent households to part with some of their assets via gift taxes as a means of avoiding prospective higher estate taxes. Thus, the remarkable upswing in French inheritance flows since the 2000s may represent a transient shift in asset transfers.

Inheritance Flows in Relation to Wealth Stock

When we turn to figure 9.2, which compares inheritance flows to total private wealth, a more consistent pattern emerges across the three nations. Over time, inheritance flows have waned, reducing their share of total private wealth from 3 to

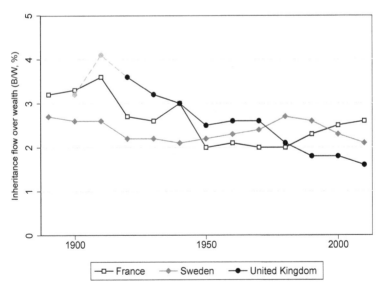

Figure 9.2 Aggregate Inheritance Flows as a Share of Private Wealth, 1890–2010 (%)

Source: Data from Piketty (2011) and Ohlsson, Roine and Waldenström (2020).

4 percent around the year 1900 to 2 to 3 percent by 2010. Among these, the UK exhibited the most pronounced decline, while Sweden's rates remained relatively stable across the century.

Declining Shares of Wealth That Has Been Inherited

Let us now turn our attention to the proportion of wealth in the economy that comes from inheritance compared to wealth that is self-made. This question and how to answer it has been debated by economists for many years, partly related to different methodological approaches to calculate the inheritance share.[3]

Figure 9.3 unveils an intriguing historical trend in five Western countries: the proportion of wealth that is inherited has notably declined over the last century. Specifically, from 1900 to the 2010s, the percentage of wealth that was inherited dropped from a range of 60 to 80 percent to 40 to 60 percent. Variances exist between countries, with France, Sweden, and the UK showing higher shares of around 80 percent, while Germany and the US had comparatively lower shares of around 60 percent.

Interpreting these findings entails consideration of each country's stage in economic development. Earlier industrializers such as France and the UK built extensive industrial and financial capital but have experienced slower growth in more recent decades, mitigating the rise of newly created wealth. In contrast, Germany and the US industrialized later and subsequently enjoyed rapid economic expansion, allowing new wealth to eclipse older, inherited wealth. Fast forward to the latter half of the twentieth century: a general uptick in economic growth across Western countries led to the quicker generation of new fortunes, diminishing the relative weight of inherited wealth. This process was especially pronounced in Germany, France, and Sweden from the 1950s.

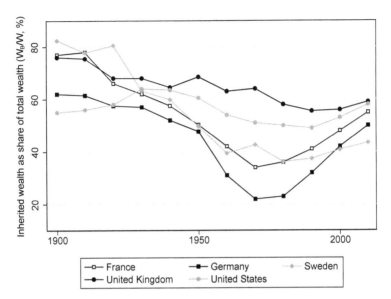

Figure 9.3 Share of Inherited Wealth in Total Wealth, 1900–2010 (%)
Source: Alvaredo, Garbinti and Piketty (2017); Ohlsson, Roine and Waldenström (2020).

The landscape has become more nuanced since the 1980s. Germany and France saw a marked resurgence in the share of inherited wealth, with Germany climbing from 20 percent in 1950 to 40 percent in 2010, suggesting a reversion to historical norms in the postwar period. In Sweden, the UK, and the US, the proportions have plateaued at their postwar levels, a trend consistent with the stability observed in overall inheritance flows and private savings rates.

In summary, the dynamics of inherited wealth share fluctuate across countries and over time, influenced by myriad factors including economic growth rates and saving behaviors. It's a complex narrative that challenges simplistic assumptions about wealth accumulation and inheritance, requiring a nuanced approach to data interpretation and policy considerations.

9.2 INHERITANCE AND ITS COMPLEX IMPACT ON WEALTH INEQUALITY

The discourse surrounding wealth inequality has increasingly come to include the complex role played by inheritance. If rich kids get their money from their wealthy parents, and this inheritance mostly goes to a select few, it is possible that the more inheritance money being passed down could lead to a greater gap between the rich and the poor.

A range of research approaches have been employed to investigate this relationship, each offering distinct perspectives. While studies relying on computational simulations predominantly suggest that inheritance serves to widen the wealth gap, empirical analyses utilizing self-reported data argue for a more balanced outcome. The latter set of studies generally find that, although individuals with greater wealth inherit larger sums, these inheritances constitute a smaller proportion of their overall net worth when compared to those of their less wealthy counterparts.[4]

Relative versus Absolute Inequality Effects in Sweden

An enlightening case study arises from a comprehensive analysis of Swedish population register data.[5] Our scrutiny of these data allowed us to examine the direct consequences of inheritances on the distribution of wealth among various socio-economic strata. Figure 9.4 presents the main results from this analysis. The left panel shows that richer heirs inherit more money. This result mirrors the well-established positive correlation of wealth across generations.

Intriguingly, inheritances have at the same time an equalizing effect on wealth inequality. The overall effect of inheriting in our sample is a 7 percent decrease in the Gini index during the 2000s. This level of equalization is actually quite large, comparable in size to the inequality fall observed in the wake of the slashing of some large fortunes during the

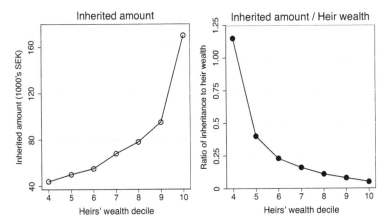

Figure 9.4 Inheritances Are Larger for Richer Heirs but More Important for Poorer Heirs

Source: Elinder, Erixson and Waldenström (2018).

dotcom crash of 2000. However, the equalizing potential of inheritances appears to be attenuated by spending behaviors, with the negative inequality effect being reduced in the years right after inheriting. Such offsetting behavioral responses corroborate longstanding economic theories propounded by John Maynard Keynes and Milton Friedman, which argue that less wealthy individuals are inclined to spend any additional income they receive.

Implications and Future Directions

While these analyses provide critical insights into the role of inheritance in shaping wealth inequality, they represent but one facet of a far more complex landscape. A comprehensive understanding of the societal implications of inherited wealth necessitates a broader purview, embracing a multitude of variables that contribute to individual wellbeing and the overall health of a society.

In conclusion, the relationship between inheritance and wealth inequality is intricate and multi-layered, defying reductive categorizations. Consequently, both scholars and policymakers would do well to approach this subject with the nuanced consideration it warrants, taking into account both its specific manifestations within distinct national settings and its broader implications.

9.3 THE GENESIS OF EXTREME WEALTH: SELF-MADE VERSUS INHERITED FORTUNES

As we extend our investigative lens to the uppermost stratum of the wealth hierarchy, we focus on a topic that is often debated: whether extreme wealth is typically self-made or inherited. Moreover, we consider the temporal aspect by exploring the evolution of this dynamic from the 1980s to the present.

Based on listings of billionaires, figure 9.5 presents a comparative analysis of the wealthiest families in Sweden and

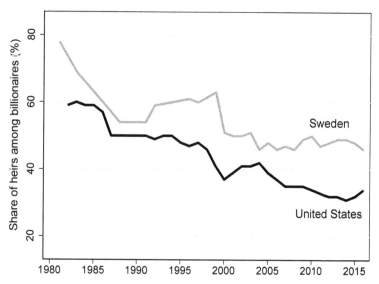

Figure 9.5 How Large a Proportion of the Super-Rich Are Heirs? Sweden versus the US, 1980–2016

Source: Waldenström, Bastani and Hansson (2018) for Sweden; Korom, Lutter and Beckert (2017) for the US.

the United States between 1981 and 2016. The dataset, culled from journalistic accounts, sorts the exceptionally wealthy into two primary categories: "entrepreneurs," denoting those who are the originators of their wealth, and "heirs," an all-encompassing category for everyone else. It is pertinent to note that this binary categorization masks a range of complexities. Among them are the challenges inherent in measuring closely held versus publicly listed wealth and the diverse roles that may be played by heirs – from passive capital accumulators to entrepreneurial transformers of inheritances. The wealth holders can be individuals or large families, and it is more difficult to observe and evaluate closely held wealth than publicly listed fortunes. For the purposes of this discussion, these complexities are set aside with the assumption that they remain consistent both temporally and cross-nationally, thereby permitting valid comparative analysis.

The Swedish data illustrate a near-even split between heirs and entrepreneurs among its wealthiest citizens in recent years. Interestingly, this has been relatively stable for the last three decades, apart from a substantial shift in the 1980s when heirs constituted almost 80 percent of this elite group. By contrast, approximately one-third of the wealthiest US individuals are heirs, while the remaining two-thirds have amassed their fortunes through entrepreneurship. The historical analysis reveals a gradual decline in the proportion of heirs. In the early 1980s, around 60 percent of the billionaires were listed as heirs, and in the 2010s the share was down to 35 percent.

While the Swedish data thus suggest a balance in wealth origins among the most well-to-do, the US tends to lean more towards self-made wealth, at least among the exceptionally affluent.[6] However, it is crucial to acknowledge the limitations inherent in the data, particularly when making cross-national comparisons or extrapolating across diverse temporal frameworks. Further scholarly investigations are necessary for a nuanced understanding of the mechanisms driving the formation of extreme wealth.

In conclusion, this analysis provides crucial, albeit tentative, insights into the origins of extreme wealth. The data reveal intriguing cross-national and temporal variations, begging for more nuanced future research that takes into consideration a multitude of variables and the specific cultural and economic contexts of individual nations. This could form the basis for more informed policy discussions and interventions aimed at managing wealth distribution in an equitable manner.

9.4 INTERGENERATIONAL WEALTH TRANSMISSION: THE ROLE OF INHERITED CAPITAL

The exchange of inheritances and gifts within families is a universal practice and serves as a vivid illustration of the correlation between capital accumulation and life opportunities across generations. While our earlier discussions have focused primarily on the disparities in outcomes – measuring inequality by the gulf between the wealthy and the less affluent – we now turn our attention to inequality of opportunity. Specifically, we explore how wealth is not just a matter of what you have but also a question of how you came to possess it. This draws our focus towards the relationship between inherited wealth and the correlation of family affluence across generations.

Collecting data that could definitively illuminate this relationship presents a formidable challenge. It requires, at a minimum, consistent information about individual wealth across at least two generations, obtained at a comparable life stage. The data intricacies are compounded when one considers the additional variable of inherited wealth, which often originates from disparate sources compared to data on lifetime wealth accumulation.

New Multigenerational Microdata on Wealth and Inheritance

To shed light on the role of inheritances for wealth mobility, some colleagues and I started a project to investigate these patterns in Sweden over the past century. At our disposal was a unique historical dataset that we gathered from different administrative sources. What was specific about these data was that they extended across several generations and contained details about both lifetime and inherited wealth of parents, their children, their grandchildren, and even their great-grandchildren. This robust dataset described important aspects observed in inheritance tax returns, allowing us to account specifically for bequests and gifts within families.[7]

Our empirical strategy adhered to conventional statistical methodologies. Initially, we employed regression models linking parental wealth to that of their children, before integrating inheritance data into the analysis. Subsequently, we conducted counterfactual analyses, excluding inherited wealth to understand its impact on the parent–child wealth correlation.

A Positive Correlation of Wealth across Generations

The results were revelatory. A strong positive correlation emerged between parent and child wealth, indicating that a parent possessing wealth 50 percent above their generational average would likely have a child with wealth 15 percent above the average in their own generation. This confirms that, while parental wealth is a significant factor, it is not the sole determinant of a child's future financial status.[8] The finding that the wealthier a parent is, the wealthier we can expect the child to become, is not new to the literature. In fact, similar significant correlations in wealth across generations have been encountered several times in previous studies in many countries.[9]

Half of Parental Wealth Transmission Operates through Inheritance

Yet the most compelling insight pertained to the role of inheritances. We found that including inheritance data in our model led to a decline of over 50 percent in the parent–child wealth correlation. This is a remarkably large reduction, and it was new to the literature when we presented it. The implication is that inherited capital appears to be a predominant factor in explaining intergenerational wealth continuity.

These findings are presented in figure 9.6. Utilizing kernel regression lines, it visualizes the parent–child wealth ranks across generations. The line marked "Baseline" delineates the established correlation when inheritances are factored in. The line labeled "Without past inheritance in children's wealth" portrays a markedly reduced correlation when

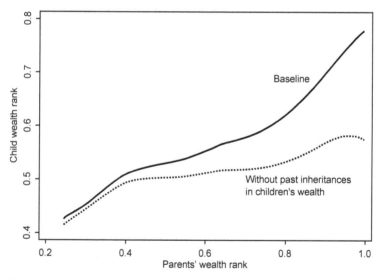

Figure 9.6 Inheritances Account for Half of the Link between Parent and Child Wealth

Note: The figure, from Adermon, Lindahl and Waldenström (2018), plots the relationship between the wealth of parents and their children when ranked according to the size of their wealth in the respective wealth distributions.

inherited wealth is excluded. Notably, the decline is most pronounced among families in the upper echelons of the wealth distribution.[10]

In summary, our findings underscore the pivotal role played by inheritances in perpetuating wealth across generations. This informs the broader discourse on inequality by highlighting that the opportunity to amass wealth is not solely the outcome of individual effort or societal structures but is significantly influenced by intergenerational transfers of capital. Further research could elaborate on these dynamics to provide richer policy insights into fostering a more equitable distribution of wealth and opportunity.

Part III
A New History of Wealth

10

Conclusions and Policy Insights

10.1 REVISING THE HISTORY OF WEALTH INEQUALITY

This book has offered a fresh look at the role of capital in Western economies, scrutinizing how wealth has been generated and distributed over time and the forces shaping it. The investigation has looked at a much longer time frame, 130 years, than is commonly the case in economics research or in the political debate on economic outcomes. This approach is intentional for several reasons. Firstly, people tend to be concerned more with trends over time than with static snapshots, making the study of long-term series crucial. While the optimal length for assessing trends is debatable, providing a comprehensive 130-year timeline allows for the examination of various potential trends. Additionally, delving deep into history offers valuable insights, as past events and policies can shed light on contemporary issues and even enhance our projections for the future.

The analysis has arrived at three central revelations, or facts as I called them in the introductory chapter. Each of them rests on a collection of evidence and research results that the book's chapters present in detail and scrutinize carefully.

First, the world is today a much richer place than it was a century ago. The value of the assets owned by households after adjusting for hikes in consumer prices has increased many times over. Even when relating the value of wealth to national income, building on both revised and newly added data series, wealth values today are at least as high as they were before World War I. This more uniform distribution of wealth relative to national income aligns better with the standard macroeconomic models of capital accumulation and economic growth.

Second, the twentieth century ushered in a democratization of wealth. Around 1900, wealth consisted mainly of agricultural and corporate assets, clustered among the rich. The past century transformed this pattern, fueled by higher education, better incomes, and policies encouraging homeownership and retirement saving. As a result, today's principal forms of household wealth are property and pension savings, contributing to a more equal distribution. In fact, without public pensions, the equalizing trend would be even more pronounced.

Third, wealth has become notably less concentrated over the past 100 years. I term this development "the Great Wealth Equalization," which is one of the book's most robust empirical results. In Europe, wealth inequality fell dramatically until the 1970s, and it has remained low since the 1980s. In the US, the historical decrease was less pronounced and was followed by an increase in wealth concentration until the 2000s. Accounting for offshore and social security wealth modifies the details but not the overarching narrative of decreasing concentration of wealth.

These discoveries prompt us to rethink some aspects of capitalism's historical narrative. In particular, they question the long-held views that unregulated capitalism, as in the nineteenth century, inherently fosters extreme capital accumulation and that wars and progressive taxation were the main equalizers of twentieth-century wealth. The world wars had significant, yet transient, impacts on wealth distribution. Moreover, countries untouched by these wars showed similar patterns. Progressive taxes played a role but were secondary to the broad accumulation of new wealth by middle-class individuals.

The documented accumulation of popular wealth points to the influence of political and economic institutions. Early twentieth-century democratic shifts expanded property rights and launched education and labor reforms that boosted labor productivity and the financial wellbeing of the working class. This led to widespread homeownership and pension savings, now the dominant forms of household wealth. Importantly, this democratization also clarifies why current wealth concentrations did not rise steeply everywhere in the West at the beginning of the twenty-first century despite the large increases in asset prices and rising wealth–income ratios. Simply put, the assets are nowadays for the most part owned by ordinary middle-class households as housing and pension funds, and whenever they appreciate that will benefit the broad masses.

To fully grasp these long-term trends affecting Western wealth, future research must focus much more on the role of institutions than has previously been the case. These institutions, which evolve gradually, have been both shaped by and influential in molding inequality. Understanding them necessitates a historical lens.

10.2 LESSONS FOR POLICYMAKERS

John F. Kennedy famously associated economic growth and inequality with the phrase "a rising tide lifts all boats." The findings in this book, which explores the long-term relationship between economic development and wealth distribution, largely support Kennedy's statement. The past 150 years saw an explosive rise in both income and wealth, coinciding with a remarkable reduction in economic inequality. This history teaches vital lessons for devising policies that foster wealth accumulation while moderating inequality.

How should policymakers approach strategies that combine both high rates of wealth accumulation and moderate levels of wealth inequality? Does the economic history of the West offer lessons to be learned in this regard? I believe it does. History is not always linear and may not move consistently in the same direction; what has been true before may not necessarily be true in the future. However, while it is challenging to suggest specific policies based on long-term trends in a few countries, there are five key lessons worth considering.

1 *Discarding the Zero-Sum Game Fallacy*
First and foremost, the narrative that the economy is a zero-sum game should be emphatically rejected. It is fair to say that the majority of academics and policymakers view rising wealth concentration negatively. They have valid reasons for this stance. However, theory does not point out what level of wealth inequality can be regarded as socially optimal. Some economic models emphasize the need for capital to reach a degree of concentration to serve effectively as a foundation for investing in profitable ventures or providing loans to others. Keynes argued along these lines when he referred to the significant wealth concentration in the late nineteenth century as being crucial for making the big capital investments that came to benefit all people.

The evidence presented in this book makes it abundantly clear that the prosperity of the richest segments of society and that of the rest can, and often do, rise in unison. Over the past 130 years, wealth per capita in Western societies has escalated almost tenfold in real terms. Since 1980 alone, it has multiplied by factors of between 2 and 3. The accumulation of wealth in the bottom groups outpaced that of top groups in the postwar era, especially in Europe and, for some periods, also in the US.

2 *Support Individual Homeownership*
Property has consistently been a profitable long-term investment, leading to less capital stock depreciation and diminishing wealth inequality by increasing middle-class ownership levels. Practical steps might include prioritizing tenant-owned apartment construction or subsidizing mortgages, though careful implementation is essential.

Two examples from US economic history demonstrate how active housing policies can yield contrasting results: the GI Bill of the 1940s was a success, while the subprime loans of the 2000s contributed to the 2008 financial crisis.

3 *Advocate for Pension Savings Securitization*
   Many countries' pension systems are underfunded, often linked to their pay-as-you-go structures, which rely on current workers' contributions and taxes to fund present-day pensions. In contrast, a funded pension system connects people's pensions to their past payments into securitized funds invested in financial markets. The postwar period has shown the funded pension system to be an extraordinary success. Today, thanks to positive asset price development in recent decades, funded pensions constitute a significant portion of household wealth. Ordinary individuals were granted the opportunity to benefit from financial market growth. Critics argue against pension securitization, but their concerns are weak. Transitioning from pay-as-you-go to funded pensions may appear costly, but some countries have gradually made this shift over twenty years. Another critique is the exposure to risk as a result of stock market volatility. However, this argument overlooks the fact that pension funds are typically well diversified to distribute risk while maintaining high average returns. Furthermore, pay-as-you-go pensions are not risk-free, as their funding weakens during economic downturns, when unemployment rises and pension fees decline.

4 *Revisit Labor Income Taxation*
   Labor taxation probably has a constructive role to play in wealth equalization. The findings of this book clearly demonstrate that an increase in the assets of the many that can be invested in their own housing or pension funds is key to reducing the wealth gap. A rise in salary after tax will more rapidly redistribute wealth to the many. Therefore, while taxation on labor income is critical to maintain public services, it has a negative impact on wealth inequality.

5 *Tax Capital Income, Not Wealth*
  Capital taxation, particularly wealth taxation, does not significantly affect wealth inequality. Historical evidence reveals that the equalization of wealth throughout the twentieth century resulted from wealth accumulation among the broad middle classes rather than taxes on wealth or capital income. Most countries have experimented with wealth taxation, but almost none continue to impose such taxes. This is because wealth taxes are fraught with practical challenges, particularly concerning business asset valuation, and generate meager revenues for governments. Capital income taxes are in this context more effective as they adjust to economic cycles and capture windfall gains.

10.3 PRACTICAL TAKEAWAYS FOR HOUSEHOLDS

Providing advice to households about their economic affairs can be difficult. This is because each household is unique and makes decisions based on their specific circumstances, taking into account various critical factors. The portfolio of the modern household is more complex than ever – a blend of traditional property, financial, and social assets. But understanding the historical shifts and current landscapes can guide informed decisions, ensuring financial stability and growth in the long run.

Home Sweet Home: The Investment Case for Homeownership
A primary takeaway is the value of homeownership. Homes don't just offer emotional comfort; they are sound financial investments too. Compared to stocks, real estate has been shown to offer similar long-term returns but with half the volatility, making it an appealing option for the majority of the population. However, the youth and the elderly, whose financial needs and horizons differ, may find renting a more flexible choice.

Mutual Funds: Democratizing Investment
The advent of mutual funds has shifted and simplified the investment landscape for ordinary people. Introduced in the late 1970s and the 1980s, these funds have quickly overtaken traditional savings and pension accounts. They offer households a diversified portfolio, reducing risks while maintaining average returns akin to individual stocks. Their rise has rendered stock market investments more accessible and manageable for the average person, essentially democratizing asset-building.

Invisible Assets: The Role of Welfare Systems
Another underemphasized asset is the individual's relationship with the welfare state. Postwar policy reforms have led to tax-funded systems that offer a range of social benefits, from pensions to insurance. These benefits, while not immediately visible, are a form of wealth that can be capitalized. They also affect private saving behavior – often reducing the need for private pension or healthcare funds. Hence, alongside focusing on accumulating personal assets, it is prudent for households to be mindful of their "social wealth" and focus on income-generating activities to enhance it.

Notes

Chapter 1 Uncovering a Positive Story

1 There are, in fact, several older accounts of the history of wealth and wealth inequality that have inspired both Piketty and me. The work of Simon Kuznets (1953) on the evolution of top income shares in the US offered crucial insights and empirical contributions that have shaped the entire inequality literature. The historical balance sheets of national wealth collected and analyzed by Raymond Goldsmith, especially in *Comparative National Balance Sheets* (1985), were important. Antony Atkinson's contributions to the study of the evolution of wealth inequality have also been central to this literature, especially his book *The Distribution of Personal Wealth in Britain* (1978), written together with Alan Harrison. A more recent key contribution is Branko Milanović's book *The Haves and the Have-Nots* (2011), which analyzes the history of global inequality over the past centuries, emphasizing and extending the Kuznets theory of inequality change.

2 See, for example, the historical exposés of long-run trends in wealth inequality offered in Roine and Waldenström (2015), Piketty and Zucman (2015), Scheidel (2017), van Bavel (2016), and Alfani (2023).

3 There are, of course, nuances in the outlines of the historical wealth inequality trends within and across countries that have been reported. For example, the *World Inequality Report 2022* (World Inequality Lab, 2022) mentions how present European wealth inequality trends are substantially lower than in history. As for the role of wars as a pivotal factor behind the equalization of wealth during the past century, this has also been investigated and emphasized by the historians Walter Scheidel (see Scheidel, 2017) and Guido Alfani (see Alfani, 2023).

4 Piketty (2014, p. 68) writes that, "Broadly speaking, it was the wars of the twentieth century that wiped away the past to create the illusion that capitalism had been structurally changed." A notable exception to the lack of empirical criticism was the series of writings by Chris Giles in the *Financial Times* in 2014.
5 See, for example, Acemoğlu and Robinson (2015), Krusell and Smith (2015), Mankiw (2015), and Weil (2015).
6 For a related account of the historical merits of capitalism in providing growth and widespread welfare gains, although not without recognizing the need for continued redistribution, see Milanović (2019).
7 See further the analysis in chapter 7.
8 A seminal study by Paglin (1975) demonstrated that, when age effects are removed from the distribution of wealth, inequality (measured as the Gini coefficient) decreases by approximately a quarter.
9 See, for example, Alvaredo, Atkinson and Morelli (2018) and Cummins (2022).
10 The method of transforming the wealth distribution of the deceased to the wealth distribution of the living thus uses so-called mortality multipliers, which are based on recorded mortality rates by age, class, sex, and sometimes socio-economic status. For descriptions of this method, see Atkinson and Harrison (1978) or Kopczuk and Saez (2004).
11 There is an extensive literature describing the methodology of measuring historical wealth inequality that has laid the ground for the analyses in this book. Several of the works are cited in subsequent chapters, but among the central contributions are Atkinson and Harrison (1978), Spånt (1979), Williamson and Lindert (1980a, 1980b), Wolff and Marley (1989), Soltow and van Zanden (1998), Wolff (1998), Lindert (2000), Kopczuk and Saez (2004), Piketty, Postel-Vinay and Rosenthal (2006), Ohlsson, Roine and Waldenström (2008), Roine and Waldenström (2015), Kopczuk (2015), Bricker et al. (2016), Wolff (2017), and Alfani (2021).
12 For extensive elaborations into the measurement of inequality, see Cowell (2011).
13 Amiel and Cowell (1999) and Ravallion (2021).
14 Tawney (1913, p. 10).
15 Several studies have inquired just how different the rich are from each other. For example, the *Wall Street Journal* reporter Robert Frank describes in his book *Richistan* (2007) how the millionaires in today's US can be divided into four different social classes based on where in "Richistan" they live: "lower," "middle," and "upper Richistanis," and, finally, the richest,

living in Billionaireville. See also Atkinson (2008) and Alfani (2023).

16 See discussions in, for example, Davies and Shorrocks (2000), Atkinson (2008), Saez and Zucman (2016), Vermeulen (2018), and Bach, Thiemann and Zucco (2019).

17 A famous example of the mismeasurement of debts among the named super-rich is the British media tycoon Robert Maxwell, whose accidental death in 1991 revealed large debts that moved him from being one of the richest men on earth to becoming virtually bankrupt (Davies and Shorrocks, 2000).

18 Clark (2008), table 14.4, p. 183.

19 See Bozio et al. (2024) for France, and Piketty, Saez and Zucman (2018) and Auten and Splinter (2024) for the US.

20 These global facts are well known. For example, Hans Rosling tirelessly explained the achievements of recent world developments; see the book *Factfulness* (Rosling, Rosling and Rosling Rönnlund 2018). Similar evidence and conclusions have been presented by Pinker (2018) and Norberg (2023).

21 Shorrocks et al. (2023).

22 Data from the World Bank, https://data.worldbank.org/.

23 See Milanović (2016, and later updates published on the internet) and, for a specific view of global earnings inequality since the 1970s, Hammar and Waldenström (2020).

Chapter 2 The History of Wealth Accumulation

1 The works of Raymond Goldsmith (1962, 1985, 1987) laid the ground for the analysis of historical balance sheets. The later contributions on which I base my series are cited in the sections where these are used.

2 The data sources for the six countries are the following: Piketty and Zucman (2014) for France and the US; Albers, Bartels and Schularick (2022) for Germany; Artola Blanco, Bauluz and Martínez-Toledano (2021) for Spain; and Waldenström (2017) for Sweden. Additional series for Germany and the US are made by Piketty and Zucman (2014).

3 For an analysis of the role of wealth in industrializing Sweden, see Waldenström (2016, 2017).

4 See Henrekson and Jakobsson (2001) and Henrekson and Stenkula (2016) for descriptions of the growth of government and taxation in postwar Sweden. See also chapter 8 for further evidence on public-sector wealth growth in Sweden and other Western countries.

5 Regarding income denominator, national income is the pre-

ferred choice. It differs from domestic output (for example, gross domestic product, or GDP) in two ways. First, it encompasses net foreign income, which includes payments to and from other countries. Second, it excludes capital depreciation, the decrease in value resulting from factors such as machinery rusting or technology becoming obsolete.

6 In particular, if the wealth–income ratio, or, rather, the capital–output ratio K/Y is lower than the ratio of the saving rate s to the sum of the economic growth rate g, population growth n, and the capital depreciation rate δ, then capital accumulation induces growth in a standard so-called Solow growth model – that is, when $K/Y < s/(g + n + \delta)$.

7 Artola Blanco, Bauluz and Martínez-Toledano (2021).

8 See Piketty (2014) and Piketty and Zucman (2014, 2015).

9 The revised series for Germany are presented in Albers, Bartels and Schularick (2022). The new series for the United Kingdom are from Madsen (2019), for Spain from Artola Blanco, Bauluz and Martínez-Toledano (2021), and for Sweden from Waldenström (2016, 2017).

10 There is a steadily growing literature on historical wealth series. Baselgia and Martínez (2024) present a series for Switzerland going back to 1900, and a recent working paper by Toussaint and his colleagues (2022) presents new data for the Netherlands back to the 1850s. These countries offer a somewhat nuanced picture of the European experience pre-World War I, showing higher wealth–income ratios than those found on the rest of the continent. It remains to be seen how this new evidence harmonizes with the rest of the country evidence, but it is clear that history offers a great variety of outcomes and country-specific effects.

11 The capitalization method is a simple technique for transforming observed capital incomes into a capital stock. If one denotes capital income Y_k and the capital stock K, relating the two by a rate of return r such that $Y_k = rK$, we get the capital stock by dividing capital income with the rate of return, $K = Y_k/r$.

12 The growth in saving rate s and national income g and in particular the s/g ratio, were used in Piketty (2014) in a theoretical derivation of the long-run level of the wealth–income ratio W/Y. Piketty called this the "First fundamental law of capitalism." The idea is that, in equilibrium, which economists call steady state, the economy is not moving. Then, the ratio of the growth rates of capital and income, s/g, will be equal to the ratio of the ratio of the levels of capital and income, W/Y. This is why Madsen (2019) refers to the lack of sudden shifts in s, g or s/g during the period 1913 to 1920 as an argument against the claim that there

should have been a sudden change in W/Y. Subsequent research has questioned the validity of the link between s/g and W/Y (see, for example, Krusell and Smith 2015).

13 See Alvaredo, Atkinson and Morelli (2018) and Cummins (2022). In their figure 4 on the wealth per adult, Alvaredo and his colleagues show that real average wealth hovered around £40,000 to £60,000 between 1911 and 1950.

14 Kuvshinov and Zimmerman (2022).

15 Albers, Bartels and Schularick (2022).

16 Artola Blanco, Bauluz and Martínez-Toledano (2021).

17 See, for example, Prados de la Escosura and Rosés (2010).

18 Previous studies of early twentieth-century stock markets have found that the trading at stock exchanges was often dominated by a few large shares. For example, see studies of Sweden by Waldenström (2014, 2016), Rydqvist and Rong (2021) and, for Berlin and Madrid, by Moore (2010). Furthermore, Kuvshinov and Zimmerman (2022) find no trend or large swings in their newly created series on the Spanish stock market capitalization during the period 1900 to 1925.

19 Waldenstrom (2016, 2017).

20 The calculation uses intermediate consumption of raw materials in home crafts, calculated by deducting intermediate consumption of raw materials in factories and handicrafts from the total supply of raw materials, which in turn is drawn from outputs of agriculture, mining, and net imports. The value added across home industries is then supplemented to the rest of the economy's value added (baseline GDP). See Edvinsson (2013) and calculations in Waldenström (2022b).

21 See, for example, Piketty and Zucman (2014) and Waldenström (2017).

22 A new paper on wealth–income ratios in Switzerland from 1900 to 2020 largely confirms this picture, with a pre-1914 ratio around 500 percent (with variation) and a large increase in recent years (Baselgia and Martínez 2024).

23 The "European" series in figure 2.6 are computed using unweighted averages. Waldenström (2024) shows that the results are similar using population-weighted averages (that is, giving more weight to the larger France, Germany and UK relative to Spain and Sweden).

24 See Goldsmith (1985, pp. 123, 300).

25 Waldenström (2017).

26 Kaldor (1961).

27 There exists an extreme situation where capital and wealth are in principle identical, namely when the country's economy is

not open for foreign trade, when there are no other stores of value than capital, and when relative asset prices do not change, so that the price of capital is fixed and capital gains do not arise.

28 Critics of the wealth valuation method argue that it creates a risk of capturing temporary market price bubbles, whereas critics of the cumulation of investments method point to the fact that these investments may be a useless mismeasure of the true market value of capital.

29 See, for example, Piketty (2014), Weil (2015), and Blume and Durlauf (2015).

30 See Milanović (2019) for a thought-provoking discussion about capitalism in history and the future.

Chapter 3 The Changing Nature of Wealth

1 The historical evidence on asset-type ownership over the wealth distribution is quite scarce. In the early twentieth century, there existed many small-scale farmers owning their own farms whose domains were also part of the aggregate agricultural account, as well as ordinary people owning deposits at their local savings bank. See, for example, discussions of the case of the UK in Atkinson and Harrison (1978) and Sweden in Roine and Waldenström (2009).

2 See Goldsmith (1985, 1987) and Piketty (2014).

3 For discussions of the historical shares of agriculture in GDP, employment, and national wealth, see Grigg (1992), Clark (2008), Goldsmith (1985), and Roine, Vlachos and Waldenström (2009).

4 In Sweden around 1900, agricultural land, including timber tracts and other forestry, represented only 15 percent of total agricultural assets. See Waldenström (2016, 2022b) for a detailed calculation of agricultural wealth.

5 For a discussion of the timing of industrialization in the Western world, see Cameron and Neal (2003).

6 There is a vast literature on Western financial history; see, for example, Gerschenkron (1962), Kindleberger (1984), and Ferguson (2002, 2008).

7 Keynes (1919, p. 19).

8 See, for example, the famous article by Galor and Zeira (1993).

9 For a path-breaking analysis of the factors that account for the emergence of modern corporate finance during the industrial era, see Barron Baskin and Miranti (1997). See also Waldenström (2014, 2022a) for analyses of the financial history of Sweden, with specific attention to the evolution of financial market returns and the structure of the bond market.

10 Pistor et al. (2002) provide a comparative history of corporate legislation in several Western countries.

11 There exist much more ambitious and more nuanced attempts to model personal wealth accumulation. For example, Davies and Shorrocks (2000) propose the model $W_t = W_{t-1} + s_t(r_t W_{t-1} + E_{t-1} + G_{t-1}) + I_t$, where W_t is wealth at end of year t, r_t is the rate of return to capital, E_{t-1} is last year's after-tax labor income, G_{t-1} is last year's government transfer payments, s_t is saving rate out of income, and I_t is inheritances or bequests (and other capital transfers) net of any dissaving in the year received.

12 Of course, over longer historical periods, breaking new land by cutting woods or draining swamps did indeed increase the supply of arable land.

13 The saving data is the saving of the entire private sector, which includes both households and corporations. Some analyses make a distinction between total private saving and household saving (see, for example, Waldenström, 2017) because sometimes the links between corporate and personal household saving take time to materialize. Savings calculated from corporate balance sheets may not immediately affect the market value of corporate equity, and in this case a deviation arises between the book and market values. Households therefore do not experience an increase in capital income as firm values do not change and household saving behavior is unaffected. Still, the book value of recorded corporate saving spills over into the estimation of total private saving and could generate divergent behavior between corporations and households, which is reflected in the two distinct saving rates. Capital gains are rarely observed directly and are calculated as a residual between total wealth growth and saving, using the wealth growth equation in the main text. In one of my studies of the Swedish historical aggregate wealth growth (Waldenström, 2017), I made a simple analysis comparing observed capital gains in the Swedish stock market and housing market over different historical periods with the estimated residual capital gains in the aggregate wealth growth analysis. The comparison showed fairly large consistencies and suggested that the aggregate model framework delivers plausible results.

14 See Waldenström (2014, 2016, 2017, 2022a, 2022b).

15 Removing corporate saving from total private saving lowers the relative contribution of savings to wealth growth from 80 percent to 65 percent in France, from 109 to 28 percent in Sweden, and from 72 to 48 percent in the US (Waldenström, 2017, table 1).

16 See Knoll, Schularick and Steger (2017) for a comprehensive analysis of the evolution of Western house prices since 1870. For discussions of the role of housing wealth in the recent increase in aggregate wealth–income ratios, see Bonnet et al. (2014), Weil (2015) and Artola Blanco, Bauluz and Martínez-Toledano (2021).

17 Results from a study by the car search engine iSeeCars.com (www.iseecars.com/how-long-people-keep-cars-study).

18 This standard procedure used by statistical agencies is called the *perpetual inventory method*. It defines the stock of consumer durables CD_t as the accumulated annual consumption flows I_t (in real terms) accounting for annual rate of capital depreciation δ, using ultimately the equation $CD_t = I_t + (1 - \delta)CD_{t-1}$.

19 Bricker, Hansen and Volz (2019). See also Wolff (2021).

20 Waldenström (2022b) shows that the stock of consumer durables has fluctuated in the past 200 years between 5 and 15 percent of total assets; it trended downwards during the 2010s and by the early 2020s had reached 5 percent.

21 For Sweden, see Kuuse (1970, chapter IV) and, for the US, see Wolff (2017, chapter 11).

22 Schularick and Taylor (2012) and Jordà, Schularick and Taylor (2016) study the historical evolution of household mortgages and its links with bank credits and macroeconomic crises.

23 Jordà, Schularick and Taylor (2016).

24 Sandberg (1978, 1979).

Chapter 4 Homes and Pensions

1 Headlines telling the German people that they are outranked in terms of wealth per capita have been seen in the media several times over recent years. The specific headline quoted comes from *Der Stern*, "Vermögensschock: Die Deutschen sind die armen Würstchen der EU" (January 5, 2018). But similar messages were found in *Süddeutsche Zeitung*, "Die meisten Deutschen besitzen weniger als andere Europäer" (December 23, 2016), and *Die Welt*, "Abgeschalgen auf Rang 19 – darum sind Deutschlands Nachbarn so viel reicher" (September 2023).

2 See, for example, Schön (2012) for Sweden and Kohl (2018) for several Western countries.

3 For discussions about the rise in US homeownership between the 1940s and 1960s, see Fetter (2013) and Kohl (2017).

4 See Fetter (2013) for discussions of how to measure the impact of housing policies as they coincided with other societal developments.

5 For a general discussion of the role of public policy in homeownership in the OECD countries, see Andrews and Caldera (2011). For discussions about the case of Sweden, see Schön (2012).

6 Despite its widespread attribution to President Franklin D. Roosevelt, there's no verified source confirming that he actually made this statement.

7 Among the studies that find evidence on the benefits of owning one's home relative to renting it are Shilling, Sirmans and Dombrow (1991), Gatzlaff, Green and Ling (1998), Harding, Miceli and Sirmans (2000), and Hausman et al. (2022).

8 See Sodini et al. (2023).

9 Pádraig Floyd, "Three-quarters of UK adults are ignorant of their pension savings," April 17, 2023, www.pensions-expert.com/De fined-Benefit/Three-quarters-of-UK-adults-are-ignorant-of-their -pension-savings?ct=true.

10 See Roine and Waldenström (2009) and a later discussion in Waldenström (2016, 2017).

11 While Atkinson and Harrison (1978) do not talk much about the role of funded pensions, they actually include it in some of their analyses (see, for example, p. 279).

12 There is some variation across countries in the structure of funded pension savings. In some countries (for example, Sweden and the UK), funds are tied to occupational pension contributions run by employers. By contrast, the French funded pensions are more closely tied to life insurance, with specified annuities being paid out in old age. For discussions of pension arrangements in OECD countries, see OECD (2021).

13 There is little research on the historical evolution of statutory pension ages in the West. OECD (2011, chapter 1) shows that it has varied largely between sixty and sixty-five since 1950, being stable in most countries in this period and increasing in some.

14 We use here "period life expectancy," which Our World in Data explains as the average number of years a newborn would live if mortality rates in the current year were to stay the same throughout its life. Historical data on statutory pension ages across OECD countries is presented in OECD (2011, table 1.1).

15 See Sinn (2000) for a discussion about the arguments for and against transitioning from pay-as-you-go pensions to fully funded pensions.

16 For an early discussion of funded capitalism, see Johnson and Greening (1999).

17 See Bebchuk, Cohen and Hirst (2017) for a critical assessment of institutional investors as corporate owners; and Appel, Gormley and Keim (2016) for a more positive assessment.

Chapter 5 The Great Wealth Equalization of the Twentieth Century

1 The *New York Magazine* article headline "Jeff Bezos's Space Flight Is One Giant Leap for Inequality" (July 20, 2021) exemplifies the view of today's super-rich and their role for the wealth distribution.

2 Of course, we should be aware that this top group has consisted of different individuals over time because of wealth mobility. Mobility in the distribution of wealth is not part of the main analysis of this book, as I also mentioned in the introductory chapter. Life-cycle mobility is a very important component for understanding who the rich are (in short, they are old), while year-to-year mobility is a smaller issue in the wealth distribution than in, for example, the income distribution (unemployment, sick leave, parental leave, studies, or capital gains all make a large difference between annual and multi-year inequality). Intergenerational mobility in wealth distribution (self-made versus inherited) is a major topic in wealth inequality analysis that I discuss in chapter 9.

3 Data sources are the following. France: estate tax returns and capitalized capital income (Garbinti, Goupille-Lebret and Piketty, 2021; Piketty, Postel-Vinay and Rosenthal, 2006); Germany: mainly wealth tax returns (Albers, Bartels and Schularick, 2022); Spain: estate tax returns, wealth survey, capitalized capital income (Alvaredo and Artola Blanco, 2023, for 1901–1958; Martínez-Toledano, 2020, for 1984–2015); Sweden: wealth tax returns, third-party reported registry wealth, capitalized capital income (Roine and Waldenström, 2009; Lundberg and Waldenström, 2018); United Kingdom: mainly estate tax returns (Alvaredo, Atkinson and Morelli, 2018; Cummins, 2022); United States: capitalized capital incomes, wealth survey (Saez and Zucman, 2016, 2020; Smith, Zidar and Zwick, 2023; Wolff and Marley, 1989; Wolff 2017).

4 We do not observe US estimates before 1913, but the available data that economic historians have produced for the nineteenth century suggest that American wealth inequality was even lower in that era (Lindert, 2000; Ohlsson, Roine and Waldenström, 2008, Roine and Waldenström, 2015).

5 The latest Swedish estimate is from 2012, and top shares seem to have increased in the years thereafter. The finding of low UK wealth inequality in recent decades may come as a surprise, but it has been reproduced using other data sources; see Cowell (2013) and the other chapters in Hills et al. (2013). Accounting

for family trusts, often used in estate tax planning, also does not
seem to matter a lot for UK wealth concentration, as discussed
by Alvaredo, Atkinson and Morelli (2018) and Cummins (2022).

6　For analyses of the evolution of wealth inequality in Canada,
see Morissette, Zhang and Drolet (2006), Brzozowski et al. (2010),
and Davies and Di Matteo (2020). For an analysis of the recent
evolution of wealth inequality in Italy, see Acciari, Alvaredo and
Morelli (2024).

7　Most of the data come from Roine and Waldenström (2015).

8　Data on long-run "observed" series come from Roine and
Waldenström (2015), while data on the shorter "observed/sim-
ulated" series come from the World Inequality Database (www
.wid.world).

9　Piketty, Postel-Vinay and Rosenthal (2006, 2014).

10　See Madsen and Strulik (2020).

11　In a related study on trends during the nineteenth century,
O'Rourke and Williamson (2005) offer a multidimensional explanation to inequality. While agricultural productivity and the
growth of the labor force contributed to rising land values, and
thus to the wealth of rich landowners, counteracting forces were
rising industrial productivity, which increased the real wages of
industrial workers, and the opening of the economy to trade.
The authors' evidence on falling transport costs, rising liberal
policy, evaporating international commodity price gaps, rising
trade shares, and the relationship between commodity prices
and factor endowments all suggest that the English economy
became much more open to trade during the eighteenth and
early nineteenth centuries, which meant that land rents were
determined more by international prices than by domestic
factors, and ultimately lowered the wealth of the landed elites.

12　Alfani (2021, 2023) examines wealth inequality trends during pre-
industrial times in several European countries, and Bengtsson
et al. (2018) study Sweden since 1750.

13　See Saez and Zucman (2016, 2020); Kuhn, Schularick and Steins
(2020); Bricker, Hansen and Volz (2019); Bricker et al. (2020); and
Smith, Zidar and Zwick (2023).

14　To see how this capitalization method works, denote capital
income y_k, wealth W, and the rate of return r. If $y_k = rW$, we can
estimate W from the observed y_k and the assumed r by dividing
both sides of the equation by r, which gives $y_k/r = rW/r = W$.

15　Nordic countries have population-wide register data on both
wealth stocks and wealth returns, offering unique opportunities to scrutinize the reliability of the capitalization approach.
Lundberg and Waldenström (2018), using Swedish data, and

Fagereng et al. (2020), using Norwegian data, find notable discrepancies between capitalized and actual wealth stocks.

16 The replication study is Smith, Zidar and Zwick (2023). In subsequent work, both research teams have revised their series, which has led to some convergence. In their latest versions, Saez and Zucman have reduced their share in 2012 from 41.8 percent to 36.7 percent, whereas Smith, Zidar and Zwick have increased their share from 32.2 percent to 34.4 percent.

17 Roine and Waldenström (2009).

18 For another recent historical exposé of the rich in Western societies, see Alfani (2023).

19 Milanović (2011).

20 Historical data on annual earnings in 1914 from Roine and Waldenström (2008) and annual stock and bond yields from Waldenström (2022a). Data on Stefan Persson's ownership share and H&M's market capitalization from open sources. Median monthly salary is 33,200 SEK, which, multiplied by twelve months and adding 50 percent in social security contributions, payroll taxes, and occupational pension provisions, gives an annual labor cost of 600,000 SEK.

21 See, for example, Bricker et al. (2016), Bricker, Hansen and Volz (2019) and Bach, Thiemann and Zucco (2019).

22 See Davies et al. (2011, 2017) and Shorrocks et al. (2023).

23 Smith, Zidar and Zwick (2023).

24 For example, *Forbes* magazine mainly uses a 10 percent value discount on closely held corporate shares. But research estimates of the value discounts are around 30 percent, and in some studies even higher (Smith, Zidar and Zwick, 2023).

25 Atkinson (2008) proposed a measure based on the returns to wealth as multiples to average incomes. The "rich" are individuals whose wealth exceeds thirty times mean income and the "super-rich" those who can live off the interest on their interest – that is, with a return to their wealth that exceeds thirty times mean income. Peichl and Pestel (2013) and Krolage, Peichl and Waldenström (2022) compare a number of measures and how they perform in historical time series.

26 See Henrekson (2015) for the 1964–2014 comparison, Cervenka (2022) for the 2021 listing, and the Swedish magazine *Affärsvärlden* 26/6 (1991) for that of 1991.

27 Hoffman, Postel-Vinay and Rosenthal (2009).

28 For the US study, see Haveman and Wolff (2005) and Wolff (2017, chapter 11). The Swedish data analysis was made using microdata from the LINDA database in 2002, employing standard variables from the wealth and income tax registers. Finally,

Brandolini, Magri and Smeeding (2010) studied asset poverty in several Western countries.
29 See Modigliani's Nobel Prize lecture for a good description of this theory (Modigliani, 1985).
30 See Paglin (1975) for the original analysis and, for example, Almås and Mogstad (2012) for applications on Norwegian data.
31 See Fisher et al. (2020).
32 See Congressional Budget Office (2022, p. 13).
33 Derenoncourt et al. (2023).
34 Wolff (2017, chapter 9).
35 Jones and Simkovich (1992).
36 Edlund and Kopczuk (2009).
37 Grabka, Marcus and Sierminska (2015).

Chapter 6 Exploring the Great Wealth Equalization

1 For a description of models explaining wealth inequality change, see Davies and Shorrocks (2000), Cagetti and De Nardi (2008), Cowell and Van Kerm (2015), and Piketty and Zucman (2015). Some recent contributions also propose some new and interesting channels, such as the role of patience (Epper et al., 2020) and risk-taking (Bach, Calvet and Sodini, 2020).
2 Lindert (1986).
3 The Paris estate tax return project is one of the most ambitious (see Piketty, Postel-Vinay and Rosenthal, 2006, 2014). The so-called TRA project sampled all French families whose family names began with the letters "Tra" over the past two hundred years and studied their social and economic whereabouts, including their wealth accumulation patterns (Bourdieu et al., 2019).
4 Soltow (1985, 1989).
5 Average wealth growth across groups was computed by combining data on aggregate wealth (chapter 2) and top wealth shares (chapter 5). Missing data for 1910 implies using 1913 in the US.
6 Bricker and Volz (2019).
7 Atkinson and Harrison (1978) and Bastagli and Hills (2013) for the UK; Wolff (1989), Artola Blanco, Bauluz and Martínez-Toledano (2021) and Martínez-Toledano (2020) for Spain; Roine and Waldenström (2009) for Sweden; and Kuhn, Schularick and Steins (2020) for the US.
8 See Kuhn, Schularick and Steins (2020).
9 In a study of the role of savings for wealth accumulation, Bauluz, Novokment and Schularick (2022) show evidence of a "savings glut" elevating high-end wealth disproportionately in several Western economies.

10 A linear regression, $Gini_i = a + b \cdot Homeownership\ Rate_i + e$ over country i using the data in the figure, produces a statistically significant estimate $\hat{b}$ of −0.04 (standard error 0.01 and t-statistic −0.04/0.01 = −3.9).

11 For examples of country-specific evidence on the negative correlation between homeownership and wealth inequality, see Bastagli and Hills (2013) and Kuhn, Schularick and Steins (2020).

12 See, for example, Piketty (2014, p. 20), but also Piketty (2001), Piketty and Saez (2003), and Atkinson, Piketty and Saez (2011).

13 Milanović discusses mainly the role of wars for income inequality trends, either over the long historical periods, in Milanović (2011), or at the global level, in Milanović (2016). For summaries of the works of Alfani, see Alfani (2021, 2023).

14 In the classical Cobb–Douglas model of the economy, capital volumes and prices are perfectly offset. That is, if the volume of capital decreases by 10 percent, capital prices will increase by exactly the same so as to keep the value of the capital stock unchanged. Note that this interplay goes in both directions, meaning that price effects also spur volume responses. In other models, for example the common constant elasticity model, the responses need not be exactly offsetting, but empirical estimates are not uniform as to the degree of the offset. For further discussions, see, for example, Rognlie (2015) and Piketty and Zucman (2015).

15 Prados de la Escosura (2022).

16 Heldring, Robinson and Whitfill (2022).

17 The analysis combines the top percentile wealth share estimates presented in chapter 5 and the inflation-adjusted aggregate private wealth data presented in chapter 2. Germany is unfortunately omitted because of a lack of frequent enough estimates during the period.

18 See Scheve and Stasavage (2010) for a formal argument concerning the link between mass mobilization and tax progressivity.

19 For instance, Malaysia's poverty rate dropped from 54 percent in 1970 to 5 percent in 2000, while South Korea's decreased from 23 percent to 4 percent over the same period. Thailand's income inequality (measured using the Gini index) also fell from 45 in 1990 to 35 in 2020. Poverty rates have plummeted: in Malaysia from 54 percent in 1970 to 5 percent in 2000 and in South Korea from 23 to 4 percent over the same period, and the income Gini of Thailand fell from 45 in 1990 to 35 in 2020. See Jomo (2006) for poverty incidence and the World Bank's World Development Indicator for Thailand's Gini coefficients.

20 A recent survey of the economics of capital taxation is by Bastani and Waldenström (2020).

21 Discussions of how to tax the rich (more) are provided by Bastani and Waldenström (2023) and Piketty, Saez and Zucman (2023).

22 For theoretical studies proposing inheritance taxation, see Cagetti and De Nardi (2009) and Piketty and Saez (2013).

23 For instance, while top inheritance tax rates in Sweden reached their zenith in the 1960s, average rates peaked much earlier, in the 1930s. The scarcity of data on historical capital returns and tax rates hampers research. Although information on top marginal rates exists, it's unclear how many individuals actually paid these rates or how deductions influenced the tax base. Economists often focus on marginal rates to fit standard models, but average rates are generally more telling for wealth accumulation. In fact, average rates often lag far behind top marginal rates and may not share the same temporal trends. For in-depth discussions and data specifics, refer to works by Du Rietz, Henrekson and Waldenström (2016) and Ohlsson, Roine and Waldenström (2020). Studies have similarly found gaps between top marginal and effective rates across various nations; see Roine, Vlachos and Waldenström (2009), Rydqvist, Spitzman and Strebulaev (2014), and Scheve and Stasavage (2016, ch. 3). See also Henrekson and Stenkula (2016) for in-depth descriptions of capital taxation in Sweden from the nineteenth century to the present.

24 This is Piketty's "fundamental law" stating that wealth inequality increases as the wedge between wealth return (r) and income growth (g), $r>g$, widens. If wealth returns are reduced by a capital tax, the wedge shrinks, and the same holds for wealth inequality (Piketty 2014, chapter 10).

25 Hubmer, Krusell and Smith Jr. (2020) find that the diminished income taxation for high earners has exacerbated wealth inequalities. One may want to qualify this conclusion given that much of the elevated US wealth concentration stems from capital gains and new entrepreneurial ventures (recall the analysis in chapter 5), indicating wealth growth among groups to whom marginal labor income tax rates hardly matter much.

26 Scheuer and Wolitzky (2016) highlight the importance of political constraints by analyzing optimal capital taxation under the threat of a radical political reform that could entail a significant redistribution of wealth. From an empirical perspective, the political economy of capital taxation has recently been analyzed by Bastani and Waldenström (2021).

27 Scheve and Stasavage (2010, 2016).

28 Henrekson and Waldenström (2016) study the rise and fall of inheritance taxation in Sweden, while Bastani and Waldenström (2021) show experimental evidence on the determinants of political support for inheritance taxation. For an overview of the evolution of taxation in Sweden, see Henrekson and Stenkula (2016).

29 Ernst Wigforss, Swedish minister of finance from 1932 to 1949, talked about society-controlled "firms without owners," and the Swedish Trade Union Federation (LO in Swedish) talked about "capitalism without capitalists." For a thorough analysis of Swedish taxation from the nineteenth century to the present day, see Henrekson and Jakobsson (2001). A specific analysis of how taxes impacted capital owners in Sweden is Henrekson, Johansson and Stenkula (2020).

30 Acemoğlu, Robinson and Verdier (2017).

31 Lindert (2004) was among the first to point out the positive growth effects of public spending. Interestingly, Acemoğlu and Johnson (2023) point to the long-run economic benefits of restraining the positions of market leaders even if that could have short-run negative effects on incentives.

32 For a formalization of this institutional model, see Acemoğlu, Johnson and Robinson (2005) and Acemoğlu and Robinson (2006). For implementation of this institutional analysis on long-run prosperity, see Acemoğlu and Robinson (2012), and see also Acemoğlu and Robinson (2015) on how institutions matter for economic inequality trends in the West.

33 North and Thomas (1973).

34 In their recent exposé of almost a thousand years of human and economic development, Acemoğlu and Johnson (2023) argue that, without political institutions restraining rulers and elites, economic growth may be captured primarily by such groups rather than being circulated more widely.

35 Hacker and Pierson (2010).

36 See van Bavel (2016), Scheidel (2017), and Alfani (2023).

37 Lindert (2004) presented an important synthesis of long-run social spending patterns and their importance for economic growth in the West. See also Tanzi and Schuknecht (2000) for a global perspective on the growth in public spending and its economic effects.

38 Goldin and Katz (2008). See also Lindert and Williamson (2016) for a further elaboration of the relationship between educational spending and economic inequality in the US over the twentieth century.

39 Mokyr (1990, 2016) and McCloskey (2016).

40 A recent study shows that human capital returns, though paid out as dividends from pass-through companies, have been instrumental in the rise of US top income inequality in recent years (Smith et al. 2019).

41 Gans and Leigh (2019) discuss how innovation and technological advances have acted to drive economic inequality, but they also point out pathways through which the productivity improvements can be channeled towards lifting the bottom of the distribution. The increasing accumulation of intangible capital and its importance for growth and distribution has further been analyzed by Haskel and Westlake (2017) and Madsen, Minniti and Venturini (2021).

42 See Goldin and Margo (1992). On unionization and the labor share of value added, see Ciminelli, Duval and Furceri (2022).

43 A fraction of taxable wealth was added to individual incomes to calculate the "taxable amount," revealing information on the size of wealth holdings by income class. For details on Swedish historical wealth data and income tax rules, see Roine and Waldenström (2008, 2009).

44 These patterns are in line with descriptions of the emergence of a class of managers and high-level professionals in interwar Sweden (Glete 1994).

45 See Beck, Demirgüç-Kunt and Levine (2007), Demirgüç-Kunt and Levine (2009), and Levine (2021).

46 Cagetti and De Nardi (2006, 2008).

Chapter 7 Hidden Offshore Wealth

1 See EU Tax Observatory (2023) for a recent estimate of the total offshore wealth and Shorrocks et al. (2023) for an estimate of the total value of financial and non-financial assets in the world.

2 There is a rapidly growing literature on the estimation of the offshore wealth possessions of Western citizens and corporations. See, for example, Zucman (2013), Alstadsæter, Johannesen and Zucman (2018, 2019), and EU Tax Observatory (2023).

3 EU Tax Observatory (2023).

4 There are many studies concerning offshore holdings of individuals and corporations. For estimates of individual asset holdings, see, for example, Zucman (2013) and Alstadsæter. Johannesen and Zucman (2018, 2019). Estimates of hidden offshore assets of corporations is a more complex area, but an indication of the scale of these operations was recently given in a study of profit shifting by Tørsløv, Wier and Zucman (2023). Notice that individual foreign possessions can be handled through legal entities,

typically corporations, but these will all the same be treated as individual wealth in this book's analysis.

5 The OECD (2014) describes a tax haven as a country with "no or low taxes, lack of effective exchange of information, lack of transparency, and no requirement of substantial activity." The EU (European Parliamentary Research Service 2018) talks about countries that "provide taxpayers, both legal and natural persons, with opportunities for tax avoidance, while their secrecy and opacity also serves to hide the origin of the proceeds of illegal and criminal activities."

6 See Zucman (2013).

7 Statistics on OECD corporate tax rates were taken from the OECD.Stat tables "Table II.1: Statutory corporate income tax rate" and "Table II.4: Overall statutory tax rates on dividend income," with reported percentage rates as of 2023 (see https://stats.oecd.org/). See EU Tax Observatory (2023) for references on what countries are and are not labeled as tax havens.

8 See Zucman (2013, 2015), Alstadsæter, Johannesen and Zucman (2019), and Martínez-Toledano (2020) for descriptions and applications of this approach to estimate offshore wealth.

9 See Roine and Waldenström (2009), for more details on the flow-based method to estimate offshore wealth.

10 Offshore wealth estimate from Zucman (2015) and global wealth amounts from the Global Wealth Report (Shorrocks et al., 2023).

11 See EU Tax Observatory (2023) and Shorrocks et al. (2023).

12 For a discussion of the change in national accounts definitions and the impact on estimated offshore wealth, see Waldenström (2022b).

13 Alstadsæter, Johannesen and Zucman (2019).

14 EU Tax Observatory (2023).

15 For the study of capital and labor income tax responsiveness, see Kleven and Schultz (2014). For the responsiveness to wealth taxation, see Jakobsen et al. (2020), Brülhart et al. (2022), and Bastani and Waldenström (2020, 2023).

16 See Martínez-Toledano (2020) and Roine and Waldenström (2009).

17 Characterizing the full extent of the Kamprad family's ownership of IKEA-related businesses is complicated, but it seems to include stakes in the IKANO bank and the Inter IKEA group.

Chapter 8 Public-Sector Wealth

1 See, for example, Feldstein (1974, 1976, 1996), Gale (1998), and Gruber and Yelowitz (1999).

2 The exact names of this unfunded wealth vary a bit in the literature and include "pension wealth," "retirement wealth," "social security wealth," and "transfer wealth." The term "social security wealth" is used here in a broad sense, containing the capitalized value of future incomes from pensions and social insurance transfers. However, in the US context, social security has a narrower meaning that does not include old-age pensions (for a discussion, see Wolff, 2011, 2017).

3 On the US, see Sabelhaus and Volz (2020) and Catherine, Miller and Sarin (2023). On Europe, see Sierminska and Wroński (2022) and Wroński (2023).

4 See Boyer and Schmidle (2009) for Victorian England, and Edebalk (2009) for Sweden.

5 In the pension debate, you often hear about defined-contribution and defined-benefit plans. Defined-contribution plans tie pensions to savings, while defined-benefit plans link them to salaries. Individuals shoulder most risks in defined-contribution plans, but defined-benefit plans spread risks among workers, shareholders, and taxpayers.

6 The first computations of social security wealth are found in the seminal paper by Feldstein (1974), who also did the analysis (Feldstein, 1976). Several studies have subsequently estimated the value and distributional properties of social security wealth for different countries, for example Wolff (2011), Frick and Grabka (2013), Bönke et al. (2019), and Wroński (2023).

7 See extensive discussions in Wolff (2011) and Cowell et al. (2017).

8 Recent years have seen an increasing number of defined-benefit pension systems being required to back their pension promises with fund accounts. The traditional demarcation between defined-benefit and defined-contribution pensions, where pensions are deposited in individual accounts and are part of the standard wealth definition, has become less clear.

9 Data are taken from Wolff and Marley (1989) and Wolff (2011) for the period 1922–95 and from Sabelhaus and Volz (2020) for the period thereafter. The recent period has also been studied in Catherine, Miller and Sarin (2023). They make similar computations to Sabelhaus and Volz (2020) but use different assumptions about discount rates when valuing social security wealth and find higher values in recent years and a flatter overall trend in wealth concentration.

10 See, for example, Piketty, Saez and Zucman (2018).

11 For a discussion of war finance in the twentieth century, see Gerschenkron (1962).

12 Waldenström (2017) on Sweden; Blake and Orszag (1999) on the UK; Albers, Bartels and Schularick (2022) on Germany.

Chapter 9 Inheritance and Wealth Inequality

1 Thomas Piketty made an important contribution when he summarized this macroeconomic accounting analysis in his survey of inheritance in France (Piketty, 2011). In that study, he also discussed a second approach to estimating inheritance flows by gathering information from probate inventories and estate tax returns, a method that is quite sensitive to aspects of tax legislation.

2 See the comparative study of Sweden, France, the UK, and the US by Ohlsson, Roine and Waldenström (2020).

3 Notable scholars offer divergent views on how inherited wealth grows and accumulates. Foremost among them is Franco Modigliani (1986, 1988), who argues that inherited wealth is compounded over time as a result of investment returns. In contrast, American economists Laurence Kotlikoff and Lawrence Summers contend that people typically spend their inheritances, leading to less accumulation than posited by Modigliani (Kotlikoff and Summers, 1981; Kotlikoff, 1988). These differing views impact the estimated share of inherited wealth in the economy. Using Modigliani's approach, which considers past inheritances but assumes capital returns are consumed, we get an inherited share of 20 to 30 percent of total wealth. Kotlikoff and Summers, however, factor in a rate of return to capital and estimate a much higher share of 80 to 90 percent. More recently, Piketty, Postel-Vinay and Rosenthal (2014) suggested an approach to account for both the growth and potential dissipation.

4 There is a longstanding research literature studying the links between inheritance and wealth inequality, with some notable contributions being Atkinson (1971), Harbury and Hitchens (1979), and Karagiannaki (2017) on the UK; Wolff (2002, 2011) and Wolff and Gittelman (2014) on the US; Boserup, Kreiner and Kopczuk (2016) on Denmark; Elinder, Erixson and Waldenström (2018), Black et al. (2020), and Nekoei and Seim (2023) on Sweden; and Fagereng, Mogstad and Rønning (2021) on Norway.

5 Elinder, Erixson and Waldenström (2018).

6 A study of longer time series of the share of entrepreneurs among the wealthiest in the US confirms this rising trend in the share of entrepreneurs (Edlund and Kopczuk 2009).

7 Adermon, Lindahl and Waldenström (2018).

8 The following table from Adermon, Lindahl and Waldenström

(2018) contains the results estimating the linear model *Child's Wealth* = $a + b \cdot$ *Parents' Wealth* + $c \cdot$ *Inheritance* + e:

Explanatory variables:	Dependent variable: Child's wealth		
	Model 1:	Model 2:	Model 3:
Parents' wealth	0.31***		0.14**
	(0.05)		(0.07)
Inheritance		0.38***	0.28***
		(0.06)	(0.07)
R^2	0.113	0.144	0.181
Observations	386	386	386

The estimated coefficients are shown in the table with associated standard errors in parenthesis below. R^2 denotes how large a share of the total variation the model explains. The asterisk denotes the level of statistical precision of the estimate: *** is significance at the 1 percent level and ** significance at the 5 percent level.

9 See Adermon, Lindahl and Palme (2021), Hällsten and Kolk (2023), and Black et al. (2020) for studies of Sweden, and Fagereng, Mogstad and Rønning (2021) on Norway.

10 The computation of the "inheritance free" measure of wealth of children uses the data on the amount inherited and the date of receipt t to construct a model of child wealth with and without inheritance. A model is $W_{iy} = a_0 + c_1 I_{iy-t} + \delta(t \cdot I_{iy-t}) + \lambda(t \cdot I^2_{iy-t}) + W^p + u_{it}$, where W_{iy} is wealth of the child i measured at the end of year y, and I_{iy-t} is the sum of the child's inheritance received on average at year $y - t$. We also interact inheritance with a quadratic in average time since receiving the inheritance. Because the inheritance terms in this regression provide a prediction of the child wealth that is due to inheritance, the residuals with the constant added back in provide an estimate of wealth net of inheritance for the individual child. This is the "inheritance free" wealth. See Adermon, Lindahl and Waldenström (2018) for details.

References

Acciari, P., Alvaredo, F., and Morelli, S. (2024) "The Concentration of Personal Wealth in Italy, 1995–2016," *Journal of the European Economic Association* forthcoming.

Acemoğlu, D., and Johnson, S. (2023) *Power and Progress: Our Thousand-Year Struggle over Technology and Prosperity*. New York: Basic Books.

Acemoğlu, D., and Robinson, J. (2006) *Economic Origins of Dictatorship and Democracy*. Cambridge: Cambridge University Press.

Acemoğlu, D., and Robinson, J. (2012) *Why Nations Fail: The Origins of Power, Prosperity, and Poverty*. New York: Crown.

Acemoğlu, D., and Robinson, J. (2015) "The Rise and Decline of General Laws of Capitalism," *Journal of Economic Perspectives* 29(1): 3–28.

Acemoğlu, D., Johnson, S., and Robinson, J. (2005) "Institutions as the Fundamental Cause of Long–Run Growth," in Aghion, P., and Durlauf, S. (eds), *Handbook of Economic Growth*. Amsterdam: North-Holland.

Acemoğlu, D., Robinson, J. A., and Verdier, T. (2017) "Asymmetric Growth and Institutions in an Interdependent World," *Journal of Political Economy* 125(5): 1245–305.

Adermon, A., Lindahl, M., and Palme, M. (2021) "Dynastic Human Capital, Inequality, and Intergenerational Mobility," *American Economic Review* 111(5): 1523–48.

Adermon, A., Lindahl, M., and Waldenström, D. (2018) "Intergenerational Wealth Mobility and the Role of Inheritance: Evidence from Multiple Generations," *Economic Journal* 128(612): F482–F513.

Albers, T., Bartels, C., and Schularick, M. (2022) *Wealth and its Distribution in Germany, 1895–2018*. CEPR Discussion paper no. DP17269.

Alfani, G. (2021) "Economic Inequality in Preindustrial Times: Europe and Beyond," *Journal of Economic Literature* 59(1): 3–44.

Alfani, G. (2023) *As Gods among Men: A History of the Rich in the West*. Princeton, NJ: Princeton University Press.

Almås, I., and Mogstad, M. (2012) "Older or Wealthier? The Impact of Age

Adjustment on Wealth Inequality," *Scandinavian Journal of Economics* 114(1): 24–54.

Alstadsæter, A., Johannesen, N., and Zucman, G. (2018) "Who Owns the Wealth in Tax Havens? Macro Evidence and Implications for Global Inequality," *Journal of Public Economics* 162: 89–100.

Alstadsæter, A., Johannesen, N., and Zucman, G. (2019) "Tax Evasion and Inequality," *American Economic Review* 109(6): 2073–103.

Alvaredo, F., and Artola Blanco, M. (2023) *Wealth Concentration at Death and Wealth Inequality in Spain: Global vs. Local Forces, 1901–2010*. Working paper, Universidad Carlos III.

Alvaredo, F., Atkinson, A. B., and Morelli, S. (2018) "Top Wealth Shares in the UK over More Than a Century," *Journal of Public Economics* 162: 26–47.

Alvaredo, F., Garbinti, B., and Piketty, T. (2017) "On the Share of Inheritance in Aggregate Wealth: Europe and the USA, 1900–2010," *Economica* 84: 239–60.

Amiel, Y., and Cowell, F. (1999) *Thinking about Inequality*. Cambridge: Cambridge University Press.

Andrews, D., and Caldera, A. (2011) "The Evolution of Homeownership Rates in Selected OECD Countries: Demographic and Public Policy Influences," *OECD Journal: Economic Studies* 2011(1).

Appel, I., Gormley, T., and Keim, D. (2016) "Passive Investors, Not Passive Owners," *Journal of Financial Economics* 121(1): 111–41.

Artola Blanco, M, Bauluz, L., and Martínez-Toledano, C. (2021) "Wealth in Spain 1900–2017: A Country of Two Lands," *Economic Journal* 131(633): 129–55.

Atkinson, A. B. (1971) "The Distribution of Wealth and the Individual Life-Cycle," *Oxford Economic Papers* 23(2): 239–54.

Atkinson, A. B. (2008) "Concentration among the Rich," in Davies, J. B. (ed.), *Personal Wealth from a Global Perspective*. Oxford: Oxford University Press.

Atkinson, A. B., and Harrison, A. (1978) *The Distribution of Personal Wealth in Britain*. Cambridge: Cambridge University Press.

Atkinson, A. B., Piketty, T., and Saez, E. (2011) "Top Incomes in the Long Run of History," *Journal of Economic Literature* 49(1): 3–71.

Auten, G., and Splinter, D. (2024) "Income Inequality in the United States: Using Tax Data to Measure Long-Term Trends," *Journal of Political Economy*, forthcoming.

Bach, L., Calvet, L. E., and Sodini, P. (2020) "Rich Pickings? Risk, Return, and Skill in Household Wealth," *American Economic Review* 110(9): 2703–47.

Bach, S., Thiemann, A., and Zucco, A. (2019) "Looking for the Missing

Rich: Tracing the Top Tail of the Wealth Distribution," *International Tax and Public Finance* 26: 1234–58.

Barron Baskin, J., and Miranti, P. (1997) *A History of Corporate Finance*. New York: Cambridge University Press.

Baselgia, E., and Martínez, I. Z. (2024) "Wealth–Income Ratios in Free Market Capitalism: Switzerland, 1900–2020," *Review of Economics and Statistics*, forthcoming.

Bastagli, F., and Hills, J. (2013) "Wealth Accumulation, Ageing, and House Prices," in Hills, J., Bastagli, F., Cowell, F., Glennerster, H., Karagiannaki, E., and McKnight, A. (eds), *Wealth in the UK: Distribution, Accumulation, and Policy*. Oxford: Oxford University Press.

Bastani, S., and Waldenström, D. (2020) "How Should Capital Be Taxed?" *Journal of Economic Surveys* 34(4): 812–46.

Bastani, S., and Waldenström, D. (2021) "Perceptions of Inherited Wealth and the Support for Inheritance Taxation: Evidence from a Randomized Experiment," *Economica* 88(350): 532–69.

Bastani, S, and Waldenström, D (2023) "Taxing the Wealthy: The Choice Between Wealth and Capital Income Taxation," *Oxford Review of Economic Policy* 39(3): 604–16.

Bauluz, L., Novokment, F., and Schularick, M. (2022) *The Anatomy of the Global Savings Glut*. Working paper, University of Bonn.

Bebchuk, L. A., Cohen, A., and Hirst, S. (2017) *The Agency Problems of Institutional Investors*. Discussion paper, Harvard Law School.

Beck, T., Demirgüç-Kunt, A., and Levine, R. (2007) "Finance, Inequality and the Poor," *Journal of Economic Growth* 12(1): 27–49.

Bengtsson, E., Missiaia, A., Olsson, M., and Svensson, P. (2018) "Wealth Inequality in Sweden, 1750–1900," *Economic History Review* 71(3): 772–94.

Black, S. E., Devereux, P. J., Lundborg, P., and Majlesi, K. (2020) "Poor Little Rich Kids? The Role of Nature versus Nurture in Wealth and Other Economic Outcomes and Behaviours," *Review of Economic Studies* 87(4): 1683–725.

Blake, D., and Orszag, M. J. (1999) "Annual Estimates of Personal Wealth Holdings in the United Kingdom since 1948," *Applied Financial Economics* 9(4): 397–421.

Blume, L. E., and Durlauf, S. N. (2015) "Capital in the Twenty-First Century: A Review Essay," *Journal of Political Economy* 123(4): 749–77.

Bönke, T., Grabka, M. M., Schröder, C., Wolff, E. N., and Zyska, L. (2019) "The Joint Distribution of Net Worth and Pension Wealth in Germany," *Review of Income and Wealth* 65(4): 834–71.

Bonnet, O., Bono, P.-H., Chapelle, G., and Wasmer, E. (2014) *Does Housing Capital Contribute to Inequality? A Comment on Thomas Piketty's Capital in the 21st Century*. Sciences Po Economics Discussion paper 2014-07.

Boserup, S. H., Kopczuk, W., and Kreiner, C. T. (2016) "The Role of Bequests in Shaping Wealth Inequality: Evidence from Danish Wealth Records," *American Economic Review* 106(5): 656–61.

Bourdieu, J., Kesztenbaum, L., Postel-Vinay, G., and Suwa-Eisenmann, A. (2019) "Intergenerational Wealth Mobility in France, 19th and 20th Century," *Review of Income and Wealth* 65(1): 21–47.

Boyer, G. R., and Schmidle, T. P. (2009) "Poverty among the Elderly in Victorian England," *Economic History Review* 62(2): 249–78.

Bozio, A., Garbinti, B., Guillot, M., and Piketty, T. (2024) "Predistribution vs. Redistribution: Evidence from France and the U.S," *American Economic Journal: Applied Economics*, forthcoming.

Brandolini, A., Magri, S., and Smeeding, T. M. (2010) "Asset-Based Measurement of Poverty," *Journal of Policy Analysis and Management* 29(2): 267–84.

Bricker, J., and Volz, A. H. (2019) *Why Has Wealth Concentration Grown in the United States? A Re-examination of Data from 1998–2016.* Working paper, Federal Reserve Board.

Bricker, J., Goodman, S., Moore, K. B., and Volz, A. H. (2020) "Wealth and Income Concentration in the SCF: 1989–2019," *FEDS Notes*, September 28.

Bricker, J., Hansen, P., and Volz, A. H. (2019) "Wealth Concentration in the US after Augmenting the Upper Tail of the Survey of Consumer Finances," *Economics Letters* 184: 108659.

Bricker, J., Henriques, A., Krimmel, J., and Sabelhaus, J. (2016) "Measuring Income and Wealth at the Top Using Administrative and Survey Data," *Brookings Papers on Economic Activity* 2016(1): 261–331.

Brülhart, M., Gruber, J., Krapf, M., and Schmidheiny, K. (2022) "Behavioral Responses to Wealth Taxes: Evidence from Switzerland," *American Economic Journal: Economic Policy* 14(4): 111–50.

Brzozowski, M., Gervais, M., Klein, P., and Suzuki, M. (2010) "Consumption, Income, and Wealth Inequality in Canada," *Review of Economic Dynamics* 13(1): 52–75.

Cagetti, M., and De Nardi, M. (2006) "Entrepreneurship, Frictions, and Wealth," *Journal of Political Economy* 114(5): 835–70.

Cagetti, M., and De Nardi, M. (2008) "Wealth Inequality: Data and Models," *Macroeconomic Dynamics* 12(S2): 285–313.

Cagetti, M., and De Nardi, M. (2009) "Estate Taxation, Entrepreneurship, and Wealth," *American Economic Review* 99(1): 85–111.

Cameron, R., and Neal, L. (2003) *A Concise Economic History of the World: From Paleolithic Times to the Present.* Oxford: Oxford University Press.

Catherine, S., Miller, M., and Sarin, N. (2023) *Social Security and Trends in Wealth Inequality.* Working paper, Wharton School.

Cervenka, A. (2022) *Girig-Sverige: så blev folkhemmet ett paradis för de super-rika*. Stockholm: Natur och Kultur.

Ciminelli, G., Duval, R., and Furceri, D. (2022) "Employment Protection Deregulation and Labor Shares in Advanced Economies," *Review of Economics and Statistics* 104(6): 1174–90.

Clark, G. (2007) *A Farewell to Alms: A Brief History of the World*. Princeton, NJ: Princeton University Press.

Congressional Budget Office (2022) *Trends in the Distribution of Family Wealth, 1989 to 2019*. Washington, DC.

Cowell, F. (2011) *Measuring Inequality*. Oxford: Oxford University Press.

Cowell, F. (2013) "UK Wealth Inequality in International Context," in Hills, J., Bastagli, F., Cowell, F., Glennerster, H., Karagiannaki, E., and McKnight, A. (eds), *Wealth in the UK: Distribution, Accumulation, and Policy*. Oxford: Oxford University Press.

Cowell, F., and Van Kerm, P. (2015) "Wealth Inequality: A Survey," *Journal of Economic Surveys* 29(4): 671–710.

Cowell, F., Nolan, B., Olivera, J., and Van Kerm, P. (2017) "Wealth, Top Incomes and Inequality," in Hamilton, K., and Hepburn, C. (eds), *National Wealth: What Is Missing, Why it Matters*. Oxford: Oxford University Press, pp. 175–206.

Cummins, N. (2022) "The Hidden Wealth of English Dynasties, 1892–2016," *Economic History Review* 75(3): 667–702.

Davies, J. B., and Di Matteo, L. (2020) "Long Run Canadian Wealth Inequality in International Context," *Review of Income and Wealth* 67(1): 134–64.

Davies, J. B., and Shorrocks, A. F. (2000) "The Distribution of Wealth," in Atkinson, A. B., and Bourguignon, F. (eds), *Handbook of Income Distribution*, vol. 1. Amsterdam: North-Holland.

Davies, J. B., Lluberas, R., and Shorrocks, A. F. (2017) "Estimating the Level and Distribution of Global Wealth, 2000–2014," *Review of Income and Wealth* 63(4): 731–59.

Davies, J. B., Sandström, S., Shorrocks, A., and Wolff, E. N. (2011) "The Level and Distribution of Global Household Wealth," *Economic Journal* 121(551): 223–54.

Demirgüç-Kunt, A., and Levine, R. (2009) "Finance and Inequality: Theory and Evidence," *Annual Review of Financial Economics* 1(1): 287–318.

Derenoncourt, E., Kim, C. H., Kuhn, M., and Schularick, M. (2023) "Wealth of Two Nations: The US Racial Wealth Gap, 1860–2020," *Quarterly Journal of Economics*, https://doi.org/10.1093/qje/qjad044.

Du Rietz, G., Henrekson, M., and Waldenstrom, D. (2012) "Swedish Inheritance and Gift Taxation (1885–2004)," in Henrekson, M., and

Stenkula, M. (eds), *Swedish Taxation: Developments since 1872*. New York: Palgrave Macmillan.

ECB [European Central Bank] (2020) *The Household Finance and Consumption Survey*, 2017 Wave, Statistical Tables.

Edebalk, P. G. (2009) *From Poor Relief to Universal Rights: On the Development of Swedish Old-Age Care 1900–1950*. Working paper 2009:3, Lund University.

Edlund, L., and Kopczuk, W. (2009) "Women, Wealth, and Mobility," *American Economic Review* 99(1): 146–78.

Edvinsson, R. (2013) "New Annual Estimates of Swedish GDP, 1800–2010," *Economic History Review* 66(4): 1101–26.

Elinder, M., Erixson, O., and Waldenström, D. (2018) "Inheritance and Wealth Inequality: Evidence from Population Registers," *Journal of Public Economics* 165: 17–30.

Epper, T., Fehr, E., Fehr-Duda, H., Kreiner, C. T., Lassen, D. D., Leth-Petersen, S., and Rasmussen, G. N. (2020) "Time Discounting and Wealth Inequality," *American Economic Review* 110(4): 1177–205.

EU Tax Observatory (2023) *Global Tax Evasion Report 2023*. Paris.

European Parliamentary Research Service (2018) *Listing of Tax Havens by the EU*. Briefing, PE 621.872, May 2018.

Fagereng, A., Guiso, L., Malacrino, D., and Pistaferri, L. (2020) "Heterogeneity and Persistence in Returns to Wealth," *Econometrica* 88(1): 115–70.

Fagereng, A., Mogstad, M., and Rønning, M. (2021) "Why Do Wealthy Parents Have Wealthy Children?" *Journal of Political Economy* 129(3): 703–56.

Feldstein, M. (1974) "Social Security, Induced Retirement, and Aggregate Capital Accumulation," *Journal of Political Economy* 82(5): 905–26.

Feldstein, M. (1976) "Social Security and the Distribution of Wealth," *Journal of the American Statistical Association* 71: 800–7.

Feldstein, M. (1996) "Social Security and Saving: New Time Series Evidence," *National Tax Journal* 49(2): 151–64.

Ferguson, N. (2002) *The Cash Nexus: Economics and Politics from the Age of Warfare to the Age of Welfare, 1700–2000*. New York: Basic Books.

Ferguson, N. (2008) *The Ascent of Money: A Financial History of the World*. London: Allen Lane.

Fetter, D. K. (2013) "How Do Mortgage Subsidies Affect Home Ownership? Evidence from the Mid-Century GI Bills," *American Economic Journal: Economic Policy* 5(2): 111–47.

Fisher, J. D., Johnson, D. S., Smeeding, T. M., and Thompson, J. P. (2020) "Estimating the Marginal Propensity to Consume Using the

Distributions of Income, Consumption, and Wealth," *Journal of Macroeconomics* 65: 103218.

Frank, R. (2007) *Richistan: A Journey through the American Wealth Boom and the Lives of the New Rich.* New York: Penguin.

Frick, J., and Grabka, M. (2013) "Public Pension Entitlement and the Distribution of Wealth," in Gornick, J. C., and Jäntti, M. (eds), *Income Inequality: Economic Disparities and the Middle Class in Affluent Countries.* Stanford, CA: Stanford University Press.

Gale, W. G. (1998) "The Effects of Pensions on Household Wealth: A Reevaluation of Theory and Evidence," *Journal of Political Economy* 106(4): 706–23.

Galor, O., and Zeira, J. (1993) "Income Distribution and Macroeconomics," *Review of Economic Studies* 60(1): 35–52.

Gans, J., and Leigh, A. (2020) *Innovation + Equality: How to Create a Future that is More Star Trek than Terminator.* Cambridge, MA: MIT Press.

Garbinti, B., Goupille-Lebret, J., and Piketty, T. (2021) "Accounting for Wealth-Inequality Dynamics: Methods, Estimates, and Simulations for France," *Journal of the European Economic Association* 19(1): 620–63.

Gatzlaff, D. H., Green, R. K., and Ling, D. C. (1998) "Cross-Tenure Differences in Home Maintenance and Appreciation," *Land Economics* 74(3): 328–42.

Gerschenkron, A. (1962) *Economic Backwardness in Historical Perspective.* Cambridge, MA: Belknap Press.

Glete, J. (1994) *Nätverk i näringslivet: ägande och industriell omvandling i det mogna industrisamhället 1920–1990.* Stockholm: SNS.

Goldin, C., and Katz, L. F. (2008) *The Race between Education and Technology.* Cambridge, MA: Belknap Press.

Goldin, C., and Margo, R. A. (1992) "The Great Compression: The Wage Structure in the United States at Mid-Century," *Quarterly Journal of Economics* 107(1): 1–34.

Goldsmith, R. W. (1962) *The National Wealth of the United States in the Postwar Period.* Princeton, NJ: Princeton University Press.

Goldsmith, R. W. (1985) *Comparative National Balance Sheets: A Study of Twenty Countries, 1688–1979.* Chicago: University of Chicago Press.

Goldsmith, R. W. (1987) *Premodern Financial Systems: A Historical Comparative Study.* Cambridge: Cambridge University Press.

Grabka, M. M., Marcus, J., and Sierminska, E. (2015) "Wealth Distribution within Couples," *Review of Economics of the Household* 13(3): 459–86.

Grigg, D. (1992) "Agriculture in the World Economy: An Historical Geography of Decline," *Geography* 77(3): 210–22.

Gruber, J., and Yelowitz, A. (1999) "Public Health Insurance and Private Savings," *Journal of Political Economy* 107(6): 1249–74.

Hacker, J. S., and Pierson, P. (2010) *Winner-Take-All Politics: How Washington Made the Rich Richer – and Turned its Back on the Middle Class*. New York: Simon & Schuster.

Hällsten, M., and Kolk, M. (2023) "The Shadow of Peasant Past: Seven Generations of Inequality Persistence in Northern Sweden," *American Journal of Sociology* 128(6): 1716–60.

Hammar, O., and Waldenström, D. (2020) "Global Earnings Inequality, 1970–2018," *Economic Journal* 130(632): 2526–45.

Harbury, C., and Hitchins, D. (1979) *Inheritance and Wealth Inequality in Britain*. London: Routledge.

Harding, J., Miceli, T. J., and Sirmans, C. F. (2000) "Do Owners Take Better Care of Their Housing Than Renters?" *Real Estate Economics* 28(4): 663–81.

Haskel, J., and Westlake, S. (2017) *Capitalism without Capital: The Rise of the Intangible Economy*. Princeton, NJ: Princeton University Press.

Hausman, N., Ramot-Nyska, T., and Zussman, N. (2022) "Homeownership, Labor Supply, and Neighborhood Quality," *American Economic Journal: Economic Policy* 14(2): 193–230.

Haveman, R., and Wolff, E. N. (2005) "Who Are the Asset Poor? Levels, Trends, and Composition, 1983–1998," in Sherraden, M. (ed.), *Inclusion in the American Dream: Assets, Poverty, and Public Policy*. Oxford: Oxford University Press.

Heldring, L., Robinson, J. A., and Whitfill, P. (2022) "The Second World War, Inequality and the Social Contract in Britain," *Economica* 89, S137–S159.

Henrekson, M. (2015) "Kapitalägare då och nu: förmögenheter, beskattning och samhällets syn," in Swedenborg, B. (ed.), *Svensk ekonomisk politik – då, nu och i framtiden: festskrift tillägnad Hans Tson Söderström*. Stockholm: Dialogos Förlag.

Henrekson, M., and Jakobsson, U. (2001) "Where Schumpeter was Nearly Right – the Swedish Model and Capitalism, Socialism and Democracy," *Journal of Evolutionary Economics* 11(3): 331–58.

Henrekson, M., and Stenkula, M. (2016) *Swedish Taxation: Developments since 1862*. London: Macmillan.

Henrekson, M., and Waldenström, D. (2016) "Inheritance Taxation in Sweden, 1885–2004: The Role of Ideology, Family Firms and Tax Avoidance," *Economic History Review* 69(4): 1228–54.

Henrekson, M., Johansson, D., and Stenkula, M. (2020) "The Rise and Decline of Industrial Foundations as Controlling Owners of Swedish Listed Firms: The Role of Tax Incentives," *Scandinavian Economic History Review* 68(2): 170–91.

Hills, J., Bastagli, F., Cowell, F., Glennerster, H., Karagiannaki, E., and

McKnight, A. (2013) *Wealth in the UK: Distribution, Accumulation, and Policy*. Oxford: Oxford University Press.

Hoffman, P. T., Postel-Vinay, G., and Rosenthal, J.-L. (2009) *Surviving Large Losses: Financial Crises, the Middle Class, and the Development of Capital Markets*. Cambridge, MA: Harvard University Press.

Hubmer, J., Krusell, P., and Smith Jr, A. A. (2021) "Sources of US Wealth Inequality: Past, Present, and Future," *NBER Macroeconomics Annual* 35(1): 391–455.

Jakobsen, K., Jakobsen, K., Kleven, H., and Zucman, G. (2020) "Wealth Taxation and Wealth Accumulation: Theory and Evidence from Denmark," *Quarterly Journal of Economics* 135(1): 329–88.

Johnson, R. A., and Greening, D. W. (1999) "The Effects of Corporate Governance and Institutional Ownership Types on Corporate Social Performance," *Academy of Management Journal* 42(5): 564–76.

Jomo, K. S. (2006) *Growth with Equity in East Asia?* DESA Working paper no. 33.

Jones, A. H., and Simkovich, B. (1992) "The Wealth of Women, 1774," in Goldin, C., and Rockoff, H. (eds), *Strategic Factors in Nineteenth Century American Economic History: A Volume to Honor Robert W. Fogel*. Chicago: University of Chicago Press.

Jordà, Ò., Knoll, K., Kuvshinov, D., Schularick, M., and Taylor, A. M. (2019) "The Rate of Return on Everything, 1870–2015," *Quarterly Journal of Economics* 134(3): 1225–98.

Jordà, Ò., Schularick, M., and Taylor, A. M. (2016) "The Great Mortgaging: Housing Finance, Crises and Business Cycles," *Economic Policy* 31(85): 107–52.

Kaldor, N. (1961) "Capital Accumulation and Economic Growth," in Hague, D. C. (ed.), *The Theory of Capital: Proceedings of a Conference Held by the International Economic Association*. London: Palgrave Macmillan.

Karagiannaki, E. (2017) "The Impact of Inheritance on the Distribution of Wealth: Evidence from Great Britain," *Review of Income and Wealth* 63(2): 394–408.

Keynes, J. M. (1919) *The Economic Consequences of the Peace*. Republished as Vol. II of *The Collected Writings of John Maynard Keynes*, 1971, London: Macmillan for the Royal Economic Society.

Kindleberger, C. P. (1984) *A Financial History of Western Europe*. London: Routledge.

Kleven, H. J., and Schultz, E. A. (2014) "Estimating Taxable Income Responses Using Danish Tax Reforms," *American Economic Journal: Economic Policy* 6(4): 271–301.

Knoll, K., Schularick, M., and Steger, T. (2017) "No Price Like Home:

Global House Prices, 1870–2012," *American Economic Review* 107(2): 331–53.

Kohl, S. (2017) *Homeownership, Renting and Society: Historical and Comparative Perspectives*. London: Routledge.

Kohl, S. (2018) *A Small History of the Homeownership Idea*. MPIfG Discussion paper no. 18/6, Cologne.

Kopczuk, W. (2015) "What Do We Know about the Evolution of Top Wealth Shares in the United States?" *Journal of Economic Perspectives* 29(1): 47–66.

Kopczuk, W., and Saez, E. (2004) "Top Wealth Shares in the United States, 1916–2000: Evidence from Estate Tax Returns," *National Tax Journal* 57(2): 445–87.

Korom, P., Lutter, M., and Beckert, J. (2017) *The Enduring Importance of Family Wealth: Evidence from the Forbes 400, 1982 to 2013*. Discussion paper no. 15/8, Max Planck Institute for the Study of Societies.

Kotlikoff, L. (1988) "Intergenerational Transfers and Savings," *Journal of Economic Perspectives* 2(2): 41–58.

Kotlikoff, L., and Summers, L. (1981) "The Role of Intergenerational Transfers in Aggregate Capital Accumulation," *Journal of Political Economy* 89: 706–32.

Krolage, C., Peichl, A., and Waldenström, D. (2022) "Long-Run Trends in Top Income Shares: The Role of Income and Population Growth," *Journal of Economic Inequality* 20(1): 97–118.

Krusell, P., and Smith, A. A. (2015) "Is Piketty's 'Second Law of Capitalism' Fundamental?" *Journal of Political Economy* 123(4): 725–48.

Kuhn, M., Schularick, M., and Steins, U. I. (2020) "Income and Wealth Inequality in America, 1949–2016," *Journal of Political Economy* 128(9): 3469–519.

Kuuse, J. (1970) *Inkomstutveckling och förmögenhetsbildning: en undersökning av vissa yrkesgrupper 1924–1959. Meddelanden från ekonomisk-historiska institutionen vid Göteborgs universitet 23*. Gothenburg University.

Kuvshinov, D., and Zimmermann, K. (2022) "The Big Bang: Stock Market Capitalization in the Long Run," *Journal of Financial Economics* 145(2): 527–52.

Kuznets, S. (1953) *Shares of Upper Income Groups in Income and Savings*. Cambridge, MA: NBER.

Levine, R. (2021) *Finance, Growth, and Inequality*, IMF WP/21/164.

Lindert, P. H. (1986) "Unequal English Wealth since 1670," *Journal of Political Economy* 94(6): 1127–62.

Lindert, P. H. (2000) "Three Centuries of Inequality in Britain and America," in Atkinson, A. B., and Bourguignon, F. (eds), *Handbook of Income Distribution*, vol. 1. Amsterdam: North-Holland.

Lindert, P. (2004) *Growing Public: Social Spending and Economic Growth since the Eighteenth Century*. Cambridge: Cambridge University Press.

Lundberg, J., and Waldenström, D. (2018) "Wealth Inequality in Sweden: What Can We Learn from Capitalized Income Data?" *Review of Income and Wealth* 64(3): 517–41.

Madsen, J. (2019) "Wealth and Inequality over Eight Centuries of British Capitalism," *Journal of Development Economics* 138: 246–60.

Madsen, J., and Strulik, H. (2020) "Technological Change and Inequality in the Very Long Run," *European Economic Review* 129: 103532.

Madsen, J. B., Minniti, A., and Venturini, F. (2021) "Wealth Inequality in the Long Run: A Schumpeterian Growth Perspective," *Economic Journal* 131(633): 476–97.

Mankiw, G. N. (2015) "Defending the One Percent," *Journal of Economic Perspectives* 29(1): 21–34.

Martínez-Toledano, C. (2020) *House Price Cycles, Wealth Inequality and Portfolio Reshuffling*. WID World Working paper, Paris School of Economics.

McCloskey, D. N. (2016) *Bourgeois Equality: How Ideas, not Capital or Institutions, Enriched the World*. Chicago: University of Chicago Press.

Milanović, B. (2011) *The Haves and the Have-Nots: A Brief and Idiosyncratic History of Global Inequality*. New York: Basic Books.

Milanović, B. (2016) *Global Inequality: A New Approach for the Age of Globalization*. Cambridge, MA: Harvard University Press.

Milanović, B. (2019) *Capitalism, Alone: The Future of the System That Rules the World*. Cambridge, MA: Harvard University Press.

Modigliani, F. (1985) "Life Cycle, Individual Thrift and the Wealth of Nations," Prize Lecture to the Memory of Alfred Nobel, December 9.

Modigliani, F. (1986) "Life Cycle, Individual Thrift and the Wealth of Nations," *American Economic Review* 76(3): 297–313.

Modigliani, F. (1988) "The Role of Intergenerational Transfers and Life Cycle Savings in the Accumulation of Wealth," *Journal of Economic Perspectives* 2(2): 15–40.

Mokyr, J. (1990) *The Lever of Riches: Technological Creativity and Economic Progress*. Oxford: Oxford University Press.

Mokyr, J. (2016) *A Culture of Growth: The Origins of the Modern Economy*. Princeton, NJ: Princeton University Press.

Moore, L. (2010) "Financial Market Liquidity, Returns and Market Growth: Evidence from Bolsa and Börse, 1902–1925," *Financial History Review* 17(1): 73–98.

Morissette, R., Zhang, X., and Drolet M. (2006) "The Evolution of Wealth Inequality in Canada, 1984–1999," in Wolff, E. N. (ed.), *International Perspectives on Household Wealth*. London: Edward Elgar.

Nekoei, A., and Seim, D. (2023) "How Do Inheritances Shape Wealth

Inequality? Theory and Evidence from Sweden," *Review of Economic Studies* 90(1): 463–98.

Norberg, J. (2023) *The Capitalist Manifesto: Why the Global Free Market Will Save the World*. London: Atlantic Books.

North, D. C., and Thomas, R. P. (1973) *The Rise of the Western World: A New Economic History*. Cambridge: Cambridge University Press.

OECD (2011) *Pensions at a Glance 2011: Retirement-Income Systems in OECD and G20 Indicators*. Paris: OECD.

OECD (2014) *Countering Harmful Tax Practices More Effectively, Taking into Account Transparency and Substance*, OECD/G20 Base Erosion and Profit Shifting Project. Paris: OECD.

OECD (2021) *Pension Markets in Focus 2021*. Paris: OECD.

Ohlsson, H., Roine, J., and Waldenström, D. (2008) "Long-Run Changes in the Concentration of Wealth: An Overview of Recent Findings," in Davies, J. B. (ed.), *Personal Wealth from a Global Perspective*. Oxford: Oxford University Press.

Ohlsson, H., Roine, J., and Waldenström, D. (2020) "Inherited Wealth over the Path of Development: Sweden, 1810–2016," *Journal of the European Economic Association* 18(3): 1123–57.

O'Rourke, K. H., and Williamson, J. G. (2005) "From Malthus to Ohlin: Trade, Industrialisation and Distribution since 1500," *Journal of Economic Growth* 10: 5–34.

Paglin, M. (1975) "The Measurement and Trend of Inequality: A Basic Revision," *American Economic Review* 65(4): 598–609.

Peichl, A., and Pestel, N. (2013) "Multidimensional Well-Being at the Top: Evidence for Germany," *Fiscal Studies* 34(3): 355–71.

Piketty, T. (2001) *Les hauts revenues en France au XXe siècle: inégalités et redistributions 1901–1998*. Paris: Grasset.

Piketty, T. (2011) "On the Long-Run Evolution of Inheritance: France 1820–2050," *Quarterly Journal of Economics* 126(3): 1071–131.

Piketty, T. (2014) *Capital in the Twenty-First Century*. Cambridge, MA: Harvard University Press.

Piketty, T., and Saez, E. (2003) "Income Inequality in the United States, 1913–1998," *Quarterly Journal of Economics* 118(1): 1–39.

Piketty, T., and Saez, E. (2013) "A Theory of Optimal Inheritance Taxation," *Econometrica* 81(5): 1851–86.

Piketty, T., and Zucman, G. (2014) "Capital is Back: Wealth–Income Ratios in Rich Countries 1700–2010," *Quarterly Journal of Economics* 129(3): 1255–310.

Piketty, T., and Zucman, G. (2015) "Wealth and Inheritance in the Long Run," in Atkinson, A. B., and Bourguignon, F. (eds), *Handbook of Income Distribution*, Vol. 2B. Amsterdam: North-Holland.

Piketty, T., Postel-Vinay, G. and Rosenthal, J.-L. (2006) "Wealth Concentration in a Developing Economy: Paris and France, 1807–1994," *American Economic Review* 96(1): 236–56.

Piketty, T., Postel-Vinay, G. and Rosenthal, J.-L. (2014) "Inherited vs. Self-Made Wealth: Theory Evidence from a Rentier Society (Paris 1872–1927)," *Explorations in Economic History* 51: 21–40.

Piketty, T., Saez, E., and Zucman, G. (2018) "Distributional National Accounts: Methods and Estimates for the United States," *Quarterly Journal of Economics* 133(2): 553–609.

Piketty, T., Saez, E., and Zucman, G. (2023) "Rethinking Capital and Wealth Taxation," *Oxford Review of Economic Policy* 39(3): 575–91.

Pinker, S. (2018) *Enlightenment Now: The Case for Reason, Science, Humanism, and Progress.* New York: Penguin Books.

Pistor, K., Keinan, Y., Kleinheisterkamp, J., and West, M. D. (2002) "Evolution of Corporate Law: A Cross-Country Comparison," *University of Pennsylvania Journal of International Law* 23: 791–871.

Prados de la Escosura, L. (2022) "Capital in Spain, 1850–2019," *Cliometrica* 16: 1–28.

Prados de la Escosura, L., and Rosés, J. R. (2010) "Capital Accumulation in the Long Run: The Case of Spain, 1850–2000," *Research in Economic History* 27: 141–200.

Ravallion, M. (2021) "What Might Explain Today's Conflicting Narratives on Global Inequality?" in Gradin, C. (ed.), *Inequality in the Developing World.* Oxford: Oxford University Press.

Rognlie, M. (2015) *Deciphering the Fall and Rise in the Net Capital Share: Accumulation or Scarcity?* Brookings Papers on Economic Activity, spring.

Roine, J., and Waldenström, D. (2008) "The Evolution of Top Incomes in an Egalitarian Society: Sweden, 1903–2004," *Journal of Public Economics* 92(1–2): 366–87.

Roine, J., and Waldenström, D. (2009) "Wealth Concentration over the Path of Development: Sweden, 1873–2006," *Scandinavian Journal of Economics* 111(1): 151–87.

Roine, J., and Waldenström, D. (2015) "Long-Run Trends in the Distribution of Income and Wealth," in Atkinson, A., and Bourguignon, F. (eds), *Handbook in Income Distribution*, vol. 2A. Amsterdam: North-Holland.

Roine, J., Vlachos, J., and Waldenström, D. (2009) "The Long-Run Determinants of Inequality: What Can We Learn from Top Income Data?" *Journal of Public Economics* 93(7–8): 974–88.

Rosling, H., Rosling, O., and Rosling Rönnlund, A. (2018) *Factfulness: Ten Reasons We're Wrong about the World – and Why Things Are Better Than You Think.* New York: Flatiron Books.

Rydqvist, K., and Rong, G. (2021) "Performance and Development of a Thin Stock Market: The Stockholm Stock Exchange 1912–2017," *Financial History Review* 28(1): 26–44.

Rydqvist, K., Spizman, J., and Strebulaev, I. (2014) "Government Policy and Ownership of Equity Securities," *Journal of Financial Economics* 111(1): 70–85.

Sabelhaus, J., and Volz, A. H. (2020) *Social Security Wealth, Inequality, and Lifecycle Saving*. NBER Working paper no. 27110.

Saez, E., and Zucman, G. (2016) "Wealth Inequality in the United States since 1913: Evidence from Capitalized Income Tax Data," *Quarterly Journal of Economics* 131(2): 519–78.

Saez, E., and Zucman, G. (2020) *Trends in US Income and Wealth Inequality: Revising after the Revisionists*. NBER Working paper no. 27921.

Sandberg, L. G. (1978) "Banking and Economic Growth in Sweden before World War I," *Journal of Economic History* 38(3): 650–80.

Sandberg, L. G. (1979) "The Case of the Impoverished Sophisticate: Human Capital and Swedish Economic Growth before World War I," *Journal of Economic History* 39(1): 225–41.

Scheidel, W. (2017) *The Great Leveler: Violence and the History of Inequality from the Stone Age to the Twenty-First Century*. Princeton, NJ: Princeton University Press.

Scheuer, F., and Wolitzky, A. (2016) "Capital Taxation under Political Constraints," *American Economic Review* 106(8): 2304–28.

Scheve, K., and Stasavage, D. (2010) "The Conscription of Wealth: Mass Warfare and the Demand for Progressive Taxation," *International Organization* 64(4): 529–61.

Scheve, K., and Stasavage, D. (2016) *Taxing the Rich: A History of Fiscal Fairness in the United States and Europe*. Princeton, NJ: Princeton University Press.

Schön, L. (2012) *An Economic History of Modern Sweden*. London: Routledge.

Schularick, M., and Taylor, A. M. (2012) "Credit Booms Gone Bust: Monetary Policy, Leverage Cycles, and Financial Crises, 1870–2008," *American Economic Review* 102(2): 1029–61.

Shilling, J. D., Sirmans, C. F., and Dombrow, J. F. (1991) "Measuring Depreciation in Single-Family Rental and Owner-Occupied Housing," *Journal of Housing Economics* 1(4): 368–83.

Shorrocks, T., Davies, J. B., Lluberas, R., and Waldenström, D. (2023) *Global Wealth Report 2023*. Zurich: UBS and Credit Suisse.

Sierminska, E., and Wroński, M. (2022) *Inequality and Public Pension Entitlements*. GLO Discussion paper no. 1212.

Sinn, H.-W. (2000) "Why a Funded Pension System is Useful and Why it is Not Useful," *International Tax and Public Finance* 7(4): 389–410.

Smith, M., Yagan, D., Zidar, O., and Zwick, E. (2019) "Capitalists in the Twenty-First Century," *Quarterly Journal of Economics* 134(4): 1675–745.

Smith, M., Zidar, O., and Zwick, E. (2023) "Top Wealth in America: New Estimates under Heterogeneous Returns," *Quarterly Journal of Economics* 138(1): 515–73.

Sodini, P., Van Nieuwerburgh, S., Vestman, R., and von Lilienfeld-Toal, U. (2023) "Identifying the Benefits from Homeownership: A Swedish Experiment," *American Economic Review* 113(12): 3173–212.

Soltow, L. (1985) "The Swedish Census of Wealth at the Beginning of the 19th Century," *Scandinavian Economic History Review* 33(1): 1–24.

Soltow, L. (1989) "The Rich and the Destitute in Sweden, 1805–1855: A Test of Tocqueville's Inequality," *Economic History Review* 42(1): 44–63.

Soltow, L., and van Zanden, J. L. (1998) *Income Wealth Inequality in the Netherlands 16th–20th Century*. Amsterdam: Het Spinhuis.

Spånt, R. (1979) *Den svenska förmögenhetsfördelningens utveckling*, SOU 1979:9. Stockholm: Fritzes.

Tanzi, V., and Schuknecht, L. (2000) *Public Spending in the 20th Century: A Global Perspective*. Cambridge: Cambridge University Press.

Tawney, R. H. (1913) "Poverty as an Industrial Problem," in Tawney (ed.), *Memoranda on the Problem of Poverty*. London: William Morris Press.

Tørsløv, T., Wier, L., and Zucman, G. (2023) "The Missing Profits of Nations," *Review of Economic Studies* 90(3): 1499–534.

Toussaint, T., de Vicq de Cumptich, A., Moatsos, M., and van der Valk, T. (2022) *Household Wealth and its Distribution in the Netherlands, 1854–2019*. WID Working paper 2022/19.

van Bavel, B. J. (2016) *The Invisible Hand? How Market Economies Have Emerged and Declined since AD 500*. Oxford: Oxford University Press.

Vermeulen, P. (2018) "How Fat Is the Top Tail of the Wealth Distribution?" *Review of Income and Wealth* 64(2): 357–87.

Waldenström, D. (2014) "Swedish Stock and Bond Returns, 1856–2012," in Edvinsson, R., Jacobson, T., and Waldenström, D. (eds), *Historical Monetary and Financial Statistics for Sweden*, vol. 2: *House Prices, Stock Returns, National Accounts and the Riksbank Balance Sheet, 1860–2012*. Stockholm: Sveriges Riksbank and Ekerlids förlag.

Waldenström, D. (2016) "The National Wealth of Sweden, 1810–2014," *Scandinavian Economic History Review* 64(1): 36–54.

Waldenström, D. (2017) "Wealth–Income Ratios in a Small, Developing Economy: Sweden, 1810–2010," *Journal of Economic History* 77(1): 285–313.

Waldenström, D. (2022a) "The Swedish Bond Market, 1835–2020," in Edvinsson, R., Jacobson, T., and Waldenström, D., (eds), *Historical Monetary and Financial Statistics for Sweden*, vol. 3: *Banking, Bonds, National Wealth, and Stockholm House Prices, 1420–2020. Banking, Bonds, National*

Wealth, and Stockholm House Prices, 1420–2020. Stockholm: Sveriges Riksbank and Ekerlids förlag.

Waldenström, D. (2022b) "The National Wealth of Sweden," in Edvinsson, R., Jacobson, T., and Waldenström, D. (eds), *Historical Monetary and Financial Statistics for Sweden*, vol. 3: *Banking, Bonds, National Wealth, and Stockholm House Prices, 1420–2020*. Stockholm: Sveriges Riksbank and Ekerlids förlag.

Waldenström, D. (2024) "Wealth and History: A Reappraisal," *Explorations in Economic History*, forthcoming.

Waldenström, D., Bastani, S., and Hansson, Å. (2018) *Kapitalbeskattningens förutsättningar: SNS Konjunkturrådsrapport 2018*. Stockholm: SNS.

Weil, D. (2015) "Capital and Wealth in the Twenty-First Century," *American Economic Review* 105(5): 34–7.

Williamson, J. G., and Lindert, P. (1980a) *American Inequality: A Macroeconomic History*. New York: Academic Press.

Williamson, J. G., and Lindert, P. (1980b) "Long-Term Trends in American Wealth Inequality," in Smith, J. D. (ed.), *Modeling the Distribution and Intergenerational Transmission of Wealth*. Chicago: University of Chicago Press.

Wolff, E. N. (1989) "Trends in Aggregate Household Wealth in the U.S., 1900–83," *Review of Income and Wealth* 35(1): 1–29.

Wolff, E. N. (1998) "Recent Trends in the Size Distribution of Household Wealth," *Journal of Economic Perspectives* 12(3): 131–50.

Wolff, E. N. (2002) "Inheritances and Wealth Inequality, 1989–1998," *American Economic Review* 92(2): 260–4.

Wolff, E. N. (2011) *The Transformation of the American Pension System: Was it Beneficial for Workers?* Kalamazoo, MN: WE Upjohn Institute.

Wolff, E. N. (2015) *Inheriting Wealth in America: Future Boom or Bust?* Oxford: Oxford University Press.

Wolff, E. N. (2017) *A Century of Wealth in America*. Cambridge, MA: Harvard University Press.

Wolff, E. N. (2021) *Household Wealth Trends in the United States, 1962 to 2019: Median Wealth Rebounds . . . but Not Enough*. NBER Working paper no. 28383.

Wolff, E. N., and Gittleman, M. (2014) "Inheritances and the Distribution of Wealth, or Whatever Happened to the Great Inheritance Boom?" *Journal of Economic Inequality* 12: 439–68.

Wolff, E. N., and Marley, M. (1989) "Long-Term Trends in U.S. Wealth Inequality: Methodological Issues and Results," in Lipsey, R. E., and Tice, H. S. (eds), *The Measurement of Saving*. Chicago: University of Chicago Press.

World Inequality Lab (2022) *World Inequality Report 2022*.

Wroński, M. (2023) "The Impact of Social Security Wealth on the Distribution of Wealth in the European Union," *Journal of the Economics of Ageing* 24: 100445.

Zucman, G. (2013) "The Missing Wealth of Nations: Are Europe and the U.S. Net Debtors or Net Creditors?" *Quarterly Journal of Economics* 128(3): 1321–64.

Zucman, G. (2015) *The Hidden Wealth of Nations: The Scourge of Tax Havens.* Chicago: University of Chicago Press.

Detailed Contents

Figures and Tables

Tables

Index

Figures are in *italics* and tables in **bold**.

Printed in the USA
CPSIA information can be obtained
at www.ICGtesting.com
LVHW012022211024
794394LV00005B/7/J